Also by Sarah Kuhn

HEROINE COMPLEX
HEROINE WORSHIP
HEROINE'S JOURNEY

HEROINE'S JOURNEY

SARAH KUHN

BOOK THREE OF HEROINE COMPLEX

DAW BOOKS, INC.

DONALD A. WOLLHEIM, FOUNDER

375 Hudson Street, New York, NY 10014

ELIZABETH R. WOLLHEIM
SHEILA E. GILBERT
PUBLISHERS

www.dawbooks.com

First Printing, July 2018
1   2   3   4   5   6   7   8   9

For the real Bea and Leah, House Koch—long may you reign.

CHAPTER ONE

I WILL NEVER be a superhero.

I glared at the book I was re-shelving in Paranormal Romance, trying to stop my negative train of thought in its tracks. Unfortunately, my negative trains of thought tend to power themselves into full-blown locomotives of motherfuckin' doom.

I'm talented like that.

The current shelf situation wasn't helping. My sworn nemesis, Nicole Yamamoto, had just hurricaned through It's Lit, the adorable San Francisco bookshop/café where I work as a re-shelving/coffee-slinging lackey, and messed up the entirety of Paranormal Romance, committing an array of heinous crimes against the basic concept of the alphabet. I had at least another forty-five minutes of organizing before things were set right, and the tedium of moving book after book from Point A to Point B had me down the all too familiar mental rabbit hole of *I will never be a superhero.*

I heaved a mighty sigh and shoved another book into place. The shelf shook a little, and I instantly felt bad. I gave the book a soothing pat. After all, it wasn't the book's fault I was in such a shitty mood—no, that honor rested one hundred percent with my big sister Evie.

I should be taking down demons as Bea Tanaka, Superheroine Extraordinaire. Instead I was rearranging books and cleaning up after pretentious slobs. All because Evie kept giving me that one little word I'd come to hate more than anything in the whole entire world: *No.*

Bzzzzzz.

My phone vibrated in my pocket and I yanked it free, glowering at the screen. Evie again. Begging me to call her. She had a constant need to make sure you weren't mad at her, to be cleared of all wrongdoing, to get you to see things her way. But I was pretty set on *my* way of seeing things, and my way said she was totally frakballs *wrong*.

That hadn't stopped her from texting me no fewer than seven times in the last hour. One of her classic "don't be mad at me" tactics.

I shoved my phone back in my pocket, gritted my teeth, and surveyed the section, trying to lull myself into a sense of calm by running my fingers along the colorful rainbow of book spines. We shelved new and used together, so some of the spines were cracked and worn, and I paused on a hot pink vampire tome that was one of my favorites. This particular copy had been read so many times its spine was creased with a series of jagged lines, giving it the appearance of aged wood. Well . . . aged, hot pink wood.

Hmm. I wonder if it would piss Evie off if I painted my room this color?

"Bebe!" A sharp voice pierced my thoughts, and I nearly jammed my finger against the book I'd been stroking. "We've got a Code Green in the café, and I need you to—wait, what's wrong?"

I turned to see my best friend and fellow bookstore lackey, Leah Kim, cocking her head at me. Her mane of curly dark hair listed to the side, and her eyebrows were raised over the clunky frames of her nerdy-cool glasses.

"How can you tell something's wrong from my *back*?" I said, shaking my head.

"I'm empathetic and shit," Leah said with a shrug. "Plus, you're fondling that book in a way that borders on inappropriate, sooo . . ." She crossed her arms over her chest, rumpling her shapeless linen jumpsuit—a garment that would have appeared vaguely cult-member-appropriate on most people, but Leah made it look downright artsy.

I let out the longest, gustiest sigh ever. "I pitched Evie again last night about me joining the official superteam. As an official superheroine. Fighting demons and stuff alongside her. Officially."

"And she said no?"

"And she said no."

My big sister was San Francisco's coolest superhero ever— I mean, she could shoot fire out of her hands, it doesn't get more badass than that. She and her superheroing partner, Aveda Jupiter (aka Annie Chang), battled demon threats large and small and kept the Bay Area safe from supernatural harm. In the past, I'd been a glorified assistant on the team, helping with research and paperwork and Team Tanaka/Jupiter's social media presence, but now I was ready for more. So much more.

"And then you had the same fight you guys always have, the fight you are destined to have forever, the one that always ends with you rage-stomping up the stairs and slamming your bedroom door, like the pouty teen she seems to think you still are?" Leah continued.

I couldn't help but crack a small smile. "Are you psychic or something?"

"Thoroughly mundane," Leah said. "Y'all are just super predictable. Do you need a pep talk?" She rolled her eyes to the ceiling, as if calling up the words. "Listen. You are a strong woman of color, your brain is gigantic and full of science, and your rainbow-dyed hair looks particularly fetching and anime-heroine-esque today. You are a beautiful, empowered, uniquely skilled flower, and you can be anything you set your mind to."

"Thank you," I said, meaning it. "Especially about the hair—I wasn't totally sure about going for the whole purple-pink-turquoise mermaid look, particularly since too much Technicolor streakage is like catnip to White Guys Who Like Asian Girls, but then I was like, *I* dig it, so who cares?"

"Preach," Leah said, holding up her hand for a high-five. "And don't forget about the little project we've got going in the back—it will definitely enhance your presentation next time you pitch Evie, give it that extra bit of oomph. Now. About that Code Green—"

"Which one is Code Green again?" I said, giving her palm a half-hearted slap. "The almond milk doesn't taste like almonds? They hate the cookie they just ate, even though they ate it in two seconds flat?"

"It's the thing where they spilled coffee all over a book they haven't paid for and are now trying to get out of paying for it," she said with an eye-roll.

"Gotcha." I nodded in recognition. "I'm on it."

I abandoned Paranormal Romance and followed Leah through the bookstore and toward the café area. Our boss, Charlotte Wilcox, had three goals in mind when she designed It's Lit: she wanted it to be open and airy (tough to accomplish in the often cramped, claustrophobic environs of the city), home to popular genres dominated by women writers (not an obvious fit for sometimes snooty San Francisco), and respectful of said genres (hence the name, It's Lit, which was supposed to be both cute and defiant). Luckily, Charlotte had tons of money from her incredibly successful local-turned-national bakery franchise, Cake My Day. That money had allowed her to secure an amazing space for It's Lit, with huge windows, tons of light, and high ceilings, and to decorate it with a plush pink velvet couch, a mish-mash of colorful throw rugs and pillows, and an ever-growing army of collectible porcelain unicorns. The store felt more like an eccentric aunt's home than a retail establishment. And the café area, with its fine selection of caffeine and baked goods, added to the comfortable vibe.

"Come on, Pancake," Leah sang out, scooping up her tiny one-eyed dog from his resting place on one of the throw pillows. "Bebe's about to take down a fiendish destroyer of books. It's gonna be awesome."

Pancake snorted and gazed up at her, looking vaguely put out. Leah liked to say Pancake, who she'd rescued two Thanksgivings ago from a local shelter, was a blend of breeds and therefore "a beautiful representation of the mixed-race experience—just like us." I was pretty sure, however, that he was one-hundred percent long-haired Chihuahua with the diva temperament to match.

As we neared the café area, I heard the dreaded customer before I saw him.

"—and as I keep saying, I *barely* dribbled anything on this book, so I don't understand why I should have to pay for it. I wasn't even considering purchasing it, merely perusing." The voice was pinched, nasal, and had the entitled air of someone who likes himself a whole, whole lot.

"Frustrated novelist grad student who ordered one latte and then sat here for three hours siphoning off the wi-fi?" I said to Leah.

"Four hours," she corrected. "And do *not* ask him about his *Saved by the Bell* tee, he doesn't even own a television. Or any devices with streaming capacity, apparently. The shirt is meant to be—"

"—ironic," I finished. "Of fucking course."

We rounded the corner and walked through the arched entrance that led into the café, a sunny space with mismatched thrift store tables and chairs. There was a handy garage door-style metal barricade that could be pulled down between the café and the bookstore area, but we hardly ever used it.

The customer in question stood over Charlotte, his long, spindly arms gesticulating expansively to make his point. Thankfully, most of the regulars had cleared out for the day. The only other people witnessing this unfortunate display were Nemesis Nicole, who was buried in a book from one of the shelves she'd ransacked, and Sam Fujikawa, my other best friend, who was sitting with a cute redhead clad in a gingham dress with a rockabilly flair. Sam and the redhead were probably on a date. Sam was *always* on a date. As Leah and I walked in, Sam caught my eye and raised an eyebrow at the increasingly loud customer.

Bzzzzzzz.

My phone vibrated against my hip again, and I jumped a little.

Goddammit, Evie, I'm working. *Don't you have someone else's dreams to crush?*

When I got home, I'd just tell her my phone died. That would piss her off even more.

I've told you a kazillion times to plug it in during your shift, she'd say. *What if there's an emergency?*

You never let me help when there's an emergency, I retorted in my head. *So what's the point?*

"I'm pretty sure you have no official policy that requires people to purchase damaged books anyway," the customer continued, giving Charlotte a piercing stare over the frames of his wire-rim glasses. "And if you do, it really should be posted somewhere."

"That's true," Charlotte mumbled, her eyes wandering to the floor. Despite her status as one of the city's most successful businesswomen, Charlotte maintained an air of mopey moroseness at all times. She'd only recently started going by "Charlotte" after her business manager suggested it sounded more serious and intimidating than her nickname, Letta. I'd hoped the Charlotte upgrade would make her *feel* more intimidating. But so far, it hadn't changed her demeanor. When it came to difficult customers, she still preferred the path of least resistance. Which meant she was two seconds from giving in and letting this guy get away with blatant book besmirching.

Well, no matter. That's why she had Leah and me. She'd had the good sense to promote Leah to store manager two years ago, and it was usually Leah who interfaced with people looking for book recs or cheerful conversation while Charlotte was off tending to her bakery empire. But for the difficult customers . . . well, my unique skill set tended to be more useful.

"Excuse me," I said loudly. I shot Charlotte a look, like, *I got this.* She gave me a grateful head bob and shuffled to the side.

The customer turned and sized me up, his eyes narrowing. He was tall and skinny and had kind of an Ichabod Crane thing going on. I watched his expression soften into amusement as he took me in: the neon hair; the black lace slip dress, ratty cardigan, and purple ankle boots; the excessive eyeliner. My aesthetic was somewhere in the realm of "cartoon character in a state of goth rebellion," and I knew he'd decided in an instant that he didn't need to take me seriously.

That's cool. When it comes to stuff like this, being underestimated works in my favor.

"Excuse me," I repeated. "I understand we've got a damaged book situation?"

"I wouldn't exactly call it damaged." Ichabod Lite nodded at the table he was standing next to, which held an empty coffee cup and a very soggy paperback. "Just got a little coffee on it," he said with an overly casual shrug. "I'm sure it'll be fine once it dries out."

"Huh." I stepped forward and leaned down to examine the book, gently lifting the cover away from the pages, as if I were a medical examiner on a primetime crime drama. The poor paperback was definitely a lost cause. The pages were barely maintaining structural integrity.

I straightened up and looked Ichabod Lite in the eye. "Looks pretty damaged to me."

He shrugged again. "Maybe it was like that before?"

I cocked an eyebrow. "Or maybe you got a little too excited reading about . . ." I snuck another glance at the cover. "Sexy wereporcupine shifters."

As he sputtered, I reached deep into my mind, focused, and finally did what I'd come in here to do.

I decided to start with a positive feeling. The joy he'd likely felt reading such a delicious book, the joy he was ashamed to express because it conflicted with his too-cool-for-school image. I felt that joy deep in my veins, focused on it, then turned it up until it was thrumming through my entire being. Then I gave him a bright smile and sent *pure joy* spinning in his direction. When I first project a feeling at someone, I usually start with a softball—like I'm an aromatherapy candle, here to gently change your mood with my delicious aura of pumpkin spice.

I saw it hit. He stopped sputtering, then frowned and shook his head, like he was trying to get free.

Oh, no, little man. You can't get free of me.

"I . . . I . . . I'm sure I would never get anywhere close to excited reading such *trash*," he finally managed.

"Oh, you did *not*," Leah hissed behind me. "Do not insult the wereporcupine shifters, you condescending, misogynist, genre-snob *garbage can*." Pancake growled. I held up a hand to stop both of them from charging Ichabod.

"And I definitely don't want to *buy* trash." Ichabod Lite paused and shook his head again. His voice was disdainful, but his face was overtaken by an ear-to-ear grin. The contrast made for a ghoulish effect. I projected joy just a little bit harder. "What the hell?" he exclaimed. "Why can't I stop smiling?"

I rolled my neck and let out a deep exhale. *'Cause I've got you in my clutches, duh.* But Ichabod Lite was clearly naturally resistant to joy and would therefore require extra wrangling. Some people need more adjusting than others. Like they have to be overwhelmed with that pumpkin spice goodness until they can't think of anything but Halloween and cozy sweaters. With extra difficult customers, I had to try projecting a few different emotions before one took strong enough hold to actually change their minds.

In the end, I couldn't make someone do something they truly didn't want to do. But I could shift their general attitude. Alter their mood. I could *persuade*.

"I mean," Ichabod Lite pressed on, even though that dopey grin was still spread all over his face. "Sure, I've thought about shitting out one of those books as a way of making a quick buck, but I cannot imagine lowering myself to such lowbrow depths, to such . . . such . . ."

"I. Will. Kill. Him," Leah muttered.

My gaze slid to Ichabod Lite's table again, scanning for clues that might help me settle on a new emotion. I noticed a pile of papers that had been scribbled all over. Hmm. I'd been half joking about him being a frustrated novelist, but maybe that's what he was? Okay, I could use that. I refocused, scrapping the joy, and went directly to the emotion favored by Asian elders everywhere, particularly big sisters who want you to cover up your light and be all boring and basic and shit: *guilt.*

"Aw, man," I said, forcing my shoulders to relax and my voice to go regretful. I gathered up the guilt, felt it deep in my bones, and sent it spinning his way. His face fell and he looked confused. "It's such a shame when a book . . . encounters coffee that way. Such a shame for the author. It's just . . ." I let out a massive sigh that would've made my ancestors proud. ". . . so sad."

"I . . ." Ichabod Lite's eyes shifted back and forth.

"Imagine if that author was you," I said, making my eyes all big and pleading and projecting that guilty feeling at him with extra gusto. "Imagine if you worked so hard on your masterpiece, on shaping those words into coherent story formation, and all of that was undone in two seconds, thanks to a full cup of coffee and a bit of clumsiness, and it's all . . . just . . . so . . . *sad.*"

"I guess," Ichabod Lite said, haughtiness overtaking his tone again. He frowned at me. I could tell he was struggling, but this guilt thing wasn't doing the trick either. Goddammit. Asian Guilt is supposed to be the most powerful force in the universe.

So what now? One thing that tended to be most effective with strong personalities was using an emotion they went to naturally, something that was an essential part of their core personality. But what was that here? What emotion had enough presence in Ichabod's daily life to make an impact?

"But I sincerely doubt this writer worked hard at all," Ichabod sniffed, drawing himself up tall. "Certainly not as hard as I've worked on *my* novel, which interweaves themes of intergenerational trauma, the suppressed rage of men, and the universality of the human condition."

"Not to mention the theme of being boring as shit," Leah said. Pancake snuffled in agreement.

I took a deep breath and focused on Ichabod—really focused on him. His skin was red and mottled, his breath huffing and puffing with such force, such outrage, such—

Wait. Of course. I should've seen it instantly.

Ichabod probably never allowed something so trite as joy into his life. And he was clearly lacking the self-awareness necessary to feel guilt over anything. No, he was definitely powered by a single thing: righteous indignation. The conviction that he was infallible, persecuted, and unfairly treated by the entire universe. I could *so* use that.

It was easy to summon my own righteous indignation, thanks to the phone that was yet again buzzing against my hip. I homed in on my annoyance at Evie and her five million text messages, her repeated mantra that I "wasn't ready" to become a full-fledged superhero alongside her, her insistence on always seeing me as the teenager I'd once been, that broken girl with an abandonment complex and extreme lack of impulse control.

I was so sick of having the same fight with her. I *was* ready, dammit. She refused to see me as I was now: a capable adult person doing capable adult things. I'd be a huge asset to her team; I could do so much. So much more than controlling irritating customers with my mind.

I gathered up everything I was feeling and projected hard, sending it spinning toward Ichabod with all the force I could muster.

Pumpkin spice all up in this bitch.

Then I met his eyes, trying to make my gaze intense and understanding all at once.

"It's so unfair, isn't it?" I said to him. "When people don't recognize all the hard work you're doing?"

"Well . . . yeah," he said, his indignation ratcheting up another notch.

"You've probably been working on your book for . . . what? Five years?"

"Seven," he seethed, shaking his head. "I've written forty-three drafts and *still*. All I get are rejections."

"So unfair," I repeated. "It's like nobody truly sees you."

"Nobody does!" he spat out. "*Nobody*. It's like I'm doing all this for nothing."

"I know how that feels," I continued.

"You—you do?" He blinked at me. Still indignant, but momentarily confused. Probably because I'd pivoted away from his favorite topic: himself.

"I put so much into the section of the store I manage," I said, placing my hand over my heart. "Organizing and curating the gloriousness that is Paranormal Romance, and for what? Nobody appreciates it. Nobody appreciates *me*. Everybody still sees me as the loser eighteen-year-old college drop-out I was when I first got this job, and I'm like, hello? I'm twenty-two now. And I've never even gotten a raise."

"That's . . . not right," he said, blinking rapidly.

"And also not true," Charlotte murmured, sounding injured. I waved a hand to shush her. I was lying my ass off for the greater good.

"No, it's not right," I agreed with Ichabod. "And that ruined book . . . well." I made my eyes go a little dark. Haunted, even. "It's from my section. That means . . ." I paused for dramatic effect and projected indignation at him extra hard. "It's gonna come out of my paycheck."

"What!" he exploded, shaking his head. "That is *so* not right. I will organize a protest in your honor. Start a petition. Write a strongly worded letter. I will . . . will . . ."

"Or," I said sweetly, still projecting righteous indignation with all my might, "there's actually a very simple way to right that wrong. You—er, the person responsible for this little coffee disaster just needs to admit it. And pay for the book."

"You're absolutely right," he huffed. "Wrongs must always be righted, hard workers must be avenged, and . . . and . . . I did it." He shook his head—again, as if trying to get free. "I did it," he blurted out again. His eyes widened, like he couldn't believe his own behavior. "I am outraged . . . at *myself*. And I should absolutely pay for it."

"Get the sequel, too," I said, unable to resist.

"Yes. *Yes*." He nodded vigorously. "And when I get home, I can start that petition—"

"No need," I said breezily. "That'll be twenty-nine-ninety-eight plus tax. Leah and Pancake here can ring you up."

"Follow us!" Leah chimed in gleefully, waving Pancake's paw at Ichabod. "You're fucking brilliant," she whispered to me as she led him back to the bookstore area. Pancake snorted in agreement. Ichabod was starting to look confused again, so I gave Leah the "wrap it up" hand motion behind his back, indicating she should proceed with the sale quickly.

I smiled as I watched them go, allowing myself a tiny victory fist-pump. I knew it was small potatoes in the grand scheme of things, but it always felt good to bend a truly jerky person to my will, to defuse their dumbassery and make my small sphere of San Francisco a better place.

"Take that, you mansplaining mofo," I muttered under my breath, making finger guns at Ichabod's retreating back.

Bzzz! Bzzzz! Bzzzzzzzzz!

The vibrations seemed extra angry and insistent. I nearly jumped out of my skin. I yanked the phone out of my pocket and saw that it was actually ringing this time—Evie had apparently escalated to a call after her texts had gone ignored. I tapped the screen and jammed the phone to my ear.

"What?" I hissed. "What do you want? Wait, save it—I know what you want. And for the record: No, I do not forgive you, yes, I am still mad, and absolutely one-hundred percent yes, I am not speaking to you for the foreseeable future, so stop texting me and save your stupid non-apologies for someone who actually cares and just *let me be mad*."

"Bea—" she began.

I hung up. Any sense of triumph I might have felt over successfully handling a difficult customer was totally ruined, washed away by the wave of rage that was pulsing through my entire body.

Honestly. I could be lauded by my co-workers and save my place of employ from losing thousands of dollars in ruined books every year and *still*. All of it was undone by a moment of my sister reminding me that she would never, ever see me as the badass superhero I was meant to be.

I flashed to Ichabod—irritating as he was, ultimately he just wanted what I wanted: for people to see him as he truly was, rather than what their initial perceptions might say. For people to give him the chance to become the complete, fully realized, totally awesome person he was meant to be and to live the truly fabulous life he was meant to live.

"I feel you, Ichabod," I muttered.

Ugh. Really? Now this whole mess with Evie had me connecting with a truly awful human being. Thanks, Big Sis.

I turned my phone off and stuffed it in my pocket for the rest of my shift.

Which I knew would piss Evie off.

No, this was not a mature action. But if my big sister insisted on seeing me as a child, then I sure as fucking hell was going to take a little bit of immature joy in acting like one.

CHAPTER TWO

I DECIDED TO spend a few calming moments in the It's Lit bathroom before heading home after my shift. Maybe a little zen would soothe me, and then I'd be able to present my arguments to Evie and Co. for the millionth time in a reasoned, totally mature way.

I suppose some people might argue with my choice of the word "mature" applied to a presentation involving so much glitter. But my series of Why Bea Should Join the Superteam posterboards required pizzazz to get my point across, and nothing says pizzazz like a shit-ton of glitter.

I slumped to the floor of the bathroom, crossing my arms over my chest and glaring at the toilet, the sink, the wall. I breathed deeply, trying to allow the cozy atmosphere of the bathroom to drain my anger. The pink lighting was gentle and womb-like, and the little dishes of potpourri strewn around the room added a not-too-overpowering floral scent. But the best part—the part customers always raved about—was the wall opposite the toilet, which Leah had set up as a sort of evolving art installation. We'd put out markers and craft supplies, and customers and staff had doodled and pasted their creations all over the wall, leaving empowering messages ("Yassss, queen—and you're ALL queens!"), reader recommendations ("Nalini Singh's latest is FIRE EMOJI"—coupled with an actual drawing of a fire emoji, in case the message wasn't clear), and tiny bits of decoration (the whimsical animals made out of cotton balls were my personal favorite).

I stared at the wall and hugged my knees to my chest. Images from the night before flashed through my brain, Evie twisting her hands together in that nervous way that indicated she was feeling guilty about "being mean" to someone. "We don't think you're ready yet, Bea," she'd said. "There are so many split second decisions that happen during this stuff, and . . . and . . ."

"And you have not exactly proven yourself to be a model of good instincts when it comes to decision-making in general," Aveda had cut in, regarding me sternly. Aveda is *never* worried about "being mean." "No offense," she added hastily, when Evie shot her a look.

They always gave me the same speech. Even though I was constantly changing *my* presentation to them. My posterboards featured a wide array of ever-changing spreadsheets and charts and fun graphics (and glitter!) showing exactly how and why I'd be an asset to the team. And okay, yes, sometimes I also got distracted by a bright, shiny new tangent and made a whole new posterboard around that and Evie just had to go and remind me that part of my problem was lack of *focus*—

Well. Anyway.

Evie and Aveda had been official co-heroines for four years and best friends for way longer than that, and their bond was so tight they had some kind of weird and totally not supernatural telepathic connection with each other. That connection had come in handy over the years as they'd battled the various demons who had swarmed San Francisco— and it was hard to imagine a time when demons *hadn't* swarmed San Francisco. It had all started thirteen years ago, when a wannabe demon queen named Shasta (or at least that was her human cover name) opened the very first Otherworld portal to the city. She'd actually been trying to take over the city for years, having staked out Earth as the realm she wanted to rule. Her raiding party of humanoid demons had come through that first portal, set on invasion. But unfortunately for Shasta, her portal was so unstable that it snapped shut immediately, killing her invasion team and sending their special demon superpowers into various human bodies—like mine and Evie's and Aveda's. It also had aftereffects, smaller portals that kept opening up and depositing smaller demons on our doorstep.

Aveda had christened herself Aveda Jupiter, beloved superheroine of San Francisco, and fought these "puppy demons"—piranha-like pests who imprinted on the first earthly object they saw. Evie had been her personal assistant for a while, but now they were legit partners, and San Francisco definitely needed them. There was only one Otherworld portal left in the city—a dark, mysterious thing located on the floor of local lingerie shop Pussy Queen. Though the portal itself was mostly closed and mostly dormant, its presence had allowed supernatural energy to leak through slowly over the years. That meant there was still a plethora of supernatural shenanigans to be had in the city, but they were unpredictable: One week might find Evie and Aveda battling mysterious invisible pests at a greeting card store ("Greetings from Ghost Town!" I'd crowed—they hadn't laughed), another might have them trying to figure out why a statue in Japantown had come to life and started attacking people.

But whatever the demon issue, they were always there, ready to save the city yet again. And I wanted to be right there with them. I knew that whenever they said no they were probably thinking back to the time I'd rebelled and sort of, kind of, temporarily joined Shasta in her evil-doing ways. All because I'd been pissed off at Evie, of course. But I'd *changed*.

How could Evie know I wasn't ready, that I'd make bad decisions *now*, if she never even gave me the chance?

Someday I'd hit on the exact right strategy, the exact right argument to convince her. Leah and I had been working for months on a special secret project, something that would send me into the kickass superheroine stratosphere.

I stood and walked over to the craft wall. I ran my fingers over the notes and cotton balls and attempts at papier-mâché.

Studying the wall was strangely intimate; like seeing everyone's secret innermost thoughts on display. Maybe it was the
anonymity of it—when you wrote down a sentiment and put
it on the wall, you never had to say it out loud. You didn't
have to sign it. You could just let it be.

And judging from some of the more colorful entries ("I
know you cheated on me, Greg, my revenge will be swift and
sweet!"), people felt like they could share things from the
very depths of their souls. I had my own increasingly expansive doodle crawling down the far right side of the wall, accompanied by various thoughts I had on various days.

I never want to be normal

I want to live an extraordinary life

*I want fabulous adventures, fabulous food, and fabu-
lous sex*

I shook my head at the doodle. All this *wanting*. Where
was it getting me, exactly? Time to make a more declarative
statement. I picked up a marker, pressed it firmly against the
wall, and wrote:

I will be the greatest superhero of all time

Then, for good measure, I added: *Just you wait*

"You know it, Lin-Manuel," I murmured.

I knew I'd come back tomorrow and find someone responding with enthusiasm to the *Hamilton* reference. Most
people wouldn't notice my bigger proclamation, and if they
did, they probably wouldn't care.

But for just a moment, it felt good to move past wanting,
to reach for something real.

🔥

I breezed out of the bathroom, all set to head home and redo
my Why Bea Should Get to Join the Superteam presentation, when I was stopped by a familiar figure.

"Hey," said Nicole Yamamoto, my nemesis. (This is how
she must be referred to at all times, a simple "Nicole" will
not do.) She placed a perfectly manicured hand on her hip
and jiggled her empty coffee cup at me. "Refill?"

Even though she'd spent the last hour pretzeled up in a café chair, reading all the books she'd so carelessly ripped from the shelves and wasn't going to buy, there wasn't a wrinkle on her perfect beige pencil skirt and crisp white blouse. The side part in her smooth sheet of black hair was so precise, it looked like she'd done it with a ruler. And she was looking at me with her usual extreme disdain, that special Nicole brand of condescension that said, *Yes, I am an important paralegal doing important paralegal things and you are a tiny flea whose purpose is to serve me even though we used to be BFFs who did gross things together like eat sand out of the sandbox. Also, your hair is dumb.*

"I'm off work, my shift just ended," I said, trying to shoot some of that disdain right back at her. "Try, I don't know, the person actually standing behind the coffee counter?"

"There's no one there," she said, rolling her eyes at me. "And I need to caffeinate before I stay up all night with the stacks of research I need to do for the case I'm working on. It's kind of important."

"Oh, I'm sorry," I said, resisting the urge to roll my eyes right back at her. "Since it's *important*, I guess I should clock back in and make sure your every need is fulfilled, eh?"

"That would be great," she said, without missing a beat. She gave me a tight, prissy smile.

I felt my shoulders tensing up. "Listen—"

"Did I hear someone say coffee? Because I have coffee." Sam Fujikawa dashed up, toting two full to-go cups. He handed one to Nicole and flashed her his patented heartthrob grin: way too many teeth showing, dark eyes sparkling in a way that seemed to imply he had just fucked that coffee six ways from Sunday.

In addition to being one of my best friends, Sam is quite possibly the cheesiest person alive.

"You don't even work here!" I protested.

"Thank you," Nicole said, fluttering her eyelashes at him. "Bye, Bea. I left those books I was reading in the café. Maybe you can put them back when you're done doing . . . whatever you're doing."

"Guh . . . *you* . . ." was all I managed to get out before she strode off, her sensible flats clicking insolently against the floor.

"Nice, I fulfilled her coffee needs, which got her to leave— you're welcome. Score another point for Team Fujikawa," Sam said, grinning and jerking a thumb at himself.

"Your whole . . . thing is too much right now," I said, gesturing at the air around him. "Cheese, cheese, *beaucoup fromage.* I'll remind you that the running score stands at Bea: 1273, Sam: 1162. You have miles to go before you catch up with me."

Sam and I had been fierce academic rivals all through high school, constantly striving to one-up each other with extra credit, advanced classes, and ballooning GPAs. We'd ended up co-valedictorians and after that . . . well. I'd skipped college and other potential life experiences in favor of hanging around the Bay Area, pursuing my dream of becoming a full-fledged superheroine alongside my big sister. Sam had stuck around and gotten a gig at the Mission Mechanic autoshop, much to the chagrin of his two older siblings. Alex and Emily—or as we referred to them, Mr. Brag and Ms. Bore—had used their giant brains to become a fancy doctor and a fancy professor, respectively, and were desperate to convince Sam to use *his* giant brain in a way that was more impressive-sounding.

We'd basically bonded over being total disappointments to our families.

But we'd kept our ongoing score—something we'd started freshman year of high school—going to this day.

"And you know," I added, "I think you should get points docked for abusing your heartthrob skills to flirt with my nemesis."

"You use your superhero skills, I'll use mine," Sam said. "And speaking of, isn't it abuse of your superheroic gifts to force people into buying stuff? Leah ended up selling that guy the whole wereporcupine series. All seventeen books."

"It's not abuse," I retorted. "I only use my power for making our community here . . ." I gestured to my surroundings. ". . . a better place. I have a *code*."

"A code that conveniently allows you to mind-control people you find especially annoying?"

"A code that ensures my place of employment runs smoothly, and snotty snobs don't get away with anything."

He gave me an amused smile. "Then why don't you project some of that mojo onto Nicole? She is, in your estimation, extremely annoying."

"Yes, but she's only annoying *me*. My code is all about assessing what's for the greater good. And in the end, I can't force anyone to do anything they don't actually want to do— that's not within the realm of my power *or* my code. So in addition to making my little corner of the world better, I freed that guy to get what he really wanted underneath all the bluster. Which was seventeen volumes of wereporcupine goodness."

Sam shook his head and passed me the other coffee cup he was holding. "Your code, much like your skill in solving advanced quadratic equations, needs work."

"I kicked your ass in calculus—except for that one time, which barely counts," I muttered, accepting the cup and taking a sip. "Ugh, this stuff is like battery acid."

"Sweet, sweet battery acid," he said. "I thought it was local and artisanal."

"It's Folgers with the label ripped off," I said, going against my better judgment and taking another sip. "Anyway, why are *you* bringing *me* coffee? Aren't you aware of how the customer-to-caffeine-slinger relationship actually works?"

He shrugged. "You looked upset. Your face gets a very particular crinkle right . . . here." He tapped my forehead. "I don't want you to prematurely age, thereby becoming a disappointment to Asian Aunties everywhere."

"I'm already a disappointment for so many other reasons," I said, batting his hand away. "Pay less attention to my stress wrinkles and more attention to your date." I took another sip of terrible coffee and started walking back toward the café area. "What is that, the third one this week?"

His smooth brow crinkled. "I . . . mmm. I can't remember."

I shook my head. "You're disgusting."

"You're one to talk," he said, elbowing me. "I'm surprised Charlotte and Leah haven't issued a ban on you dating customers."

"I am a master of the drama-free breakup," I said with a shrug. "So we always *retain* those customers. Also, I don't straight up lose track of how many dates I've been on within a given time period."

"There was that time you double-booked yourself, though," he said, giving me a sly grin. "Guy with permascowl and way too much hair gel in the café. Girl with big sad eyes and flowery caftan in the bookstore. And you, running back and forth like you were in a hijinks-packed sitcom, trying to keep them from finding out about each other."

"That was . . . unfortunate," I admitted. "But back to *your* date. Is she another calendar groupie or did you attract her on the street after releasing an extra hefty dose of sexy mechanic pheromones?"

He laughed. "Calendar. That thing is the bane of my existence."

"Riiight," I said, giving him a look. "So awful. You must hate being you."

He just shrugged, his grin widening. If there was one thing Sam Fujikawa did *not* hate, it was being Sam Fujikawa. He'd achieved a certain level of local fame—though not really the kind his siblings were hoping for—a couple months ago, when he'd been featured in the latest edition of the Bay Area Hunky Hot Hotties calendar, a grand San Francisco tradition that plucked twelve of the region's studliest local business owners, photographed them in various states of undress, and ranked them from January to December. The thing sold like hotcakes, and all proceeds went to charity. Sam was Mr.

March, and his photo was actually quite tasteful: his blue mechanic's coveralls unbuttoned and shucked off to the waist, the better to show off his broad, muscled shoulders and ridiculous abs. And he'd been smiling that heartthrob smile, jet-black hair tousled just-so and falling rakishly over his forehead.

Since the calendar's release, Sam had been inundated with admirers—though he never went out with any of them twice.

"She left," Sam said. "My date. Our conversation was not exactly sparkling. No matter what topic we were on, she kept trying to steer me back to the organic beauty products she makes in her basement." He frowned. "I think she was mostly trying to get me to buy some. Or sell some? Maybe dating is part of her complicated pyramid scheme."

"How dare she," I said, feigning outrage. "You don't *need* any beauty products."

"Anyway," he said, rolling his eyes at me. "Why don't you and Leah come over tonight. I'll make katsu."

Sam had learned how to make katsu from his uncle, who owned Curry On in Japantown—home of the best pork katsu curry you'll ever have. My mouth watered just thinking about crispy panko breading surrounding perfect juicy pork drowning in a pool of spicy, soul-nourishing curry.

"I'm in," I said, doing my best not to drool. "Curry me up. After I work on my Why I Should Be a Superhero presentation for a few hours, of course."

"Of course." Sam pulled his phone out of his pocket and tapped on the screen. "Just gonna make a grocery list . . . oh. Wow."

"Wow . . . what?"

"Something's going down at the waterfront," he said. "And your sister's in the middle of it."

"What?" I squawked again. "Show me."

I leaned over his shoulder and studied the screen, which contained a video someone had shot only minutes ago. It was blurry, shaky, and clearly taken from far away, but if I squinted, I could make out three tiny figures poised by a long, blue stretch of waterfront: Evie, Aveda, and their frequent superheroing colleague Shruti Dhaliwal. Evie held up her hands, shooting bursts of flame. Aveda stood a few feet away from Evie, the fire dancing above her head—she was probably using her telekinesis to move it around, sending it toward . . . I frowned and squinted harder. They were being menaced by large, blurry gray blobs that looked like . . . stone? Big rocks that were kicking up some crazy-ass waves? What was happening?

"Twitter says they're at the Wave Organ," Sam said. "That sculpture near the Exploratorium? Supposedly, the waves pounding against it creates some kind of music. Though to be honest, I've never heard anything."

I studied the image, wheels in my brain turning. Could Evie have been calling me earlier because she'd had a change of heart and wanted me to join her on this superhero excursion? I hadn't let her get a word in, after all.

That seemed unlikely. But it didn't mean I couldn't once again reach past wanting and seize an opportunity that was staring me right in the face.

If I really showed Evie what I was made of—in the heat of battle—maybe it would make her forget her well-intentioned speeches about how I wasn't ready. *Showing* her I was ready would be a hell of a lot more convincing than any presentation, no matter how much glitter I put on my posterboards.

I snatched Sam's phone and dashed back into the books area of the store, my eyes never leaving the screen.

"Bea." Sam's voice was completely exasperated as he followed me, but I barely heard him.

"I need you to give me a ride somewhere," I said. "Go get your car, okay? It'll be way faster than trying to public transpo it to the waterfront."

"*Bea,*" he repeated.

I stopped and faced him, tearing my eyes from the phone screen. "Look," I said. "You're going to try to convince me to do what you think is 'the sensible thing,' and we both know I'm not going to do that because neither of us are exactly known for doing 'the sensible thing,' which is one of the reasons we're such good friends. So can we just skip that part and get to the part where you give me a ride because we *are* such good friends?"

He let out the longest sigh ever and headed for the exit. "Fiiiiiine."

Satisfied, I continued my march over to Leah. "Hey," I said, once I reached her. "You know that thing we've been working on in the back? It's showtime."

🔥

"Is that a *cape*?"

Sam was trying to drive and look at me in the passenger seat at the same time, and it wasn't going very well. I'd requested he pull around to the front of the bookstore while Leah and I prepared the creation we'd been working on for months.

Even though I was in a hurry to get to the scene of a supernatural emergency, I'd taken a moment to pose in front of the mirror in the back room of It's Lit, glorying in how the cape swished behind me, how the material looked like a beautiful rainbow kaleidoscope when the light hit it just right. Leah had also fashioned a tiny superhero cape out of the same fabric for Pancake—"just in case you find yourself in need of a sidekick"—and he ran around next to my feet, barking officiously as I posed.

Sam had tried to argue with me again when I got in the car, insisting he didn't actually have time to give me a ride because he had to go to the grocery store for katsu supplies. I'd countered that if I didn't get to the waterfront as soon as possible, I couldn't help save the world, and then we wouldn't be having katsu *ever again*.

I won. Bea: 1274. Sam: 1162. My lead was awesomely definitive.

"It is indeed a cape," I said, using the passenger side mirror to adjust my glorious cape's collar closure. "I know conventional wisdom is that capes get caught in stuff when you're trying to kick evil in the balls, but Leah and I constructed this one to be aerodynamic, so it flows *with* me rather than impeding my movements."

"It is . . . something," Sam managed, sneaking another sidelong glance at me. "And the rest of the outfit?"

"Similarly designed and constructed to give me the best range of movement possible while also withstanding the ever mercurial San Francisco climate," I said. "And pretty stylish, no? The combination of Leah's art brain and my science brain is like *magic*."

"Damn," Sam said. "The two of you would make a kickass superhero team in your own right. Just call me if you need someone to be the face of the operation, I'll be happy to add my charisma to your Justice League set-up."

"All I need is your car," I said, waving my hand at him in regal fashion. "Drive on, driver."

Satisfied with my cape collar, I ran my palms over the rest of my costume, smoothing out stray wrinkles. I was wearing a short dress that mimicked the cut of my usual slip dress fare and heavy duty leggings—both made out of a special material Leah and I had devised to enhance my aerodynamicness. It was a shimmery rainbow of colors with highlights of blue and purple, to match my hair. We hadn't quite gotten around to footwear—that was next on the agenda—so I'd topped the costume off with my purple ankle boots. They weren't perfect for superheroing purposes, but they'd do in a pinch.

"Drop me off as close to the waterfront as possible," I said. "Like, right about . . . here."

"You'll still need to run a ways to get to the Wave Organ," Sam said, pulling over into a tiny sliver of space that wasn't exactly a parking spot. He cast a doubtful look toward the water. "Are you sure you don't want help—"

"How are *you* going to help me?" I said, poking him in the arm. "Gigantic stone monsters stomping the waterfront aren't going to care about your *charisma*."

"But—"

"Bye!" I sang out, leaping from the car and slamming the door behind me.

He frowned and looked like he wanted to say *much* more, but then the car behind him started honking, which set off a honk chain reaction. He gave me one last thoroughly exasperated look and drove off. I guessed he was going to look for a parking spot, but *ha!* The only places to park around here were grimy tourist lots that stacked cars like sardines, and no way would Sam risk a scratch on his precious automobile. He'd spent a good three months restoring and upgrading the engine and it was pretty much his baby.

I took a few deep breaths, bounced up and down on my toes a couple times, then took off, running down the dirt path by the water. On an ordinary day, it would have been a lovely stroll with a beautiful view. The Golden Gate Bridge peeked its way through the fog, a bright orangey-red exclamation point of a photo backdrop for tourists. The water, a mermaid-worthy blue-green, lapped against the craggy landscape that passes for beach in Northern California. And the wind swept my hair around in a way that probably would have looked glamorous if I'd been smiling for a sunny day selfie instead of sprinting toward the scene I could see in the far-off distance: those giant gray blobs menacing three tiny figures.

I tried to pick up speed, ignoring the way the ground smacked against the thin soles of my boots, making my feet and legs ache. My breath wheezed in and out and my lungs burned—I was definitely no athlete. But hey, neither was Evie. And she still managed to do a ton of kickass superheroing.

As I got closer, the gray blobs started to come into focus— they were definitely made out of some kind of stone. What the hell? Had giant stone monsters invaded from the Otherworld? The Otherworld had giant stone monsters now?!

I found myself darting around people running in the other direction—civilians, I realized, trying to escape whatever terror these massive stone monsters were dishing out. I dodged a woman wearing a sunhat and toting a giant camera, then dodged again when her camera swung around and nearly bonked me on the head. Clearly a tourist.

"Don't go over there," the woman screeched at me as she ran past.

"Something awful's happening! Those big rocks are trying to *kill people!*" chimed in a guy wearing an Alcatraz sweatshirt. Also a tourist.

"But Evie and Aveda and their superteam have got it under control—we should stay out of the way!" called out a teenage girl with a giant backpack. Hmm. Could be a tourist or just an angsty youngster with a lot of literal baggage.

"Oh, it's cool, I'm part of the superteam!" I said breezily— well, as breezily as one can bellow something. But they were already gone, replaced by a new set of civilians just trying to get out of the damn way.

"My friend!" a woman wearing several fannypacks shrieked, gesturing in the direction of the stone monsters. "You have to help me find my friend, we were looking for her wallet and now I can't find her—"

"I assure you, we're working to evacuate all civilians." Lucy Valdez—weapons expert and personal trainer to Team Tanaka/Jupiter—gave the woman a reassuring smile. She was bringing up the rear of the tourist crowd, trying to herd them away from the water. "Please head to the evacuation point. Perhaps your friend is there already." Lucy turned and spotted me. "Bea! Darling, why aren't you at the bookstore? Come on, we're evacuating people to a safer location. Rose cordoned off an area by the Palace of the Fine Arts—"

"I'm not going to a safer location, I'm going to help," I said firmly, nodding in the direction of the action.

"That sounds like a perfectly dreadful idea, but I suppose there's no talking you out of it," Lucy said, cocking an eyebrow. "We'll be waiting if you change your mind." And with that, she raced off, another wave of civilians hot on her heels.

I doubled down on my focus and tried to run faster, to

wind myself through the crowd more efficiently. These boots were probably going to be toast. I could already feel a hole forming where the sole met the ball of my right foot. Too bad, they'd been my favorites.

I finally reached my sister and her friends and skidded to a stop right behind Evie, wheezing so hard I had to rest for a moment, doubling over and putting my hands on my knees. Leah and I had made sure the costume material was moisture-wicking, but that didn't mean it had the power to stop me from sweating altogether. I felt sticky all over.

"I'm here, Sis," I managed between wheezes. "I'm here."

"Bea?" Evie said, whipping around and giving me a quizzical look.

"Bea!" Aveda echoed, frowning at me with extreme disapproval. "What are you doing? You need to get clear of this area! Find Lucy and Rose, they'll guide you to a safe spot."

"I don't need a safe spot," I insisted, but none of them seemed to hear me. I stumbled back a few steps and managed to stand up straight, taking in the scene. "I'll just take a few minutes to observe, analyze, and strategize," I said, making my voice a bit louder. Again, none of them responded. I hoped at least Aveda had heard me since she was always droning on about how important it was to hone your observational skills in order to enhance your on-the-spot battle-planning. I wanted her to see how I totally actually listened whenever she lectured, that I was dedicated to becoming the best heroine I could be. But she just kept ignoring me.

My eyes swept over the Wave Organ. A swooping, multi-level sculptural marvel constructed of graceful pipes and squat pieces of concrete, it looked a bit like a smaller, nerdier, deconstructed version of Stonehenge. It was built into a little piece of land that juts into the ocean, giving it the dreamy feel of an almost-island. I'd never seen it in person before now, but I knew it was a favorite locale of the Bay Area's finest graffiti artists—and I could glimpse wild scribblings of blue and black and purple on some of the more hidden areas.

The stone monsters lurching through the ocean looked like they were trying to destroy the Organ and anyone around it. There were about a dozen of them, tall as giant redwood trees, towering over Evie and Co. Their movements were slow and labored as they made their way through the water. But even though they weren't particularly fast or graceful, they were still gigantic enough to be threatening, kicking up major waves and occasionally swooping dangerously near anyone in the vicinity.

Evie was poised in the center of the team's formation, at the very edge of the piece of land that juts into the water, hands raised, shooting her fire into the air. Aveda stood next to her, brow furrowed in ferocious concentration as she stared at the fire. The flames danced in the air, then joined together in one bright chain—it looked like Aveda was using her telekinesis to form a makeshift wall out of Evie's fire. Maybe to surround the stone monsters?

I homed in on the monsters themselves, trying to pick up extra details. They were big and blocky and made up of an assemblage of geometric shapes—squares, rectangles, and the occasional swooping cylinder . . . wait a minute . . .

I turned to look at the Wave Organ again. And realized half of it was gone.

"Um. Hold up," I called out. "Did the Wave Organ, like, come to life, inflate itself to gigantic proportions, and start menacing tourists?"

"Pretty much exactly right, Bea. At least part of it did," Shruti said, glancing over her shoulder to give me a bright smile. Her long dark hair was unfurled and twisting, trying to wrap itself around one of the monsters, and I saw that she already had some of them in her grasp. Shruti had the ability to grow her hair at will and grab on to stuff with it, and her power got stronger the more she used it. "Wow, I love your outfit!" she continued. I beamed and stood up a little straighter. Coming from Shruti, who ran one of the city's coolest vintage boutiques, that was high praise. (I was also still nursing the tiny remnants of a crush I'd had on her when I was younger; Leah had, of course, teased me mercilessly for falling into the "pining hopelessly for older sibling's friend" trope.) Her next words, however, undercut things a bit. "It reminds me of that X-Men panel where Kitty Pryde debuts her Sprite costume," Shruti added. "With all the colors and the stripey legwarmers and the roller skates?"

"Preeee-senting the all-new, all-different, altogether stunning Sprite!" Evie chimed in, shooting another fireball into the air with relish. They both laughed.

"Hey, hey," Aveda barked, expertly moving Evie's fireball to join the existing chain. "What have we said about keeping the giggly banter to a minimum when we're in the midst of battle?"

"*You* said that," Evie retorted. "We did *not* agree. Giggly banter totally cuts through the tension and helps us get in the zone—whoa, watch out Shruti, to your left!" One of the stone monsters had freed itself from Shruti's hair and was lurching toward her, kicking up a huge wave in the process.

"Oh, crap!" Shruti exclaimed, flinging out her hair to once again wrap around the monster.

I frowned. I remembered that panel, too, from a comic I'd stolen from Evie's stash when we were kids. Kitty's costume was, in my opinion, fabulous, but the moment was meant to poke fun at her—the young upstart playing at what she thought being a superhero was. In other words, I did *not* take it as a compliment.

"All right, team, what's our next move?" Evie said. "We have them sort of trapped . . ." She gestured to the scene. Aveda was telekinetically holding the ring of fire around some of the stone monsters while Shruti kept the rest in place with her hair. "They seem to be scared of the fire, but whenever I try to hit them with it directly . . . it doesn't destroy them, it just leaves, like, the tiniest of dents. We can only keep them trapped this way for so long and we're all gonna get tired eventually."

"We can get Scott out here," Aveda said, referring to her mage husband. "Maybe he has a spell that will do something?"

"Yes, but calling Scott means one of us has to stop what we're currently doing," Evie said, wincing as one of the stone monsters batted against her fire, kicking up another huge wave. "And who knows if he can actually get here in time?"

"I could call," I said, fishing my phone out of my pocket. "Or text." None of them responded. Really? I was so unimportant I couldn't even make a freaking *phone call* for them? I started punching in a text to Scott anyway.

"Okay," Aveda said, blowing out a long, frustrated breath. "First things first: let's get those people safely to land. Then we'll worry about destroying these monstrosities."

People?

My head jerked up from my phone, and I studied the stone monsters more intently—and saw that the two farthest from land appeared to be dotted with groups of tiny specks. I squinted, trying to get a better look.

Oh. Holy shit. There were *people* trapped on those two giant stone monsters. People holding on for dear life as the monsters swayed and lurched and made their way through the water. People in danger of falling to their death.

"Fuck!" I blurted out.

"Bea!" Evie, finally deciding I was worthy of her notice, swiveled her head to give me an exasperated look. "Can you get to safety, please?"

"I'm here to help!" I protested, drawing myself up tall.

"You can help by getting out of the way," she retorted.

"Evie, if you can make your ring of fire bigger to encompass all of these giant stone things—and Aveda, if you can keep holding the fire in place—I can try using my hair to lift these folks off and bring them to shore in clusters," Shruti said. "It will take a while, but . . ."

"But that seems to be our best option at this point," Aveda said with a grim nod.

I watched as Evie raised her hands and shot more fireballs, bright and beautiful. They arced gracefully as Aveda swept them together in a chain, then added them to the ring hanging in the air, expanding it outward. It wrapped around the giant stones, a truly dazzling sight.

Shruti's hair danced out over the water, reaching for the clump of people trapped on one of the monsters. She started wrapping it around them one by one, bundling them together. Their screams got louder as the monster lurched to the side, sending them sliding along its surface.

"It's all right," Shruti murmured, her hair wrapping more tightly around the screaming people. "Just stay calm, please. And trust me."

I swallowed hard as I scanned the scene. It felt like everything was frozen in this terrible moment, like Evie and Aveda and Shruti were taking things so slowly and deliberately, performing very careful surgery on a massive level, and one wrong move would destroy everything. And here I was on the sidelines, small and insignificant, doing nothing. There was nothing I *could* do. Anything I might try had the potential to totally disrupt their operation. I toyed with the hem of my cape. Why had I even bothered? They were a well-oiled machine and they didn't need me, no matter how many posterboards and glitter bombs I hit them with—

"Help!"

I whipped around. The voice was coming from behind us—away from the water, the danger, the stone monsters. I frantically scanned the waterfront, homing in on the source— a teenage girl with stringy hair and big scared eyes, hugging a notebook to her chest. Had she not evacuated with the rest of the civilians? And why was she screaming for help when she was safe on the shore?

I turned back to Evie and Co. They were still absorbed in their complicated operation. Well, no matter. Here was something I could do. Even if it just involved comforting a civilian who didn't appear to be in actual danger.

I dashed up to her, wincing as gravel poked through the hole in my sole and rattled around in my boot. Leah and I definitely needed to work on footwear.

"Excuse me, civilian," I said, trying to sound all official-like. "You need to evacuate this area. We are working very hard to . . ."

I trailed off as she shook her head at me, a frown overtaking her face.

"Help," she whispered, pointing at the giant stone monsters.

"Yes, I know, they're terrifying," I said. "Which is why—"

CRAAAAAASHHHHHHH

I whipped around to see a massive wave careening through the water as one of the stone monsters crashed through Evie and Aveda's fire wall, sending the people on top of the monster sliding all over the place.

"Shit!" Aveda spat out. "Shruti, grab as many people as you can. Evie, let's try to expand it again—"

But now the monsters had figured out that Evie's fire only caused them minimal damage, and they started busting through in earnest, kicking up more waves and displacing the people clinging to them. The screams intensified, mingling with the crashing of the waves. And the monsters were stomping their way toward shore, the ground shaking underneath us as they got closer.

CRASH CRASH CRAAAAAAAAASHHHHH

I stood in front of the girl, shielding her with my body. Shit. Fuck. What else could I do? I heard Aveda barking at Evie and Shruti, but the actual words faded to a distant burble as the monsters got closer and closer, looming over us like gigantic stone Godzillas. I saw Shruti snatch up the last group of people and move them to shore, but shore wasn't much safer at this point . . .

Maybe I could emotionally project at the monsters, like I

did with humans? *Stop*, I thought at them desperately, even though that wasn't an exact emotion. *Just . . . stop. You want to stop.*

They just kept going. Of course.

CRASSSSSSHHHHHHHHH

"Help," the girl whispered behind me.

Dammit. Maybe this was why Evie could never see me as a real superhero. I mean, all I could *really* do was get people to feel a little differently. What good was that in a situation like *this*? When we were dealing with monstrous, supernatural creatures who were nothing like humans, totally immune to my projection, to my . . . my . . .

Wait a minute.

Something came to me in a flash, a wispy memory from years before: Aveda telling me there was *another* component of my power, something I didn't fully understand, something I'd only used once . . .

"Shruti," I called out. "You got all the people to shore, right?"

"Affirmative," she called back, her voice strangled.

"Okay, then," I murmured to myself. "We're gonna give this a go."

CRASH CRASSSSSHHHHHHHHH

The stone monsters were kicking up such major waves, it looked like the ocean was embroiled in a thunderstorm. And they were really closing in on us. I saw Evie's fire darting around, desperately trying to contain the monsters, only to get extinguished by waves.

I pushed down my mounting fear and focused on a feeling of *rage*. I remembered how angry I'd been last night, when Evie and Aveda had told me *no* yet again. My indignation at their dismissal when I showed up here. I gathered it up, channeled it through my veins, felt the rage down to my very bones.

Then I opened my mouth and screamed.

I screamed long and loud, putting my whole body into it, ripping my throat to shreds. I screamed as much as my breath would allow, balling my fists and squinching my eyes shut and bending backward and sending all of my vocal power in the direction of the monsters menacing the shore. I screamed and I screamed and I screamed.

And when I opened my eyes, the monsters crumbled to dust in front of me.

They disintegrated on the spot, like a bunch of mini avalanches cascading into the water.

Silence blanketed the waterfront, eerie after so much chaos. Evie, Aveda, and Shruti turned to me, their jaws basically on the ground. I turned to see if the girl behind me was okay, but she was gone. Apparently she'd finally taken my advice and evacuated.

"What . . ." Aveda began. But she couldn't seem to think of what came next.

"Goddamn," I murmured, a slow smile spreading over my face. "That actually worked."

MAISY KANE PRESENTS: BUZZ BY THE BAY

By Maisy Kane, Half-Demon Princess Editrix

Hiya, 'Friscans! It never ceases to amaze me how many of y'all have been following me on this little ol' blog, in all its iterations, for so many years now! Some of you have asked me how I manage to track all the latest happenings in the Bay *and* run a smashingly successful lingerie boutique *and* play host to the only Otherworld portal in the whole freakin' city. Dear readers, what can I say? Some of are just born with the gift of multitasking and it is our duty to share that gift with you (especially if you are maybe not so good at it—kiss-kiss, I'm sure you have many other delightful talents).

As usual, most of my reader questions this week are about our fair city's incredible supersquad, Evie and Aveda! Thanks to my close, personal friendship with the girls, I am gosh-danged stoked to be able to exclusively reveal that the rumors are true: the best-selling comic book miniseries based on EVEDA's exploits is about to become an *ongoing series*! Gasp! My skin is clear, my crops are flourishing, and I feel no pain! Really, it's so lovely to witness my dear friends getting the recognition and fame they deserve and to see them win over new fans from all over the world! There are even rumors about Hollywood sniffing around, and who wouldn't want to see this duo of powerful WOC besties kicking ass and taking names on the big screen?! Rest assured that your pal Maisy will keep you updated on any and all developments in that area—I've already picked out what I'm wearing to the premiere!

In the meantime, please enjoy my exclusive gallery of shots from today's Wave Organ battle! Pussy Queen's own Shruti Dhaliwal played an integral role in saving civilians from these menacing stone monsters and I could not be prouder! And as many of you have noted on social, there was a new face in the midst: Evie's little sister, Bea Tanaka, offered up a superheroic assist in the form of a jaw-dropping, stone-shattering scream! It may interest you to know that your pal Maisy witnessed her deploy this unique talent before: back during the climactic battle against the evil Shasta. My goodness, that was one for the ages!

We haven't seen Bea do much superheroing since then, however—could this mean that she's finally following in Big Sis's footsteps?

Dear readers, I'll keep you updated—it's hard to imagine anyone but Evie and Aveda as our ultimate queens, but maybe our favorite squad has room for a new princess!

CHAPTER THREE

"I CAN'T BELIEVE we forgot about your sonic scream." Aveda gave me an approving nod. "Or is it a Canary Cry?" She nudged Evie. "Help me out with the correct nerd term, here."

"That's really only the second time I've deployed it," I said, shrugging and trying to look modest. "And the first time was kind of an accident."

"Right," Aveda said, her brow furrowing. "We should have you do some tests in a safe, controlled environment—"

"Annie." Evie gave us an exasperated look that seemed to say: *Please don't get Bea all excited and think I'm going to agree to actually let her be a real superhero, even after that undeniable display of kickassery. I am still this team's resident stick-in-the-mud, after all.*

Out loud, she just said: "Let's not get ahead of ourselves, okay?"

Evie, Aveda, and I were walking back to Tanaka/Jupiter HQ after dropping off Shruti at Pussy Queen, where she maintained a pop-up version of her fabulous vintage boutique. We first got to know Shruti back when Evie was shopping for a wedding dress—which turned out to be demonically possessed, because of course it did. Shruti became a sort of on-call member of the team, but she preferred to keep things part-time so she could tend to her local fashion empire.

Evie and Aveda both wanted to take an Uber, citing pinchy high-heeled boots (Aveda) and outright laziness (Evie), but I argued that it was really only a few blocks and walking helps shake out those last bits of battle adrenaline. And that as the indisputable day-saver, I should get to pick our mode of transport. (Even though gravel was still rattling around in my hole-y boot and I kept having to shake my foot around to try and get it out.)

My sonic scream, as Aveda had called it, was part of a power level-up I'd gotten when a supernatural earthquake rocked San Francisco during one of Evie's battles against wannabe demon queen Shasta five years ago. At the time, I hadn't known I possessed any kind of superpower at all. I mean, I had noticed that sometimes people got a little cheerier around me when I was happy and a little grouchier when I was going through a day from hell, but I'd always figured that was a result of having, as my mother used to put it, "a big personality." Since I'd started using my power more in recent years, I'd discovered I could control the emotional projection much better—that my moods didn't simply leak out all over people, that I could harness feelings and send them out as I pleased.

Evie had finally realized I had powers—and that they'd gotten an enhancement—when I'd screamed during the climactic battle with Shasta and shattered one of her evil force fields. But we'd never quite gotten a handle on how my power level-up works. Supposedly I could do more with my power if I vocalized the emotions I was projecting in a certain way. And of course I'd experimented with that for a bit, but I hadn't gotten very far with it—it was too vague, too nebulous, and I didn't usually spend my days encountering gigantic, supernatural stone monsters that needed shattering. Until now.

"I'm just saying, that was very kickass, Bea," Aveda said, smiling at me. "A truly show-stopping—and evil-stopping—moment."

"So does that mean I'm ready to join the superteam?" I said, perking up. "'Cause I think y'all would have kinda been shit out of luck if I hadn't been there today, right?"

"We'll talk about it," Evie said. She gave me a slight smile.

"You did great. I'm not trying to diminish that, I just don't want us to make any snap decisions before we've had a chance to talk about everything that needs to be talked about."

I chewed on that as they walked ahead of me, side by side. Evie and Aveda always made for an interesting study in contrasts. Evie preferred the low-maintenance superhero look, and was clad in her usual jeans and sneakers, topped off with a t-shirt with a cute cartoon hedgehog on it. Her dark brown curls floated freely around her face—that face that looked like it was made up of the same components as mine, but perhaps assembled in a different order. (She also has freckles, which I've always been sort of jealous of.) Aveda was wearing a flashy concoction of black leather and silver spandex—and of course her fabulous boots, which had become something of a trademark. Her long black hair was pulled into a sleek power ponytail, the better to show off her flawless bone structure.

As we reached the front door of the lower Haight Victorian that served as our HQ (and our home), Evie turned to me, a shadow passing over her face. "Um, before we discuss anything related to superheroing, there's actually something else I need to talk to you about. I kept trying to call you earlier, but—"

"I hung up on you," I said. "Sorry. I was *really* mad."

"I know," she said, gnawing on her lower lip. She suddenly looked like she was a million miles away. "It's okay. Let's go inside and we'll talk there."

"You got it, Big Sis!" I sang out, throwing open the front door. Damn, I felt *so good* after my triumph. Like I'd finally proved I could be a superhero after talking about it forever. Sam and Leah had watched the whole thing on social media and sent a slew of congratulatory texts, gifs, and emojis to our group text chain. I couldn't wait to recount my adventures for them in even more detail, to really convey the *drama* of it all. I started imagining how I'd tell the story as we filed into the foyer and Aveda slipped off her pinchy boots and let out a big sigh of relief and I—

"Beatrice?"

We all turned. And my jaw nearly hit the floor. Because standing there in front of me was pretty much the last person I ever expected to see gracing the halls of Tanaka/Jupiter HQ.

"Dad," Evie said through gritted teeth. "You were supposed to go take a walk or something, so I'd have time to talk to Bea. We didn't want to freak her out with a big shock, remember?"

"Oh, I know, dear, but you were gone for so long," Dad said, giving her that smile that still had an unmatched ability to charm. I was trying to process the rest of his features, what he looked like now, but I couldn't seem to get past the fact that he was actually *here*. "So I came back, made myself some tea. Your husband didn't seem interested in talking to me, though. I tried to explain that it's very important to have a true and deep bond with one's father-in-law, but—"

"But you have to understand that his basic knowledge of said father-in-law mostly involves you being an absentee loser who doesn't give a shit about your children and can't even be bothered to respond to an occasional email," Evie said, letting out a long sigh and pinching the bridge of her nose.

"Yes," Aveda snarled, putting her hands on her hips and glaring at Dad. "You have not treated Evie well, Mr. Tanaka, and Nate loves her more than pretty much anything and anyone. As do I. So maybe you should *consider*—"

"It's all right, Annie," Evie said, holding up a hand and turning to me. "I'm sorry, this is what I was trying to call you about."

"Bug," my dad said, his eyes softening as he took me in. "You've grown up so much. Oh, my little Bug."

I felt myself stepping forward, hugging my dad. He was saying something else? But I was in a weird fugue state, where everything happened in a blur, and I couldn't tell what was real and people's words were just a bunch of "mwah-mwahs," à la Peanuts cartoon adults. Was I dreaming? Or living in a hallucination? Were we actually still at the water-front and the evil force behind the giant stone monsters had trapped us in some sort of ultimate fantasy holodeck situation?

Then Evie snapped at Dad to go wait for us in the kitchen, and he left and she turned to me all concerned and asked if I actually wanted to talk to him . . .

"Of course I do," I said, my words robotic. "But, um. I need a moment. Alone. To process and stuff."

"Okay," Evie said, patting my shoulder. "You know, if you'd just answered your phone earlier . . ." She bit her lip, as if to suppress her automatic urge to scold me.

"Did he say why he's back?" I said.

"He wants to talk to us about something—he refused to say what until both of us were here," Evie said, her eyes narrowing in suspicion. I couldn't really blame her; Dad had not exactly shown himself to be a reliable parent. "Don't get your hopes up for a big, sentimental reunion, though—you know how he is."

"I know," I said, my voice snappier than I'd intended. "I'm aware that he hasn't been around for most of my life, Evelyn. You don't need to remind me, I was *there*."

"I—" She looked like she wanted to scold me again, then stopped and shook her head. "I know that. I'm sorry." She gave me a tired smile. "Take all the time you need. Come to the kitchen when you're ready."

"Okay. I'll be right back." I waved vaguely toward the stairs. "When I'm done processing."

I scampered up to my bedroom, shut the door behind me, and took in a few deep, cleansing breaths.

So. Dad was back. I could barely wrap my head around that concept. I hadn't seen him in a decade, so I was pretty used to a Dad-less state of being. He'd left when I was twelve—right after Mom died, claimed by cancer. Shattered with grief, he'd wandered the globe ever since, in search of something that would make him feel whole again.

Evie and I had gotten various postcards over the years,

always from some romantic international location and always with some starry-eyed single sentence scrawled on the back ("Peace, love, and llamas" from Peru was still my favorite). We knew he'd eventually hooked up with a self-proclaimed lifestyle guru named Yogini Lara and that he traveled the world with her doing meditation and other deep exercises in mindfulness.

From the beginning, Evie had dismissed all of this as a total crock of shit, and I couldn't really blame her—Dad left her with a bitchy-ass tween to raise (hello!) and a boatload of responsibilities that never should have been hers. At the same time, I couldn't help but be impressed by his finding a way to deal with Mom's death that worked for him. I had never quite managed to do the same. I always felt like there was a big, gaping hole inside of me. The overwhelming sadness I felt when we lost her had faded to a dull ache over the years, but it was always *there*.

If Dad had found something that let him outrun the pain, who was I to judge? And yes, I suppose I'd harbored this childish fantasy that he'd return someday and realize that his daughters would make him way more whole than traversing the world and doing endless yoga with some faux-woke white lady ever would. But that day never came, and then Evie got badly injured saving San Francisco from a wannabe demon queen, and Dad had barely even responded to my email about it. Your oldest child who you've spent most of your life ignoring is at death's door and you can't even spring for a plane ticket? Now *that's* a total crock of shit. So for the past few years, I'd put him out of my mind completely. He wasn't coming back, so why bother thinking about him like he was a real person?

Except now he was back. And he was real. Apparently.

But what did he want? Could it be that after years of claiming to go on a bunch of ill-defined quests, he'd realized he barely knew his own daughters and wanted to make amends? Or was that just another childish fantasy?

I took another few deep breaths until I felt reasonably

calm. I'd just proved myself as a badass superheroine and totally slayed some giant stone monsters, hadn't I? What was a little family drama compared to that?

I straightened my spine and headed back downstairs. The door to the kitchen was shut, and a small crowd of three was assembled outside. Of course. At Tanaka/Jupiter HQ, there's *always* someone all up in your business. Sometimes I liked that—the sense of big family chaos, the sense that something was always *happening*. Other times, I felt like I was surrounded by a bunch of dysfunctional weirdos who couldn't figure out their own lives but had no problem telling me how to live mine.

"Are you sure you want to go in there?" Scott Cameron gave me a teasing grin as he leaned against the doorframe. "Things are . . . well, 'tense' would be the understatement of the year. Decade. Maybe century."

"Move," I commanded, waving a hand. "I need to keep Evie from setting Dad on fire."

Scott laughed, but I could see concern percolating in his gentle blue eyes. "You know you don't have to talk to him, right, Bug? Him just showing up like this doesn't automatically entitle him to your time."

In addition to being one of the only people in the world who could get away with calling me by my hated childhood nickname, Scott was our resident mage and husband to Aveda Jupiter. Both roles required a metric fuckton of patience, and normally I appreciated the extra level of care and empathy he gave to his interactions with people—the way he tried to make you comfortable in situations that had the potential to be the exact opposite. But right now, I felt coddled, treated like the child everyone was so intent on seeing me as. And after all I'd accomplished today, that simply wasn't gonna fly.

"I'm fine," I said, making my tone breezy. "You may let me pass."

"Scott!" Aveda shook her head at him, ponytail twitching with annoyance. "Let her go in. Evie needs back-up. And it can't be me, because I will telekinetically throw that man out the window. Actually, I probably don't even need telekinesis. I could lift him, right?"

"Yes, sweetheart, I imagine you could," Scott said, slipping an arm around her shoulders and giving her a smile that was a perfect mix of amused and adoring.

"I do not believe that would be a productive use of time," Nate Jones interjected, his brow crinkling as he crossed his arms over his burly frame. Nate was Evie's half-demon husband, my brother-in-law, and our resident physician and demonology expert. (He was also the son of the evil Shasta, but they had not exactly had the most loving of relationships.) "Physical violence would only escalate the tension between Evie and her father, when the actual end goal is—"

"She was kidding," Scott said hastily. "Right, Annie?"

"I most certainly was *not*," Aveda muttered. "I mean, he can't weigh more than, what? A hundred-fifty, tops?"

"Guys, this is all so helpful, really," I said. "But if you'll excuse me, I need to get in there and stop Evie from committing patricide via incineration. Oh, and talk to my dad for the first time in forever."

"If you're sure, Bug," Scott said, squeezing my arm. "We'll give you some space for Tanaka family time."

"Best of luck," Nate added. "I tried to engage Evie in meaningful conversation when your father first showed up, but she was not, ah . . . receptive." He rocked back on his heels, his expression turning apprehensive. "So. On Aveda's advice, I have an array of soothing candles ready to be lit, I have added several more decorative pillows to our bed, and I have stocked up on that bizarre ice cream she likes—the one with the breakfast cereal in it."

"Good man," I said. "You're doing everything right. I'll see you on the other side."

I squared my shoulders and marched through the kitchen door. Scott was right about the tension. I felt it as soon as I walked in—I half expected all of our kitchen appliances to be covered in a thin layer of ice. Evie and my father were seated across from each other at the kitchen table, staring at each other in complete silence. Like they were in the middle of a particularly fraught set of business negotiations and were waiting to see who would blink first.

"Bug!" My dad leapt from his seat and enveloped me in a hug. "There you are." He pulled back, grasping my shoulders, eyes searching my face. "You're so . . . well. You've grown up."

"Yes, Dad," Evie said, her voice dry as sandpaper. "That's what happens to kids when you abandon them for a decade. They get older."

"Well," Dad said, clearly trying to keep his jovial tone going. "Well, well, well."

Now that I had more time to take him in, the first thing I noticed was that I was taller than him. I'd gotten all the tall genes from Mom's side of the family, so I suppose that should have come as no surprise, but . . . when had that happened? The second thing I noticed was that he looked shrunken in every sense of the word. He'd never been a big man, but now his wrinkled skin seemed to stretch painfully over his small frame—like it had the consistency of tissue paper and would rip if I so much as sneezed on him. His clothes hung loosely over his body and his fingers resting on my shoulders felt about as substantial as twigs. Seeing him so feeble poked at the delicate places in my heart, the places that could never seem to give up on him entirely. Maybe he was feeling his own mortality, realizing everything he'd missed out on. Maybe he wanted to make up for that. I knew Evie would never give him a chance, but I . . . I couldn't help it. That little spark of hope flared in my chest.

"You look so much like your mother," he said, the last word catching in his throat.

The defenses I'd built up before marching into the kitchen crumbled in an instant, my eyes misting over. I was thrown back to being seven again, cuddled up in a blanket in the warmth of our tiny suburban kitchen. I remembered Dad sitting across from me, passing me a cup of hot cocoa, and brandishing a tiny carved wooden figure.

"Your mom made that," he had said, his eyes shining with pride. "She said she was just fooling around with some old scraps she found at the swap meet, can you believe it?" As I turned the figure over in my hands, marveling at the detail, his voice turned tender. "You're just like her. You see so much beauty—so much *possibility*—in ordinary things."

The warmth I'd felt then swelled in my chest now. "Thank you, Daddy," I said, giving him a small smile. I couldn't look at Evie. She was probably rolling her eyes.

"Sit down," he said, settling back into his chair and gesturing to the seat between him and Evie. "There's something I want to talk to you Tanaka girls about."

"And I guess a letter co-signed by Yogini Lara wouldn't suffice this time," Evie muttered, examining her nails. It was weird how the presence of our father had both of us regressing so quickly. If I was an easily manipulated seven-year-old, Evie was definitely the sulky teen she'd been so many years ago.

"I thought it would be best to do this in person," Dad said. "Also, Yogini Lara told me my inner selves have aligned to the point where seeking in-person closure is definitely the healthiest option."

Oof. I felt a tiny pinprick in my happy seven-year-old's bubble.

"In any case," Dad said, forging on just as Evie was opening her mouth to interrupt him, "I have something for you. Both of you."

He reached into his pocket, pulled something out, and set it on the table. Evie and I leaned in to look. It was a key: small, silver, delicate—and attached to a tiny loop of velvet ribbon.

"Okaaaay," Evie said, sulky teenage voice still in effect. I could tell she was intrigued in spite of herself. "And what's this, exactly?"

"It's the key to a box of some of your mother's belongings," Dad said. "I didn't know until very recently that it existed. I thought all of Vivian's things were gone."

Evie snorted, and I knew we were having a rare moment of sisterly connection, both remembering the exact same thing at the exact same time: Dad right after Mom died, plowing through our house with glassy eyes, boxing up everything she'd owned to give away. He didn't want anything around, not a single solitary reminder. Evie and I had managed to salvage a few things, including Mom's wedding gown. But the majority of our physical memories of Mom had disappeared almost as soon as she did, thanks to Dad's purging crusade.

"You girls remember that swap meet where Vivian had her crafting booth? One of her old swap meet friends found the box and the key when she was cleaning out one of her closets last month," Dad said. "The box itself was too fragile to send, and I guess she tried to reach you by emailing through Evie and Aveda's official website, but no one wrote back."

"We should probably hire an assistant," Evie muttered, twisting her fingers together and glaring at the kitchen table. "We're kind of behind on answering those emails."

I noticed she left the "Ever since Bea threw a massive tantrum and stopped helping us out around here, doing all the bullshit nobody else wants to do" part unsaid.

"So she sent me the key and said I could come pick it up any time," Dad said.

Evie and I exchanged a look, our rare mind-meld still in effect. Was this real? More memories of Mom out there in the world? It seemed too good to be true.

"This friend—Kathy Kooper—also sent instructions for a pick-up," Dad said, rummaging around in his pocket. "Ah. Here we go." He set a worn slip of paper with cramped handwriting on the table. "I believe this is the current location and operating hours of the swap meet. From what I understand, it's really grown over the years. Kathy said she'd hold on to the box until one of us comes and claims it."

"So let's go!" I blurted out, my spark of excitement flaring. "All three of us. A Tanaka family road trip! To, um, Oakland," I added, reading the slip of paper. "Okay, so it won't be a very long road trip, but that's still a good forty-five minutes away, depending on traffic. We can borrow Lucy's car, load up on crappy snacks—ooh! Do you still like corn nuts, Daddy? Did you know they make this ranch flavor now that's kind of gross, but also weirdly delicious, and I think you would totally love it—"

"Bug." Dad held up a hand. His expression had gone distant. "I'm sorry, but I have to leave right away. Yogini Lara has already traveled to our latest meditation spot, and I am behind in my studies with her. I must—"

His voice faded to a burble, and I felt the excited seven-year-old inside of me shrivel up and die. I'd let myself be drawn in by the promise of him, by the stupid hope that he might actually want to spend time with me.

Evie, of course, had known better. And once again, I couldn't bear to look at her, because her expression was going to be an unbearable mix of *Oh, Bea* and *I told you so*. I slumped back in my chair, letting Dad's words wash over me, my spark of hope extinguished.

I'd gone into the kitchen thinking I was going to save our family reunion from combusting—but as it turned out, I was the one who needed saving.

CHAPTER FOUR

I BEGGED OFF katsu dinner with Sam and Leah that night, sending a text to our group chain claiming that the rest of Team Tanaka/Jupiter wanted to celebrate the day's big win with a fancy meal—and since I'd been so integral to said win, my presence was required. That was an outright lie. We were actually having a totally boring, non-celebratory meal, with everyone at varying levels of grouchy over the afternoon's dad drama. But I didn't feel like facing my friends and explaining the whole sordid saga of why I was in a bad mood. Said saga made me look, in my estimation, pretty frakballs pathetic.

Leah texted me back immediately, asking what was wrong—apparently I was just as bad at hiding my feelings in texts as I was in person. Sam texted back congrats on my kickassery, followed by a string of emojis, followed by a gif of a Pokémon group hug.

That made me feel even more pathetic—because it meant he saw through my breezy text, too. Otherwise he would have followed all of that up with some dumb joke about how even my Canary Cry was no match for his undeniable super-powered charisma and didn't I remember how he'd beaten me at calculus during sophomore year, blah blah blah. I could always count on Sam to never feel sorry for me. And the lack of dumb jokes meant he was *definitely* feeling sorry for me.

I slumped at the dinner table, imagining a cartoon rain cloud scribbled over my head. Evie and I were both picking sulkily at our food. Aveda, Nate, Lucy, and Scott were making careful small talk. Lucy's girlfriend, Rose, head of the San Francisco Police Department's Demon Unit, was working late and hadn't been able to join us. I missed her stoic, solid presence—Rose was the kind of person who could soothe your soul with a simple nod.

I stabbed at a clump of rice with my chopsticks. It actually might've made me feel better if Team Tanaka/Jupiter *had* been having a fancy celebratory dinner, but Team Tanaka/Jupiter didn't tend to indulge in those kinds of shenanigans. Well, okay, so Evie and Aveda sometimes liked to have a drink and sing-along at their favorite seedy karaoke joint, The Gutter, but I was always pushing for something more fabulous, like a themed costume/dance party with funny photo booths and a dessert buffet. I mean, didn't saving the world merit that kind of celebration? As usual, nobody listened to me. But on tonight of all nights, I wished we were having a massive celebration, big and loud and over-the-top enough to squash the ache around my heart.

"Hmm . . ." Nate was looking at his phone, his brow furrowed. "Sorry. I know we're all in the middle of, uh . . ."

"Processing the emotional upheaval caused by a certain absentee father's all-too-brief appearance?" Lucy said, arching an eyebrow.

"Yes," Nate said. "But Rose just sent me the results of her team's Wave Organ scan."

"We know the cause, do we not?" Aveda said, waving her chopsticks around. "All roads lead back to the Pussy Queen portal, as usual."

"That's what I'm finding troubling," Nate said, setting down his phone. "Rose's team did a thorough scan of the area and the origin of the supernatural energy . . ." He shook his head, trying to make sense of it. ". . . is *not* the Pussy Queen portal."

"What?" Evie pulled herself out of sulky teenager mode, her head snapping up. "How is that possible?"

"Where did it come from, then?" Scott asked.

"We don't know—the results were inconclusive." Nate leaned forward in his seat, his frown deepening. "Rose and her team have cordoned off the area and will be doing a more comprehensive set of scans tomorrow. For now, the pieces of the Wave Organ that broke off, came to life, and shattered appear to have reverted to their normal state: reconstituted, normal-sized, and not trying to kill anyone. But I think we can all agree the Organ is going to need to stay off-limits to the public until we figure this out."

"Every supernatural oddity we've encountered for the past four years has originated from that portal," Lucy said, shaking her head in wonder. "What does this mean?"

"Certainly nothing good," Aveda muttered, setting her chopsticks down. I could practically see the wheels turning in her head as she started assessing, strategizing, battle planning for this new threat. She was probably mentally slotting a few extra workouts into her already formidable schedule as well.

Nate rested his elbows on the table and steepled his fingers. "There's something else I want to bring up that may or may not connect here. When I first heard about it, it seemed like a blip on the oddity radar, but—"

"But there are no 'blips' on the oddity radar," I said, echoing something he'd said to me once when we were combing through endless amounts of data relating to a rogue demon we'd had to chase down a few years ago. "Only oddities ranging from 'huh, kinda weird' to 'WTF.'"

"Yes," he said, giving me a half-smile. "In any case, a colleague from my demonology grad program recently relocated to Maui—she's from there—and she sent me an email last week describing something that I thought was unusual, but not necessarily cause for alarm. But now . . ." He frowned again. "I'm not sure."

"Okay," Aveda said impatiently, making a circular "hurry up" motion with her chopsticks.

"My colleague, Kai, takes a very early morning walk on her local beach every day," Nate said. "One morning a few weeks ago, she heard cries for help and saw a man struggling in the ocean. She swam out and dragged him to shore. He seemed relatively disoriented and told Kai he couldn't swim. So she asked why he'd gone out so far. And he said . . ." Nate looked up at the ceiling, trying to recall the exact details. ". . . that he'd felt like something was calling to him. That one second he'd been strolling along the beach, the next he'd had this undeniable urge to walk out into the water, and he couldn't stop himself. It was like a compulsion."

"Was he perhaps indulging in some early morning mind-altering substances?" Aveda said with a snort.

"That's what Kai thought," Nate said, his mouth quirking into a half-smile. "She called the paramedics to the scene, but the person who'd walked into the water was unhurt. Nothing seemed all that out of the ordinary." He paused, his frown returning. "Until it happened again the following week."

"What, the same fool walked into the water again?" Aveda said, her eyes widening incredulously.

"A different person," Nate clarified. "But they described the same kind of compulsion to Kai, and it was the same near-drowning. It made Kai wonder if there's something supernatural at work. But if there is, she's not sure where to even begin investigating. She already checked in with local police and hospitals and there haven't been any other incidents along that stretch of beach recently—so perhaps it was only those two cases. I'm going to talk to Rose, see if it's possible to get someone dispatched to scan the area. But it does raise some interesting questions—"

"Well, yeah, it does," I couldn't help but interrupt. Despite my mopiness over Dad, my seven-year-old excitement bubble was inflating in my chest again. I love puzzles, mysteries. Stuff that seems impossible to explain on the surface. Tangled formations with a bunch of seemingly disparate pieces that need to be taken apart, examined, and somehow put back together again. A good twisty puzzle—whether it's in the form of a complex quadratic equation that needs solving or a complicated piece of electronic equipment that needs fixing or a head-scratching demon mystery that needs untangling—is one of the only things that can fully hold my attention for a decent period of time. "I mean, we've never heard of supernatural happenings anywhere else in the world. The Bay Area has always been totes unique in that respect. If the Pussy Queen portal is no longer the only source of supernatural energy leaking into our world . . ." I gnawed on my bottom lip, my synapses firing a mile a minute. "That could be interesting. Super, super freaking interesting."

"Like the demons have figured out *other* ways to come through?" Evie said, her brow crinkling. "That seems more like a recipe for disaster than anything."

"I could go to Maui," I blurted out. "I mean, with Rose or whoever's doing the scan. I'd love to get some firsthand observational data on the area, see if there are any factors that might be contributing to—"

"I thought you wanted to be promoted to full superhero," Evie said, her voice weary. "Right here, in San Francisco."

"I do," I said. "This could be a superhero mission, an away mission—"

"And what about your job at the bookstore?" she said. "You're always talking about how short-staffed you guys are. Are they really going to be okay with you flitting off to Hawaii?"

"I can get time off. Charlotte will give it to me. I mean, I never take vacation days. But wait, let's back up." I leaned in, regarding her keenly. "What's this about me being promoted to full superhero?"

"Like I said before, we'll talk about it later," Evie said, scrubbing her hand over her face.

"It's later *now*," I said, trying to keep the whine out of my voice. But honestly, it felt like every single person I'd encountered today had tried to dismiss me in some way. Ichabod Lite, when he'd seen my clothes and hair and assumed I wasn't worth taking seriously. Nemesis Nicole, who *never* thought I was worth taking seriously. Evie, Aveda, and

Shruti, when I'd showed up at the Wave Organ, ready to help. My dad, when I'd practically begged him to stay just a little bit longer. And now we were back to Evie on the Let's All Dismiss Bea Merry-Go-Round.

I set down my chopsticks and met her eyes. "I don't think there's any denying I saved the day," I said. "Y'all would have been toast without my sonic scream."

"Or is it a Canary Cry?" Aveda muttered. "I never got an actual answer on that."

"That is true," Evie said, activating her soothing, placating tone. "And like I said, we'll talk about it later. With everything that happened with Dad today, I really think it's best if—"

"Why is it always about what *you* think?" I said. "Why are you the grand arbiter of when we talk about things and when we don't? Because this is about *me*. And for the record, I'm just as fucked up as you are about Dad. Maybe even more, since you, in all your usual infinite wisdom, already knew that was going to end badly, and I was the one dumb enough to have any kind of *hope*."

My voice cracked on the last word, and I swallowed hard and glared down at my plate. Rage was roiling through me now, a thick, toxic churn of angry bile.

"I know that," Evie said, her voice shaking as she struggled to keep control. Considering how much we bickered, it was a small miracle she hadn't set me on fire by now. "I'm trying to look out for you, to take care of you—"

"I don't need you to take care of me," I snapped. "Stop trying to act like you know what I need better than I do and talk to me like an actual adult."

The rest of the table had fallen silent while we fought. Even Aveda, never shy about sharing her unsolicited opinion, wasn't chiming in.

"Fine," Evie said, throwing down her own chopsticks and glaring at me. "Let's talk about this now. Aveda and I have discussed it—"

"We have?" Aveda said, her brow furrowing.

"We have," Evie said firmly. "And the answer is still no. You're not ready yet."

"But . . . but . . . how?" I squeaked. "How can I *get* ready? Because nothing I do seems to be good enough for you. You know, you and Aveda weren't exactly perfect when you became superheroes, but you learned on the job—and it helped both of you with your, excuse me, fucking boatload of issues. It helped you become the awesome people you were meant to be. Why don't you want that for me, too?"

My voice cracked again and the last word came out plaintive. I swallowed hard, trying to regain my rage.

"Because I don't know if this is what you actually want!" Evie shot back. "Because you're always getting distracted by whatever the shiny thing of the moment is and you dive headfirst into stuff without thinking. One minute you're in college, the next minute you're dropping out. One minute you're totally into helping Nate with data collection and science stuff, then suddenly you're over it. Then you have this job at a bookstore, and it's the best thing ever. Then, just kidding, the annoying customers make it the most annoying thing ever. Then you claim to want to be a superhero more than anything in the world—but oh, hey, here's this thing in Maui over here! Oooh, something shiny!"

"That's not fair," I said through gritted teeth, blinking back tears.

"I had so many hopes for you," Evie said, her voice tight. "I worked my ass off so you wouldn't be as fucked up as I was. And now—"

"Just say it," I hissed. "Say I'm a disappointment. But you have a pretty easy way of giving me the chance to be something more, if you would just listen—"

"I'm done listening," Evie said. She didn't sound mad, just exhausted. Like I'd wrung everything I could out of her. "You can't join the team, Bea. Stuff like this . . ." She gestured between us. ". . . just proves you're not ready."

"That's not fair," I said again. "That's—"

"It doesn't have to be fair," Evie snapped. "It's my decision, and it's final. Who wants dessert?"

I stood up from the table so fast, I nearly knocked my chair over.

"It's always *your* decision," I hissed. "And you love that, don't you? Lording your power over me. Acting the part of disappointed parent. Treating me like a baby."

"You're *acting* like a baby," she growled.

"Well, I'm not," I said, drawing myself up tall and glowering at her. "I'm not a kid anymore."

For one wild moment, I was tempted to emotionally project something onto her. I don't know what. Something that would show her how unreasonable and unfair and dismissive she was being. Something that would make her feel *bad*. But I couldn't do it. I'd used my powers on Evie once before, and I'd sworn never to do it again. That, too, was part of my code. So instead, I narrowed my eyes at her and said the thing that I knew would hurt her most.

"And despite what you seem to think, despite the way you're always acting, despite the delusion you've been under for the past ten years: you are *not my mother.*"

🔥

I am a champion stewer.

Evie had—at least in the past, before she became all superheroic and shit—always tried her damndest to shove down, repress, and control her feelings. I, on the other hand, luxuriated in them. I always burrowed into a good sulk, like a gopher burying myself in my own little dirt hill of bad feelings. When Mom died, I felt like every cell in my being was screaming in agony, every minute of every day. It had faded to a dull ache as the weeks passed, and then I was blank, deadened, empty—wrapped in an eternal sulk. And I'd luxuriated in that, too. Pulled that feeling close and held it tightly. Because if I let go of it, I'd have to admit my mother, the one person who had understood me above everyone else, was gone.

Mom and I always had a special bond. I was my parents' accident baby, born almost a decade after what was supposed to be their only child. But Mom always went to great lengths to make sure I never *felt* like an accident, an afterthought, an add-on. Dad and Evie had been tolerant of (but kind of annoyed by) the places my boundless curiosity tended to lead me. Mom, on the other hand, actively encouraged me to follow my occasionally out-of-control imagination. I still remembered one day in particular, when I'd been seven. My dad had this collection of vintage radios, radio receivers, and other electronic equipment. He liked to spend his weekend afternoons restoring and carefully cleaning them, and then he'd display them on a pristine shelving unit in the den. My eyes had nearly popped out of my head when I'd seen him remove the back panel of one of his receivers with a tiny screwdriver. Suddenly there was this whole world I'd been previously unaware of, stuffed with crisscrossing wires and gears and what looked like a kazillion moving parts. And then he'd replaced the panel and just like that, this new world disappeared.

I couldn't get that world out of my head, so later that day, when everyone else was otherwise occupied, I'd snuck back into the den, dug out my dad's tiny screwdriver, and carefully removed the back panel of the receiver I'd seen him tinker with. Of course once all of those glorious wires and gears were exposed to me again, I hadn't been able to leave them there—I'd needed to explore. So I'd taken the whole thing apart.

Mom had found me sprawled on the floor with the receiver in pieces around me, carefully examining each one, trying to figure out how the whole shebang functioned. Dad probably would have yelled at me. Evie probably would have been super irritated I'd made such a mess. Mom just surveyed the scene, then plopped herself down on the floor next to me.

"Well, Bug," she'd said, her voice soft and musical. "What's all this?"

I'd very seriously explained what I'd worked out: that the inside of the radio receiver was its own special universe, and I *needed* to know how it all functioned together. I'd shown her which wires connected where, and what made things switch on and off. She spent the rest of the afternoon on the floor with me, listening. I could still remember how she looked at me as I described every detail: like I was a marvel. Like me taking apart one of my dad's prized electronics was something wonderful, rather than the sign of an alarmingly destructive child. She'd even explained the whole thing to Dad later so I didn't get in trouble.

No one had looked at me that way since. I was an annoyance, a pest, a disappointment—always.

But I could still stew with the best of them, and that's what I did after my fight with Evie. I retreated to my bedroom and flopped on the bed, letting the bad feelings wrap around me like vines. My bedroom was, in my humble opinion, the nicest, coziest room in the Victorian. I'd painted the boring white walls a soft lavender and hung up a few of Leah's paintings and mixed media works. She'd done this amazing series of fantastical creatures rendered in bold, abstract lines and somehow made them look at once ferocious and whimsical. I had her fanged mermaid and her murderous Pegasus, and I loved them both very much. Various half-done tinkering projects—bits of electronics and one of my dad's old radio receivers, left behind when he set off on his wandering—were strewn everywhere, along with discarded posterboards from my presentations to Evie and Co. I'd strung twinkle lights everywhere they'd fit, giving my room a fairyland vibe.

If you're going to wallow around in your bad feelings, why not do it in fairyland?

I stewed for about an hour before I got bored, wandered over to my messy work table, and started toying with one of my projects-in-progress. I'd been trying to construct an electric paintbrush cleaning gadget for Leah, something she could stick her brushes in when she was done working and then return to later to find them all nice and washed. I'd

played around with fitting cleaning bristles together in a
plastic canister, and I'd figured out how to automate them so
they would rotate, but I was having a hard time finding a
balance—the rotation needed to be strong enough to provide
a thorough cleaning, but gentle enough to leave Leah's delicate art implements intact.

I gnawed on my lower lip, fiddling with the wiring again.
My brain settled as I worked through the problem, experimenting with different rotation speeds, trying to find the one
that was just right. Or maybe I should switch out the bristles
entirely? Would another material be more effective?

I was so engaged in my project, I didn't hear the soft knock
on the door. Evie shuffled in, looking tired. I didn't say anything as she crossed the room and sat down on my bed.

"I'm sorry," she said without preamble. "You're right,
Bea. I was being unfair."

I was still facing my desk, so she didn't see the shocked
expression cross my face. I set aside my not-quite-finished
paintbrush-cleaning gadget and went to sit next to her. She
flopped onto her back, and I followed suit, both of us staring
up at my constellation of twinkle lights.

"I didn't mean to go all Tiger Mom and put my own fantasy aspirations for you above what *you* want," Evie continued. "The bottom line is I just want you to be happy. Really,
that's it. But sometimes when I see you . . ." She trailed off,
and I could practically hear her thinking, *How do I put this
in a way that doesn't sound totally jerky?*

"Flitting from thing to thing?" I supplied. "Diving into
potentially exciting adventures without thinking them
through even a little bit? Getting distracted every time
there's something new and shiny?"

"I'm sorry," she said again.

"No," I said, focusing on a particularly dazzling cluster of
twinkle lights. "Look, you're not wrong. About all that. And
I'm sorry, too. I said the worst thing I could think of to you."

Somehow it was easier for us to talk like this, not looking

at each other, mesmerized by the web of lights. Maybe we should conduct all our conversations this way.

"Let's call it a draw in this latest round of the sister feels dust-up," Evie said gently. "But there's something else you said earlier that I can't stop thinking about." She hesitated. "About Dad. You said you were dumb enough to have hope. Bea, I . . . I don't think that's dumb. I *love* that so many times, you choose hope. Even when it's not the obvious choice, even when the odds are stacked against it. I love that you can find that hope. You were like that when you were a kid. I mean, you believed in Santa Claus until you were eleven."

"Or maybe I just realized that meant double the presents," I muttered.

But she was right. I'd believed in Santa Claus, the Easter Bunny, and the Tooth Fairy well past the age most kids buy into such things. I *had* been convinced they were all part of a secret cabal, though, and switched off roles every year.

"I saw you lose some of that when we lost Mom," Evie continued, her voice soft and wistful. "I was afraid maybe you'd lost it forever—that ability to hope. But it seems like it's come back the last few years. I mean, you've kept pushing for this superhero thing, even though Aveda and I have said no like a zillion times."

"I guess over the years I've felt like pieces of myself have come back together," I said. "But there's a piece of who I'm supposed to be that I'm always kind of looking for, you know? You're right; I do get distracted by shiny things. My brain always feels like it's overwhelmed by so many thoughts and I can't keep up with all of them." I flipped over on my side to face her. Her face was open, earnest. She was really listening. "I want to have that purpose, like you do. Like Aveda does. I want to be able to *focus* on something that actually excites me. I want to be a superhero."

Evie studied my face for a long time, like she was finally trying to see me for who I was now, rather than the broken twelve-year-old she'd been saddled with all those years ago.

"Okay," she said.

I goggled at her. "What . . . really? That's it?"

"What, you want a parade?" she said, nudging me playfully. "Aveda and I discussed it. We're willing to give you a chance to superhero alongside us on a trial basis. We'll take it one step at a time, see how it goes."

"Like an internship?" I said, cocking an eyebrow.

"Sort of," she said, laughing. "Don't quit your day job. We'll work around it. And we do have some guidelines: you have to actually *listen* to us. And you have to use your power responsibly. No changing people's moods or shattering whatever you want just for the fun of it. I know you, ah, use your power on some of your bookstore customers and I don't love that—and this is a much higher-stakes situation."

"You got it," I said. I still couldn't believe this was happening. "You *so* got it."

"And in return," she said, "I will try my darndest to stop Momming you. I will try to see you—and treat you—like the adult you actually are."

"Can I get that in writing?" I arched an eyebrow.

She laughed again, and threw an arm around my waist, resting her head on my shoulder.

"I love you," she said. "Never forget that."

"I love you too."

Warmth surged between us, and I smiled, reveling in this rare bit of sisterly bonding. In the back of my mind, I knew the peace probably wouldn't last—but just for a moment, it was nice to lie there in silence, watching the twinkle lights blink across the room.

CHAPTER FIVE

I DON'T KNOW what I expected out of my first official day of superheroing, but it was most definitely not the illustrious Aveda Jupiter barging into my room at six a.m., throwing open the curtains, and depositing herself on my bed with the kind of gusto that comes from being a hurricane-like force of nature who is great at kicking ass and bad at listening.

"Buh . . . ?" I sputtered, sitting up and rubbing sleep from my eyes. I'd fallen asleep with a huge, dorky smile on my face and dreamed of fighting an army of gigantic stone monsters that quaked with fear at my presence, then crumbled to gravel at my feet (which, in my dream, were now shod in more durable purple ankle boots with magic hole-proof soles).

"Time to get up, Bea," Aveda said, clapping her hands together. "Didn't you use to be an early riser?"

"Yes, when I was a teenager," I retorted, shielding my face from the onslaught of light pouring in through the window. "My aging body can no longer handle this ungodly hour."

"Nonsense," Aveda sniffed. "This is the hour when I get the most done—because everyone else is still asleep. Now that you are an official superheroing intern here at Jupiter/Tanaka, Inc., you have duties to attend to. And those duties start *now*." She flashed me one of her trademark imperious looks. "You and I are going to head down to Pussy Queen, meet up with Rose, and see if there's anything weird going on with the portal—perhaps it will give us clues about yesterday's Wave Organ dust-up."

"I have questions," I said, holding up an index finger. My

brain was slowly waking up. And it was confused. "One: Is Pussy Queen even open yet? Two: I thought we'd determined the source of the supernatural energy yesterday was *not* the Pussy Queen portal, so why do we think it will give us any clues? And three: where's Evie?"

"Pussy Queen will open at any hour for Aveda Jupiter," Aveda declared, straightening her shoulders. "And yes, we did determine that, but given that the PQP has been the source of all supernatural hijinks for the last four years, it's worth examining in person to see if there's *any* connection. Finally: Evie's still in bed. But she gave me full authorization to take you on this mission and instruct you as necessary." Aveda beamed at me, rubbing her hands together with something that looked way too much like glee. "This is so exciting. We've never had an intern before." She cocked her head at me, her expression turning earnest. "I'm glad our Evie finally signed off on this. As you are and always have been her responsibility, it was her call—and I've told her since the beginning that I'd back her up, whatever she wanted to do. That's part of being on a superhero team—you must always present a united front." She glanced around the room, her brow creasing. "Do you have a notebook or something? I have many important lessons to impart and you might want to write them down."

"I think I'll be all right," I murmured.

"In any case," Aveda continued, "after yesterday's amazing display at the Wave Organ, I believe you deserve this chance. And I am thrilled to provide you with my expert guidance on your journey."

"Wow. Thank you, Aveda," I said, genuinely touched.

She gave me a small smile. I realized then that despite all the time I'd spent fighting to join the team, I hadn't thought much about how Evie, Aveda, and I might work together as a unit. Aveda and I had always had a sort of odd relationship— we'd known each other nearly our whole lives, but we'd become part of each other's worlds solely because of Evie. I didn't know that we had much in common beyond her. We had spent one infamous night getting drunk off our asses, back when I was a rebellious sixteen-year-old and she was supposed to be looking after me, and I'd introduced her to the wonders of the cocktail known simply as "mix everything in your liquor cabinet together." But that had mostly been yet another scheme of mine to get back at Evie for some infraction I couldn't even remember now.

Aveda was sort of like an overly dramatic Auntie I admired from afar: I'd always appreciated her tenacity and confidence and penchant for fabulous boots. Maybe this was our chance to bond?

"Give me a few minutes to get dressed," I said, attempting to shake off the last of my sleepiness. "Then I'll be ready for this mission."

"Excellent," she said, hopping up from the bed. She started toward the door, then turned back to face me, going all serious. "And Bea—"

I leaned in eagerly, wondering if she was about to share something momentous that would totally kick off our epic bonding.

"You really should bring that notebook," she finally said. "I have *so much* to teach you."

"Good morning to you!" Maisy Kane sang out, throwing open the door to Pussy Queen. A twee meowing chime sounded as Aveda and I filed in and Maisy locked the door behind us. "Only our most VIP guests are allowed in at this hour," Maisy continued, making a big show of adjusting the flowery calligraphied sign that declared the store closed. "But of course I am always at your service, Aveda Jupiter." She beamed at Aveda and clapped her flaky gray hands together, her ghoulish glowing eyes sparking with excitement. Aveda gave her a tight smile. Maisy had briefly been one of evil wannabe demon queen Shasta's minions and was turned into a demon-human hybrid in the process. She'd since reformed and built Pussy Queen into one of the most successful small businesses in the city while maintaining various versions of her popular blog.

Aveda has never trusted her, though, and with good reason: Maisy loved nothing more than using her blog to fan the flames of juicy (and usually very exaggerated) gossip—and as one of the city's beloved superheroines, Aveda was often at the center of said gossip.

Maisy might have been annoying, but there was no denying she had good taste: her shop was peppered with creative displays of beautiful lingerie. Lacy wisps of panties were attached to a makeshift clothesline near the front of the shop; colorful scraps of stationery hung next to them, inscribed with explanations of the design origins of each piece. In one of the back corners, a trio of mannequins wearing "superheroine-inspired" looks posed dramatically, flexing their plastic biceps. Another corner housed Shruti's pop-up version of her boutique, racks packed with beautiful vintage dresses.

And smack-dab in the middle of the room was the infamous portal, a malevolent black pit disrupting the shiny pink and white tile of the floor. The portal had opened during Evie's climactic battle with Shasta—the one where I'd let loose with my big scream for the first time—and Maisy maintained it as a tourist attraction, complete with silk ropes cordoning off the area and a "do not touch" sign.

"We need to examine the portal," Aveda said, straightening her spine and giving Maisy a commanding look.

"Indeed, indeed," Maisy said, ushering us to the center of the room, where Rose Rorick was already crouched down, waving a scanner over the jagged black insides of the portal. "Right this way, ladies."

I winced a little as we walked over. I'd forgotten about the broke-down state of my purple ankle boots and jammed them back on my feet this morning in my rush to keep up with Aveda. The sole definitely had nothing less than a full-on hole now, and full-on pebbles had made their way inside, jabbing into the bottom of my foot. I shook my leg around, trying to rid myself of annoying boot debris.

"Aveda, Bea," Rose said, nodding to us as she got to her feet. She turned to me and gave an extra head bob of recognition. "Congratulations on your superheroine promotion," she continued, cracking a small half-smile—which, for her, was the equivalent of an ear-to-ear grin. "Lucy told me. I can think of no one more deserving."

"Thank you so much!" I said, a warm glow blooming in my chest.

"What's this, Bea's officially on the superteam?" Maisy—always in search of a good scoop—cocked her head at us. "Because my readers will definitely want to know—"

"No," Aveda snapped, positioning her body in front of mine, as if to shield me. "She's just starting out, Maisy, she needs to be able to find her way without your intrusive bullshit."

"Ah, but she's in the public eye now, is she not?" Maisy said, giving me a shrewd look. "Surely her superheroing antics are fair game for—"

"Covering newsworthy heroics is fine," Aveda said, crossing her arms over her chest. "Writing long, speculative screeds about her personal life or tearing her down with snarky fashion 'critiques' about whatever she's wearing are not."

Maisy pressed a hand to her chest and made an injured face. "I would never—"

"Yes, you would," Aveda said, her eyes narrowing. "That's what you *do*."

"My angle would be *very* complimentary," Maisy retorted. "All about how a former problem-child baby sister overcame her bratty ways and ascended to sidekick status."

"Doesn't sound very complimentary to me," I muttered.

"Leave us alone so we can work," Aveda said, making shooing motions at Maisy.

Maisy looked like she wanted to retort, but settled for turning on her heel and huffing off.

"That's one of my most important superheroing lessons, Bea," Aveda muttered, her gaze following Maisy as she stalked across the room and started tidying up one of her displays. "Be on the lookout for users who want access to your fame and will relentlessly pick you apart for their own personal gain."

I nodded, trying to take it in. Maybe I should have brought that notebook after all. During my posterboarding, I'd of course thought about the fun parts of superhero fame—the love and adoration of devoted fans, the eventual trading cards and comic book covers featuring me in my glorious sparkly outfit. But I hadn't considered the darker side of being well-known that so often plagued Evie and Aveda.

Even though my sister had experienced a meteoric rise to fame the past few years, I'd remained fairly anonymous. I'd run Team Tanaka/Jupiter's social media for a while, but that was all about shining the spotlight on them, not me, and I hadn't really been interested in developing my own online presence—I wanted to achieve full fabulousness before I put it out there for all the world to see.

Sure, some of the more hardcore EVEDA fans had figured out that Evie Tanaka had a younger sister and that she worked in a bookstore, but the ones who managed to track me down mostly just came into It's Lit and hovered and gawked and whispered. They almost never got up the nerve to actually approach me.

But it was very likely all of that was about to change. What would that be like? Zillions of fans lined up out the door of It's Lit? Catty comments from the Nemesis Nicoles of the world, side-eyeing my loud hair color choices and judging me for who knows what else? Hot takes from people like Maisy that made me feel like I had yesterday, when Evie and Co. had dismissed me as a Kitty Pryde-esque upstart in a goofy costume?

I turned that idea over in my head. I remembered some of the nastier feedback so-called "fans" had posted about Evie and Aveda when I was running their social. I needed to figure out how I was going to deal with that sort of thing. I probably should have thought all this through when I was preparing one of my many presentations, pushing so hard to join the team. I could practically hear Evie lecturing me about jumping headfirst into something without considering any of the consequences.

Well. What did the imaginary Evie know—always popping into my brain to scold me? And why was I letting her suck every ounce of fun out of my big accomplishment? I'd pushed to join the team because I *knew* I was ready. If I could handle the supremely annoying likes of Ichabod Lite and Nemesis Nicole every single freaking day, surely I could handle whatever this superhero gig might send my way.

"Bea?" Aveda shot me a quizzical look.

"Sorry," I said, snapping out of my reverie. "Thanks for the tips, Aveda. You don't need to worry about me, though. I'm not—"

"A baby—yes, I know," Aveda said, one side of her mouth quirking into an amused half-smile. "But you are my intern, and that means I must guide you as best I can. Aveda Jupiter never does anything less than her absolute best. Now. Let us turn to the task at hand." She nodded at Rose. "Shall we get to scanning?"

"Let's do it." Rose brandished the scanner—a clunky gray bar that looked a bit like the hand-held metal detectors wielded at airports by TSA officials. The scanner was part of an array of tech that had been developed back when demons burst through the first Otherworld portal. The initial hope was that these gadgets would be able to detect and predict portals before they opened, but they mostly just sensed lingering supernatural energy, and they were capable of telling us when portals were closed and staying that way. That didn't mean they hadn't been useful over the years— whenever a scanner detected something supernatural, it did a quickie analysis of the elements contained in the energy. If those elements required further analysis, someone (usually Nate or one of Rose's more experienced team members) took the results to a lab to examine more closely.

But the scanners had definitely gotten worn and dated over time. The results they provided had always been kind of unreliable, but now they were straight up wonky. I knew Rose and Nate had been working to get funding to assemble a new development team—they wanted to update the scanners and some of the other demon-related tech. I'd always been fascinated by these bits of tech and itched to get my hands on them and take them apart. I imagined Evie would use that as yet another example of me getting distracted by shiny things—and now that I finally had a chance to prove myself as a superheroine, I'd best focus on that.

"What have we got?" I said to Rose, nodding toward the scanner. As soon as the words left my mouth, I realized I sounded ridiculous—like I was trying to imitate some grizzled crimebuster I'd seen on TV.

"Nothing. I haven't started yet," Rose said, exchanging an amused look with Aveda. My face flushed—we were back to problem-child Kitty Pryde territory. At least neither of them patted me on the head or let loose with an "*aww!*"

Rose held out the scanner, tapped a button, and held it over the portal. I kept my eyes glued to the scanner. If there was supernatural energy present, we'd get a flash and a loud beeping sound and then things would get *really* exciting, and hopefully everyone would forget about me acting like an inexperienced dork. But the early morning silence permeating the store was disrupted only by Maisy shuffling around and rearranging a display on the other side of the room.

"Hmm," Rose said, studying the scanner. "So there's no active supernatural energy present—"

"—and the code you're getting in the read-out area is the code you usually associate with the Pussy Queen portal," I said, leaning over her shoulder and tapping a series of numbers flashing across the small black screen at the top of the bar.

"That's right," Rose said, nodding. "The lack of beeping and flashing means we're in the presence of *dormant* supernatural energy—the portal itself—but this code—"

"—is what's helped you and Nate theorize that all supernatural encounters the past few years have originated from

PQP," I said. "Because this code is always present whenever there's been some kind of incident or attack."

"Correct," Rose said, giving me another half-smile. "Even though the portal itself isn't doing anything terribly interesting, our working hypothesis is that its presence has allowed supernatural energy to leak through from the Otherworld. Or at least that's been the case for the last four years."

"Ever since we dumped our little puppy demon friend back in after it caused all that trouble at Evie's wedding," I said, side-eyeing the portal. "'Cause prior to that, it gave us pretty dead readings, right?"

"Yes, but that could also be due to the unreliability of the scanners," Rose said, shaking her head ruefully. "In any case, the readings we got from the Wave Organ yesterday . . ." She frowned. "They were entirely different from anything we've seen the past four years. What showed up on the read-out was mostly a bunch of garbled, random characters."

"And at least from where I'm standing, it doesn't look like there have been any changes to this portal," Aveda said, casting a suspicious gaze at the black pit on the floor.

Its insides resembled a glittering, jagged crystal, and every time I looked at it, I saw a gaping mouth full of way too many teeth, trying to suck the rest of the room inside.

"That's my conclusion as well—at least for now," Rose said. "I'm going to go join my team down at the Wave Organ and see what they've found—they're doing more thorough scans of the area today, and we're hoping they'll tell us something we can—"

"Rose!" I shrieked, flapping my hand at the scanner. It still wasn't giving us any red flashes or loud beeps, but a bunch of numbers flashed across the read-out area, scrolling by faster than I could catch them.

Rose turned back to the scanner, her eyes nearly bugging out of her head. "Wow," she said, her voice jumping ever-so-slightly from its usual even tone. "What's *this*?"

"I'm ready for it, whatever it is," Aveda snarled, going immediately into her fighting stance. "Show yourself, asshole!"

she exclaimed into the empty air. "I've taken down invisible demons, and I will do it again!"

"Still no beep or flash," I said, holding up a hand. "That means no active supernatural energy, but what is *that* a code for?"

"I have no idea," Rose said, her brow furrowing as she studied this new barrage of numbers. "Of course, it could be a glitch. But this is so strange. Do you think Nate could take a look? I really need to get down to the Organ."

"I'll take the scanner to him, you go to your team and do what you need to do," Aveda said, holding out a hand. "Oh, and Bea, this is another good lesson for you to write down: A heroine is only as good as her team. We must endeavor to always support each other in order to accomplish the maximum amount of superheroing possible."

"What's this about teamwork?" We turned to see Shruti strolling up to us, beaming. As usual, she was wearing a fabulous vintage frock—emerald green with lacy cap sleeves and a full skirt. "Hello, all," she continued. "Don't let me disturb you, I came by to do inventory before the shop opens."

"Bea's joined Evie and me on an official superheroing internship basis," Aveda said. "I am instructing her on all the finer points of how to get the job done."

"Ah, fabulous," Shruti said, clapping her hands together. "And is this your first official mission, Bea?"

"I guess it is," I said.

Wow. I hadn't even thought about that. I should have done something to mark the occasion—but Aveda had roused me so unexpectedly early, I'd barely had the chance to down a granola bar and a glass of orange juice before leaving the house. I hadn't texted anything to my group chain with Sam and Leah—usually the first thing I did when something momentous happened. In fact, I'd stayed up so late hashing things out with Evie, I hadn't even talked to them about my new gig.

"And how does it feel?" Shruti prompted.

I bit back my first instinctual reply, which was: *Kind of boring, actually?*

I mean. Aveda had dragged me out of bed super early, we'd come over here and taken one piddly scan, and I'd spent almost the entire time feeling like everyone was still determined to treat me like a baby even though I was a shiny, full-fledged superheroine now.

I guess I'd expected a little more excitement? A little less of the "*aww*" face from people who were supposed to be my colleagues? And I *definitely* could have done without Maisy calling me a problem child. The only thing that was even a little bit interesting were those weird numbers that had popped up on Rose's scan. But . . . I could still *make* things exciting, couldn't I? Slap some glitter on this outing and make it at least as fabulous as my posterboard presentations.

"Um. It's great!" I said, making my tone as perky as possible. "In fact, let's take a commemorative selfie so I never forget this awesome moment."

I whipped out my phone and Aveda, Rose, and Shruti gathered around me. I framed us so the portal was in the background and snapped away, trying to give the camera my best powerful superheroine expression. Then I sent the picture to Sam and Leah. I didn't include any explanation; I wanted to tell them everything in person. But this would definitely get them intrigued, thereby setting up my story for max drama potential.

It was only later, when I looked at the picture again, that I realized I was the only one attempting any kind of powerful superheroine expression. Everyone else was turned toward me, smiling indulgently—and they totally had the "*aww*" face.

CHAPTER SIX

"**I THINK THE** cape should have a more dramatic collar,"
Leah said, sketching it out as she talked. "It will really frame
your face in all those publicity shots—they're taking official
publicity shots of you, right? To announce that you're joining
the team?" She looked up from her drawing inquisitively.

"The only thing that can improve a cape is more drama," I
said, trailing my fingers over the drawing. "But you know, I
don't think we're doing PR pictures or anything like that. This
is a trial period, after all. I still have to prove myself worthy."

"You can do it, Bebe," Leah said, nodding defiantly at her
sketch.

I smiled at her, my heart brimming with affection. I'd
booked it over for my shift at It's Lit after Aveda and I had
finished up our mission and I'd meant to wait for Sam to
show up before I fully spilled the beans—but Leah had a
million questions about the mysterious photo I'd sent, and I
couldn't resist telling her everything. She'd been so excited,
letting out a squeal and sweeping me into a bone-crushing
hug. Then she'd settled in to add more flair to our costume
design. All this had re-set my mood and now I was back to
being excited about my new superheroic status.

I may have the ability to shift people's mental states, but
Leah's infectious enthusiasm is the true game-changer.

The store was pretty quiet, so I spent most of the morning
creating a display of paranormal romances featuring scien-
tist heroines. Then I trawled the internet for different kinds
of bristles I could test out in my paintbrush cleaning gadget.

Finally, I did my weekly dusting of Charlotte's porcelain unicorns, making sure all their horns looked sufficiently sparkly. Through it all, my gaze kept wandering to my phone, hoping for a Bat Signal-type call from Evie or Aveda about some exciting new mission. That hadn't happened yet, so now I was "helping" Leah. She was perched on a stool next to the register, her various drawings spread out in front of her. I was sort of half-sprawled on the front countertop, fantasy images of my grand superhero exploits playing on a loop through my brain.

"What do you think, Pancake?" Leah said, waving her sketch at the dog, who was lounging on his special pillow next to the register. Leah had embroidered the pillow with adorable images of various breakfast foods, and customers were always trying to buy it from her. But it was one of a kind, for Pancake and Pancake only. Pancake, for his part, snuffled indifferently, then went back to napping.

"So blasé," Leah muttered, shaking her head at Pancake's snoring form. He was wearing his little superhero cape again, and it wrapped around him like a cocoon. "Maybe we should add bacon to your costume. Then he'd care."

"Not a bad strategy," I said, laughing a little and allowing my eyes to wander around the mostly empty store. My gaze landed on a cute girl perusing Paranormal Romance—she had close-cropped, irresistibly mussed black hair and striking dark eyes that were super-seriously scanning the book she'd picked up. She was dressed in a cool leather jacket and studded boots and . . . I cocked my head, scrutinizing her more closely. She had paint smudges on her hands. Maybe she was an artist?

I looked from her to Leah and back again. It had been my ultimate goal to set Leah up with her perfect love match since the day we met—which was just after I'd had another fight with Evie about my decision to drop out of college. Well, technically I'd decided not to go at all. I had *preemptively* dropped out. I'd been offered a full scholarship to San Francisco State (the only place I'd applied), but I'd declined it at the last minute, figuring I didn't really need to go to a bunch of classes that were just going to bore me anyway since I already knew what I wanted to do with my life. I wanted to be a superhero. And some other kid who really wanted that scholarship and that opportunity should have it instead.

Evie had been furious and HQ turned into a war zone for a while. After one of our particularly explosive fights, I'd been moping down the street, thinking maybe I'd drown my sorrows in ice cream or something. But all thoughts of sugar-related wallowing had evaporated when I saw the It's Lit window. It featured a display of Cozy Fall Comfort Reads—books cuddled together on a bright orange and red papier-mâché couch with tiny papier-mâché cups of cocoa in front of them, topped off with tiny cotton ball marshmallows. It was totally adorable and warmed my cranky heart. And right in the middle was a tome that was my favorite of all time, its cover a brilliant rainbow of neon hues.

Walking into the store felt like walking into a hug, all that light filtering in through the big windows and casting gentle shadows on the cushy pink couch and the whimsical porcelain unicorns. Leah was behind the counter, sketching. She didn't have Pancake yet, but sometimes I imagined him there retroactively, giving me his disdainful one-eyed stare.

"Hey," I said to her. "I wanted to ask about one of the books in the window, um . . . the really colorful one?"

"Ooooh!" she said, looking up, her eyes sparkling. "That one's fucking brilliant. It's a little older than a lot of the titles we sell—but, you know, the tale of a female dragon shape-shifter/biology professor who devises a cure for the plague that's nearly wiped out the dragon population—"

"—and ends up finding love with the reformed dragon-hunter who's supposed to kill her—"

"—is timeless!" we'd shrieked together, then dissolved into giggles.

"Seriously, though, it's like the author bottled up pure joy in book form," Leah said, swooning.

"Yes!" I said. "I read it when I was eleven and what's always stuck with me is how happy I felt while I was turning the pages."

"Eleven!" Leah said, one eyebrow shooting up over her glasses frames. "A little young and innocent for some of the, um, mature scenes in that book, no?"

"My mom gave it to me!" I said, laughing.

"Daaaaaaamn," she exclaimed, thumping a fist on the counter. "Your mom sounds cool as hell. Does she still rec awesome-yet-possibly-inappropriate books to you?"

"Um . . ." My expression froze the way it always did when someone unwittingly referred to my mother in the present tense. I still had my precious copy of the book she'd given me, my name scribbled on the inside cover. I was always looking for additional reading copies so I could keep this original book all nice and perfectly preserved—one of the few mementos I had left of Mom.

"Oh, no!" Leah said, her face twisting in regret. "That was a wrong thing to say, I can tell. No need to explain *why* it was a wrong thing to say—let's save that for later in our friendship."

"How do you know we're going to have a friendship?"

"I can just tell." She held her fingertips to her temple and narrowed her eyes. "I think we have some kind of Hapa telepathic connection going on. No words need to be spoken, we just understand each other instinctively."

"Ah, the understanding that comes from being asked 'what are you?' by supposedly well-meaning people across the board," I said, cocking an eyebrow.

"Indeed." She held up her sketchbook, so I could see what she was drawing. "I'm trying to create this fierce Blasian mermaid heroine—Black and Korean, like me. I figure when people give me the 'what are you?' spiel, I can hand this to them and it'll explain everything."

"She's incredible," I said, marveling at the bold lines, the mermaid's arresting stare. "You're an amazing artist. Do you think you could give her a Japanese-Irish mermaid friend to hang out with?" I gestured to myself.

"But of course," she said, laughing.

"Did you do the window display, too?" I asked.

"I did!" she said, grinning proudly. "And let me tell you, getting those cotton ball marshmallows just right was a *bear*."

We'd ended up talking for three hours, and she'd sold me the window copy of the dragon-shifter lady book. The next day, Leah had recommended me for a job at the store—which I'd enthusiastically accepted. It had seemed like a good way to have my own thing, away from Team Tanaka/Jupiter, while I prepared for my eventual superheroing career—particularly since Evie and I were at such odds. Soon, I was picking up more and more hours at the store and spending way less time at home. I quit doing all the grunt work and assistant-type tasks I'd been assigned at Jupiter/Tanaka, Inc. I even stopped helping Nate with all his demonology research stuff. I'd always truly enjoyed that part of it, but I felt like I had to draw a firm boundary with Evie and Co.—if they were ever going to see me as anything but a convenient add-on to the team, if I was ever going to forge a superhero identity that was mine and mine alone.

This meant Leah and I spent every waking hour together, and *that* meant I was constantly impressed by her huge, open heart, by the way she put so much love into the world without knowing if she was going to get it back.

I really *wanted* her to get it back. That's why I was so determined to find her a love match. And since I'd accomplished another one of my ultimate goals in getting promoted to superhero . . . maybe I could make it two for two?

I glanced at the cute girl in Paranormal Romance again and focused, concentrating on a feeling of desire. Desire to approach this front counter. Openness to conversation. To making a new friend. A *really cute* new friend with wild curly hair and a gigantic heart. Then I sent it spinning in the girl's direction.

I set it at a gentle pulse—firm, but not too over the top. The girl looked up from the book she was perusing and cocked her head to the side, like she'd just heard a particularly interesting song. I kept the pulse going.

Come on, come on . . .

The girl turned and started walking toward us and I did a tiny internal fist-pump.

"Hi," she said, smiling brightly as she strolled up to the counter. "My name is Reshma and I, uh . . ."

Leah looked up from her sketch. Pancake raised his head and regarded Reshma suspiciously. Ugh, don't fuck up my matchmaking, Pancake.

"You want to buy that?" Leah said, gesturing to the book in Reshma's hand.

Reshma glanced at the book and her brow crinkled, like she'd forgotten she was holding it.

"Uh, yes?" she said.

"You sure about that?" Leah said, chuckling and holding out her hand for the book. Reshma passed it to her, still looking vaguely confused. "Ah," Leah continued. "This is a good one: it has man-eating fairies. So. Much. Blood."

"That sounds cool," Reshma said, perking up again.

"Tell you what, if you don't like it, bring it back and exchange it for something else," Leah said, ringing her up. "My customer satisfaction guarantee is that you will wholeheartedly love whatever book you choose to spend money on here."

"Wow, thanks!" Reshma said. Her expression was still somewhere between bright smile and confusion. She gave Leah a final nod as she took the book and headed out.

"She was cute," I said, examining my nails.

"Bebe." Leah shook her head at me in exasperation. "Stop trying to set me up."

"What!" I tried for an indignant face. "I would never—"

"You do," she said, laughing. "Every freaking week. You compel some poor guy or girl to come up to the register and they have no idea why they're here."

"I just want you to have the fabulous romance you

deserve," I said. "A romance worthy of all the tomes you love in this bookstore. Something to make our favorite dragon-shifter lady proud." Pancake sniffed in agreement.

"I want to get with someone who likes me for me, no mental manipulation required," Leah said, arching an eyebrow.

"They would like you for you," I protested. "All I'm doing is encouraging them to come up to the counter and be, like, open to friendship. I can't *make* them like you if they're truly not into it. And even if I could do that, I wouldn't. Because, gross. Also totally against my code. But anyone who's around you for more than two seconds *should* like you. 'Cause you're awesome."

She tried, unsuccessfully, to suppress a smile. "Why don't you focus on your own love life?"

"I don't have one," I said. "Unless you count 'string of fun, sexy encounters with people who can never hold my interest for more than two seconds as a love life."

"Everyone's on their own journey," she said, shaking her head at me. "As long as that's what you want, I'm totally for it. We all deserve our dragon-shifter lady happy ending."

I grinned at her. I liked to think I was already living my dragon-shifter lady happy ending, at least when it came to romance. I had been so shut down and grieving in my teen years, I'd never opened up to any kind of hormonal adolescent explorations. There simply hadn't been room for it in my landscape of pure pain. But once I'd started the gig at It's Lit, I'd suddenly found myself meeting so many attractive people, and most of them wanted to talk to me about books, which made them even *more* attractive.

There'd been Noah, who was soft-spoken and academic and engaged in intense conversations with me about the mechanics of wereporcupine shifter mating rituals. I'd lost my virginity to him in the bookstore's cramped stockroom on a deliciously sleepy summer afternoon full of hazy sunlight and meandering conversations about all the ways certain kinds of fantastical creatures could be truly stimulated. (After a while, though, it seemed to be all he wanted to talk about, and I had interests beyond yeti erogenous zones.)

Then there was Jasmin, who was athletic and constantly caffeinated and had a thing for a long-running series of doorstopper novels about ancient covens of witches bending space and time. She always wanted to go on big, outdoorsy adventures—which were fun, but kind of same-y after a while. After her came Preeti, a cute-as-a-button stand-up comedian who liked to party and hated sleep—and who I ultimately had to stop seeing because I *love* sleep. And then Cade, a ridiculously hot dude model for romance novel covers, who was the strong, silent type—and ended up being a little too silent for my liking.

And the list went on. I always loved the initial stages of dating and hooking up: the thrill of discovery, the excitement of that little magnet pull of attraction, the delight in figuring out what kind of pleasure you most enjoyed giving each other.

But after that first fizz wore off, I always found myself bored and wishing I was hanging out with Sam and Leah instead of trying to entertain this person I didn't actually know super well. As I'd bragged to Sam, I had a flawless record of drama-free breakups, though, which meant all of my exes still patronized It's Lit—no muss, no fuss.

I'd like to think my favorite dragon-shifter lady would be proud of my ability to have so much pure, no-strings-attached fun.

"Let's get back to your cape," Leah said, turning to her sketches.

"Are you guys out of scones or what?" Sam strolled up to the register, coffee cup in hand.

"Where did you come from?" I said. "And did you serve that to *yourself*? Have you declared the café area a total free-for-all, customers-do-whatever-they-want zone at this point?"

"I came in the café entrance. And there's no one actually

working in the cafe," he said, shooting me and Leah a pointed look. "So I had to take matters into my own hands."

"We're doing important stuff over here, Sammy," Leah said, her tongue poking out between her lips as she focused extra hard on her drawing. "Bebe's been promoted to full superhero—"

"Pending a trial period," I interjected.

"—and we need to make sure she's ready and raring to go," Leah said.

"Wow," Sam said, cocking his head to the side, surprise overtaking his face. "So that's what that picture was about this morning. Congratulations. I know you've been wanting that for a while."

"I have. And no need to look so shocked, dude. My heroing work in yesterday's stone monster battle was real A-plus stuff."

"Oh, it absolutely was," he said, some semblance of his usual cocky grin returning. "How was the big celebration last night?"

"Yeah, you missed some primo katsu action, Bebe," Leah said. She pressed her fingers to her lips, kissing them in exaggerated fashion. "*Mwah*."

"Oh, it was . . . um. It was great!" I said quickly, my smile becoming a little more forced. I'd forgotten about Team Tanaka/Jupiter's completely awkward, not-at-all celebratory dinner. Not to mention the dad drama that had come before it. Normally I would have downloaded about the dad stuff to Sam and Leah, but my excitement over being promoted had temporarily displaced my disappointment. Now it came rising back up again, mixing in with the excitement. Extreme emotion stew.

Replaying the night before also reminded me of something. Before Evie and I had gone to bed, I'd volunteered to trek over to the Oakland swap meet—now known as the Grand Lake Market—to pick up Mom's mysterious box of belongings from her old friend, Kathy Kooper. Evie had wanted to come with me, but she and Aveda had a personal appearance at Shruti's boutique that was set to take up most of the afternoon.

"Sam, I need a ride somewhere," I said, poking him the arm.

"What, like, now?" He set his empty coffee cup on the countertop and goggled at me.

Leah flicked the cup and made a tsk-ing sound. "No food trash by the register." Pancake snorted in agreement—or maybe he was snoring, I couldn't tell.

"Yes, now," I said, glancing at my watch. "My shift's over in five minutes and I need to go to the Grand Lake Market."

"You need to go all the way to the East Bay?" he said, incredulous. "That is a *trek*, Beatrice."

"I know, we have to cross a whole dang bridge," I said. "Come on, it'll be fun. Like a road trip. And they have tons of good food at the Market. We'll get elephant ears."

"I have things to do—"

"No, you don't," I said sweetly. "Your shift on Thursdays is in the morning. Therefore you are done with work. Therefore you have plenty of time to drive me to the East Bay and back."

"Sounds like a convincing argument to me," Leah said, not looking up from her sketch.

"Thank you!" I said, sashaying toward the bathroom. "I'll go freshen up and then we can go. Back in a jiff!"

I was out of earshot before he could protest. I shut myself in the bathroom and scrutinized my eye makeup in the mirror, then ran my fingers through my hair. What would we find in this mysterious collection of Mom's possessions? The thought provoked a little flutter in my stomach. I had twelve years of memories of Mom, of course (well, twelve-ish, it's not like I remembered my illustrious newborn era). But they seemed to get more hazy and fragmented as the years went by. I remembered a cascade of wavy dark hair and sparkling green eyes and a voice that sounded like music when she was happy and like iron when she was raging. Evie always liked to teasingly note how much I looked like Mom when I was totally pissed off.

"You've got that Tanaka Glare," she'd say, mostly admiringly.

Sometimes I wondered if time altered these scraps of memory, made them larger than life, distorted them as they faded and as we held on to them harder. Maybe whatever was in this box could provide us with something more solid.

Yeesh. Way to go all philosophical, Bea. It's probably just a bunch of junk.

I ran my fingers through my tangled hair one more time, then turned toward the confession wall, idly scanning to see what sentiments had been added today.

Someone complaining about their mean boss.

Someone extolling the virtues of acknowledging inner beauty.

Someone gleefully noting, "I AM NASTY AND I LOVE IT," accompanied by a doodle of a smiley face with devil horns.

And over on the far right side, it looked like someone had responded to my manifesto from yesterday—

I did a double take. I'd been expecting passionate expressions of *Hamilton* fandom or maybe for someone to write out more lyrics. But there, in small, neat, cursive script was a more thoughtful response. I stepped closer, scrutinizing it. Under my proclamation of, *I will be the greatest superhero of all time, Just you wait*, someone had written:

You're on the right path, my darling—the way you used your mental gifts to take down that awful man yesterday was truly a marvel to behold.

Well, that was nice, but . . . a shiver crept up my spine. How did this rando *know* exactly what I'd done? To the casual observer, it should've looked like I was placating a difficult customer in a very mundane way—by talking him down. Only Leah, Sam, and Charlotte had known what I was actually doing, and this didn't sound like any of them. There hadn't been many casual observers. Sam's date. Nemesis Nicole. Neither of them were aware of my power. At least as far as I knew. And beyond all that, how had the person responding to me here *known* I was the one who'd written this "just you wait" manifesto in the first place? Like everything else on the wall, it was unsigned. Anonymous.

I frowned at the wall, as if I could will the scribbled words to reveal more information. Did I have a stalker? A stalker who wanted to leave me extremely complimentary messages on the bathroom wall? That didn't seem like stalker behavior—

"Bea! We need to go!"

I whipped around to see Sam burst in, looking put out.

"Hey!" I snapped. "You can't just barge into the bathroom like that! What if I had been naked?"

"Why would you be naked?" he said, shaking his head. "Come on. If you want to get to the East Bay and back before rush hour, we need to hurry."

"I . . ." I turned back to the wall. My mind was racing, I had no idea what to make of this, and I felt like I was being pulled in a zillion different directions at once.

"What?" Sam said, sidling up next to me. "You . . . what?"

I turned to face him. So much had happened in the last twenty-four hours, and I felt like I was drowning in an even more complex stew of emotions, like a tsunami of conflicting feelings was crashing through my entire body. It reminded me a bit of how Evie said she felt before she'd gotten control of her fire, when her stew of feelings had caused her to do stuff like burn down an entire library.

Well. Unlike her, I'd never been one to bottle things up.

"My dad visited last night," I said abruptly. "Yes, the one I haven't seen in ten years, and yes, I totally thought maybe he was gonna stay for longer but of course he took off right away, and then Evie and I had a huge fight but we made up and that's when she said I could officially become a superhero, but also my dad gave us the key to a box of my mom's stuff that we didn't know existed, and I have to go to the Grand Lake Market to get it and *then* . . . I saw that someone had written this in response to a thing I wrote yesterday, and it wasn't you, was it? Because it's super weird. And I'm just having a lot of feelings right now. I'm so stoked about being a superhero, but I'm also kinda fucked up about my dad, and then this thing on the wall makes me feel . . . well, weird, like I said. Just weird."

I stopped to take a breath. Sam blinked at me, then shifted his gaze to the writing on the wall.

"I did not write that," he said slowly. "And it doesn't sound like Leah or Charlotte, so . . ."

"So I have a mystery admirer," I said, trying to make my tone light.

"Yeah." He frowned. "Let's talk in the car, see if we can figure out who it might've been. And Bea . . ." He met my eyes. "That's a lot. With your dad and everything. Do you need . . . a hug?" He held his arms out.

I just stared at him. And then, improbably, felt a giggle bubbling up in my throat. He looked so serious standing there, arms outstretched, his face settling into a more sober version of the smolder he had in his half-naked calendar shot.

The giggle escaped—I couldn't help it. He looked way too ridiculous.

"Sorry, I'm sorry!" I exclaimed, clapping my hands over my mouth.

"What the hell," Sam said, his arms falling to his sides. "I'm trying to be all sensitive and shit, and you are totally ruining it."

"I know," I said, still giggling. "I appreciate the effort, I really do, but you looked so much like Calendar Sam just now, and I know the effect Calendar Sam has on almost every breathing Bay Arean who likes men, but I just . . ." I dissolved into giggles again, leaning back against the bathroom wall.

"You truly know how to wound, Beatrice," Sam said.

I stood up straight, wiping my eyes. "I don't need Calendar Sam. I actually can't think of *any* instance wherein I would need Calendar Sam. But I'll take Supportive Friend Sam."

"And what would Supportive Friend Sam do in this situation?" he said, cocking an eyebrow.

"Drive me to the East Bay, of course," I said, giving him a winning smile and sweeping toward the bathroom exit.

CHAPTER SEVEN

THE GRAND LAKE Market is a mish-mash of stuff that doesn't really go together. There's food ranging from junky to artisanal, crafty knick-knacks, and a lady who sells nothing but obviously counterfeit t-shirts for big pop culture franchises. There's also a seasonal carnival with its own separate entrance that sets up adjacent to the Market during the warmer months. It was chugging merrily along today, the bright, primary colors of the Ferris wheel pinwheeling lazily through the sky.

By the time Sam and I reached Kathy Kooper's booth, I had already purchased a tiny glass-blown unicorn for Charlotte, a t-shirt with the words STAR WARS plastered over a picture of a Klingon for Leah, and an elephant ear for me and Sam to share. In theory, anyway.

"I've eaten almost all of this," I said, waving the pastry under his nose. "Are you cutting carbs or something? Don't want to mess up those muscles?" I poked his arm with my sticky, sugar-covered finger.

"You crammed like eighty percent of that thing in your mouth so fast, I didn't have a chance to get to it," he said, giving me a look that was somewhere between amused and exasperated. "You are the worst food sharer in the history of ever."

"A-ha! Bea: 1275, Sam 1162," I crowed triumphantly.

"Anyway," he said, rolling his eyes and gesturing to a booth across from where we were standing, "is this the place? Do you need to gear up emotionally before we approach?"

"I'm all good," I murmured, my eyes locking on the stand. I shoved the last twenty percent of elephant ear in my mouth.

"Let me hold your . . . uh, stuff," Sam said, reaching for the bag containing the souvenirs I'd gotten for Leah and Charlotte. "In case whatever she has for you requires both hands."

I took in the details of the booth as we walked up, trying to soak them in. I was hoping the visual of the booth would jog my memory, causing more visions of Mom to materialize. Kathy Kooper's booth was a bit of a jumble, a collection of three tables pushed together in a "u" shape and covered with a rickety looking tent to shade everything from the sun. Her wares included jewelry made out of old buttons and keys, a collection of handmade glass vases, and some knitted scraps that looked a bit sparse and tuft-y. These were haphazardly spread over the colorful scarves that served as tablecloths.

I had a flash of standing behind one of those tables as a kid, savoring the sugary goodness of an elephant ear and listening to Mom's bright jangle of a laugh as she assembled her various crafts. I also remembered then that Kathy's knitted wares were made of cat hair she gathered herself. Even as a kid, I thought that was kind of gross.

Kathy's booth was next to a stand selling giant pretzels—probably pretty good ones, as they had attracted quite the crowd. A dude in a giant pretzel mascot costume stood out front, passing out flyers.

"Giant pretzels!" he bellowed, just in case the costume, the flyers, and the sign proclaiming GIANT PRETZELS SOLD HERE didn't convey the purpose of the enterprise. "Come get a pretzel as big as your head!"

"Let's get one of those before we leave," I said to Sam.

"How are you still hungry?!" he countered.

"Hey!" Kathy Kooper yelled at the guy in the pretzel costume. "Quit encroaching on my territory! You're only allowed to have an out-of-booth mascot if you stay within the hundred-foot radius allocated to you by the Market."

"The crowd is taking up all the space where I'd normally stand," Pretzel Guy sniffed. "It's not my fault our pretzel delights are so popular."

"No, but it is your fault you're such a freakin' pill," Kathy muttered.

"Um, hi . . . Ms. Kooper?" I said, as Sam and I approached.

Kathy turned away from the pretzel man and goggled at me, her eyes widening. "Is that tiny Beatrice?" she exclaimed. "Oh my goodness. You've grown up so much! And please call me Kathy. We're all adults now, aren't we?"

"Yeah, I guess we are," I said. "Thank you." *Thank you?* What the hell. What was I thanking her for? I suddenly felt ultra awkward, like I didn't know what to do with my hands or my feet or my whole entire body. How are you supposed to act around your dead mom's friend?

Kathy was another part of my mom's life I remembered in flashes, but seeing her in person helped make the picture a little more clear. She was a tall white woman with long scraggly blonde hair, piercing blue eyes, and a tendency to wear a lot of velvet and whimsical hats. I recalled her being loopy and scattered, and she hadn't cared much for kids, keeping Evie and me at arm's length most of the time. But she and Mom had been close—another wisp of a memory danced through my head, Mom murmuring to Dad that Kathy didn't have many other friends. Her cats, her crafts, and the booth at the swap meet were her whole world.

I realized then that I hadn't said anything for several seconds, leaving a gulf of awkward silence between us. Kathy didn't seem terribly affected—she was still beaming at me. Maybe she felt more comfortable around me now that I was a (sort of) grown-up.

"I'm Sam," Sam said, stepping forward and holding a hand out. "Bea's friend." He flashed a softer version of his heartthrob grin and gestured to the assortment of jewelry and knits on the tables. "I love your stuff, it's all so creative."

"Oh, thank you!" Kathy said, her hands fluttering around.

"I collect all the cat hair myself. Gives it that special art-isanal touch."

"I can see that," Sam said, grin still in place.

"Mmm," Kathy responded, flushing a bit. She gave Sam a not-at-all-subtle once-over.

Oh, brother. I shot him a look. Did he really have to deploy that charm on *everyone*? It didn't exactly seem appropriate in this situation. On the other hand, I guess he'd filled that awkward silence I'd left sitting there. And Kathy was certainly enjoying whatever show he was putting on, her gaze lingering on the way the thin cotton of his t-shirt hugged his broad chest.

"So my dad came by with this key . . ." I said.

"Yes! The key!" Kathy said, tearing her eyes away from Sam's pectorals. "I've been holding on to Vivian's box for you, let me go get it."

She shuffled over to a corner of the booth sectioned off by a janky cardboard partition, disappearing behind the cardboard then returning with a small, colorful container about the size and shape of a shoebox.

"Here you are," she said, passing it to me.

I couldn't help but run my hands over it reverently. It was covered in a rainbow of old wallpaper scraps, each one painstakingly glued in place and overlapping to create a collage effect. And on one side was the tiny brass keyhole, scuffed and weathered with age.

"Wow," Sam said, peering over my shoulder. "It's beautiful."

I whipped around, ready to tell him to turn off the smooth-ass charm for two seconds, but then I saw that he was smiling at me openly and earnestly. No trace of smarm or *beaucoup fromage*.

"Thank you, Ms.—Kathy," I said. "Evie and I really appreciate you holding on to this for so long."

"Of course," she said, smiling at me. "It's something Vivian had asked me to give to you girls, back when she was in the hospital. Then I misplaced it, couldn't remember where

I put it for so many years. I'm sorry we fell out of touch, Beatrice. I'm just so *busy* here, it's hard for me to have a social life. But perhaps now we can reconnect."

"Yeah," I said, hugging the box to my chest. "That would be nice."

"I know you're probably dying to get a look at what's inside, so . . ."

She made a little shooing motion, as if to say: You don't have to hang around and make small talk with me instead of doing what you actually want to do, and I totally get it.

I felt a rush of warmth for her.

"Nice lady," Sam said, as we headed out.

"So nice you had to flirt with her, though?" I cocked an eyebrow at him.

"I was filling in an awkward conversational gap. You're welcome," he said, flashing his cheesy grin. "And by the way, that makes it Bea: 1275, Sam: 1163."

"I don't know why you should get a point for *that*," I said. "Come on, let's get that pretzel before we leave."

The crowd around the pretzel stand had dissipated a bit, but there was still a line, which Sam and I dutifully got into.

"Pretzels! Giant pretzels!" the guy in the giant pretzel costume bellowed right next to my ear.

"Yes, we get it," I muttered under my breath.

"So are you gonna crack that open as soon as we get to the car?" Sam said, nodding at the box. "Or do you and Evie need to open it together?"

"She said I could take a peek," I said, clutching the box tighter to my chest. "Though I think honestly it's because she knew I wouldn't be able to wait."

"Pretzeeeeeeellllllls!" yelled Pretzel Guy.

"I don't know if you heard, but they have pretzels," Sam said.

You don't want a pretzel.

What the hell? The thought popped into my head so unexpectedly, I jumped. Where the fuck had that come from? I was starving.

Um. Yes, I do, I thought. *My mouth is watering from the overwhelming scent of salty, carby goodness floating through the air. Plus, even if I didn't want one before, listening to this costumed guy's constant pretzel refrain has basically inceptioned the idea into my head.*

You don't want a pretzel.

The thought ran through my head again. It was a soft whisper, like maybe my subconscious was trying to tell me I wasn't really hungry or something?

But I am, I thought firmly. *I'm totally hungry. That elephant ear was not at all filling.*

You don't want a pretzel.

What. The. Fuck.

Where was that voice coming from? Why was I arguing with . . . myself?

"Bea?" Sam nudged my arm.

I blinked, like I was coming out of a trance, and realized we'd made it to the front of the line.

"Um, yeah, can we get a pretzel, please?" I said to the man behind the counter.

"Make it two," Sam said. "Otherwise this is going to turn out exactly like the elephant ear situation."

I didn't respond. I was stuck on this weird thought that had inserted itself into my brain. Even now, it was still playing underneath everything, a creepy, repetitive whisper.

You don't want a pretzel. You don't want a pretzel. You don't want a pretzel.

"Yes, I do!" I said out loud.

"What?" Sam cocked his head at me as the pretzel man passed us our salty treats. "Who are you talking to?"

"Um, no one," I said. "Sorry. Something weird's going on and . . . You know what, let's just get to the car."

We walked back to Sam's car in silence, munching our pretzels. The anti-pretzel soundtrack in my head had gone silent once I spoke out loud, and it didn't return. What on earth had that been?

"Are you sure nothing's wrong?" Sam said, as we got into

his car and buckled our seatbelts. "You look like you're somewhere else entirely. Or worrying about something really hard."

"Oh . . ." I tapped my forehead. "Crinkle?"

"Crinkle," he confirmed. "What's up?"

"This weird thing happened back there. I . . ." I paused, chewing my lower lip. I . . . what? Heard a voice in my head suggesting I wanted the opposite of what I actually wanted? Was I somehow projecting emotions onto *myself* now? I mean, I had been through a lot today. Maybe I was halluci-nating? Like, hallucinating weird thoughts into my own brain? "I think I got too much sun," I said. "I started feeling wonky while we were waiting in line."

"It's always fifteen degrees warmer in the East Bay," Sam said. "Well, make yourself comfortable. Our pretzel side trip took enough time that we're about to hit the peak of Bay Bridge traffic. On the plus side, that means you have tons of time to explore whatever's in there." He motioned to Mom's box, resting in my lap.

I focused on the box, trying to brush off the weirdness of my pretzel moment. Now that I was about to actually open the thing, I felt a sense of momentousness. Like whatever was in there was about to reveal the deep, untold secrets of my ancestral past and change my life forever. I smiled at the thought. Evie would have teased me for being overly dra-matic.

As Sam started the car, I fished the key out of my pocket and inserted it in the tiny lock. The whole contraption felt creaky as I twisted it, like the key would break off and get stuck in the lock if I made a wrong move. Yes, I guess I could have just busted it open. But ruining Mom's careful wall-paper collaging seemed wrong—and given that I had so few tangible memories of her, I wanted to preserve as much as I could. The box made an ominous squeaking sound as it opened.

"It's . . . wow. It's a bunch of letters," I said, sifting through the pile of paper that greeted me. "I think . . ." I plucked one free and studied it, making note of the names at the top. "I think these are for us. For me and Evie. Mom must have known she was terminal at this point and . . ." I trailed off, swallowing hard, the words on the paper blurring as my throat clogged and tears filled my eyes.

Sam didn't say anything. Just reached over the gearshift and put one of his hands on top of mine.

"Ugh." I pulled away and scraped a hand over my eyes. "Sorry. I don't know what I was expecting, but it wasn't this."

I looked at the letter again, determined to actually read it through.

My darling Evie, my darling Bug,

I want you both to know that I'm mostly at peace with being near the end. My life has been a great adventure and the best part is how joyful it's been—how every corner was packed with so much happiness. My one regret is that I won't get to see you become the brilliant, beautiful women I know you will be. I hope you both remain as strong-willed as you are now—that you travel the world, find great love, and live life to its fullest. And that you also live with so much joy and with few regrets. I will love you both forever no matter where my spirit ends up. Love, Mom

I wiped away more tears. The writing looked so familiar. I'd thought I didn't remember my mom's writing at all, but maybe I did. Maybe I had the same hazy memories of her writing as I did so many other things related to her. But . . .

I frowned, scrutinizing the letter further. This was a different kind of familiar. It was the kind of familiar where you've *just* seen something, so it's fresh in your mind, and it's sort of weird that you're seeing it again so soon. Like when you see the same random stranger at the movies who you saw earlier when you were out shopping.

And all of a sudden, it hit me.

I gasped, my heart seizing up like I'd just been stabbed in the chest with an icicle.

"Sam." My grip tightened on the letter, making the paper crumple. "We have to go back to the bookstore." I brandished the letter at him, forcing myself to say the words I couldn't quite believe. "This handwriting. It's . . . it's the same as the handwriting on the weird message in the bathroom."

"The one from your possible stalker?" he said.

"Yes." I shook my head at the letter, trying to come up with a scenario where any of this made sense. "Apparently my dead mother is stalking me."

CHAPTER EIGHT

I BOLTED FROM the car as soon as Sam parked, zipping through the front door of the bookstore and into the bathroom.

"Hello to you, too!" Leah yelled after me. Pancake barked in agreement.

I flicked on the light and crossed to the craft wall. My hands shook as I held up one of Mom's letters next to the message from my mysterious stalker. On the drive back—which had been a frustrating exercise in bumper to bumper traffic and that special brand of Bay Area aggro that only seems to surface during rush hour—I'd studied that same letter over and over. There was a huge pile of letters to explore, but I couldn't seem to get beyond that first one. Not until I got back to the It's Lit bathroom and confirmed this complete and total weirdness. My brain was stuck in a holding pattern, unable to process anything beyond that.

But now there was no question. The letter I was holding up was an exact match to the stalker message on the wall. There was that swooping curlicue at the bottom of the "S," that angular corner on the "E." My chest contracted, and my stomach twisted itself into a knot. My whole world felt like it was tilting on its axis.

What the frakballs fucking fuck.

"Bea!" Sam hustled into the bathroom. Leah was hot on his heels, Pancake cradled in her arms. "Well?" he said, as they crowded around me.

"It's the same writing," I said, my voice faint. I held up the letter. My hand was still shaking, and Sam reached over and gently extricated it from my grasp. "Someone with my mom's *exact same writing* left me a freaking message on the bathroom wall."

"Okaaaaay," Leah said slowly. "Let's calm down for a minute. Bebe, try those breathing exercises I showed you the other day—"

"I don't want breathing exercises!" I blurted out. "I want . . . I want to know what this means. Ugh." I shook my head, trying to get my thoughts on some semblance of a logical track. "Sorry, Lee. I don't know how to deal with this."

"It's okay, you're having emotional overload, I get it," Leah said, taking the letter from Sam. "Let's take a big ol' step back and try to examine this from a semi-logical point of view. Could this be writing that's just very similar but not exact?" She held the letter up, next to the writing on the wall. "Damn. That's pretty exact, actually."

"I mean, even if it's just someone who figured out how to copy my dead mom's writing, that's still extremely creepy," I said, rocking back on my heels.

"Do you have cameras in here?" Sam asked, gesturing around the bathroom.

"Ew, no!" Leah and I said in unison, swiveling to shoot him identical "gross" faces. Pancake gave him a disdainful side-eye.

"Sorry," he said, laughing a little. "That would be, of course, totally invasive, pervy, and privacy-violating and not something you would ever do as a legit business. I'm just trying to think of ways to figure out how this showed up."

"We do have a security camera right *outside* the bathroom, though," Leah said, handing me back the letter. She scritched Pancake's ears thoughtfully. "We could review that footage, see who comes in and out."

I nodded, trying to grab on to this solid method of practical, real world investigation. I reached out and ran my fingertips over the writing, lingering on the swoop of an "S."

Somewhere in my gut, I knew whatever was behind this was *not* a practical, real world kind of thing. I mean, how many logical explanations for this could there be?

Nate and I had developed a bit of a big concept theory back when I'd been working with him on demon data collection and analysis. Essentially it boiled down to: Don't twist yourself in knots trying to deny the fantastical. Because if it really *seems* like something involves, say, the supernatural machinations of a wannabe demon queen trying to take over San Francisco, or a bunch of literal bridezillas attempting to ruin your sister's wedding . . . well, in our line of work, that's often *exactly* what it is.

And . . .

I ran my fingertips over the wall message again. It really did sound like Mom. That kind of gentle, encouraging statement was exactly the kind of thing she'd have said to me as a kid. A hopeful flutter bloomed in my chest. Could this mean Mom was out there somewhere, trying to reach me? I didn't even know how that would be possible, but I couldn't bring myself to squash that flutter of hope. Then again, hadn't I just been telling myself not to deny the impossible? In our supernaturally infested city, there had to be a decent number of explanations for how and why this could totally be happening. At least as many as the boring, wonder-killing explanations for why it was impossible.

Mom, are you out there?

"I'm calling Evie," I said, taking my phone out of my pocket and punching in her number. "Maybe the team can come down and do some scans of the bathroom. Or at least take a look and tell me if they have any ideas on how to proceed."

"Bea!" Evie exclaimed upon answering. She sounded overexcited, out-of-breath. "Wow, you're actually calling me? Like, on the phone? Like, you kept your phone charged long enough to make a real, honest-to-god phone call?"

"Yes," I said. If she'd been standing in front of me, I would've stuck out my tongue. "Why do you sound like you've been running a marathon? You hate running. Wait."

My eyes narrowed in suspicion. "Did I interrupt you and Nate? Again? I've told you, *please* don't answer your phone when you're in the middle of—"

"No," she said, cutting me off. "We're not doing . . . that. Annie and I are on our way to the Wave Organ. A civilian who was on the scene yesterday claims their friend has gone missing."

"Missing?" My brow crinkled. "I thought we saved everyone."

"Me too," Evie said. "I'm not sure what's up, but we're meeting Rose down there. She and her team have been scanning the area, and I think they're actually going to set up a twenty-four-hour patrol, since we still don't know exactly what caused the attack yesterday."

I felt a stab of annoyance. I'd been watching my phone like a hawk all day (well, except for those few hours when I was at the Market, stuffing my face with various junk foods and hearing weird voices in my head). And now something exciting was finally happening, so why hadn't Evie or Aveda sent me the Bat Signal?

"I'll meet you down there too," I said. "This is part of my superheroing duties now, right?"

"Yes," Evie said. I could hear the smile in her voice. "But if you're still working, I understand—"

"Nope, I'm done," I said quickly. "Though . . ." I remembered why I'd called her in the first place. "I have some other weirdness to discuss with the team, whenever we're done with this mission." My eyes wandered over to the writing on the wall. Investigating Mom's mysterious message could wait, particularly since we couldn't think of tactics beyond looking at hours of boring video footage. No one seemed to be in imminent danger or missing. And when you're a superhero, you have to constantly balance one crisis against the other and figure out what requires your most immediate attention. (At least, that sounded like something Aveda would say.)

"Got it," Evie said. "We'll be there in fifteen. See you then."

I hung up and gave Sam my biggest, sweetest, toothiest grin.

"Let me guess," he said. "You need a ride."

The Wave Organ looked different today. That was to be expected, given that half of it wasn't coming to life and growing all giant and attacking everyone. As Nate had mentioned, it had reconstituted itself and was just sitting there, benign and blocky as ever. But the current surrounding seaside atmosphere made it look different than it did in everyday tourist photos, even. Rose and her team had the area cordoned off with yellow police tape and people actually seemed to be respecting that and staying far, far away. Darkness was falling, the sun disappearing over the horizon, and the police tape fluttered gently in the breeze. That whole stretch of waterfront felt abandoned, eerie—like we were living in the beginning of a Hitchcock movie, just waiting for shit to get really and truly fucked up.

I shivered as a particularly bone-rattling gust of wind whipped through me, pulling my cape more tightly around my body. I was glad I'd changed into my official superheroing outfit before leaving It's Lit—the extra bit of insulation Leah and I had built into the material was keeping me from going full-on popsicle.

I'd expected a whole crowd of gawkers or a fresh batch of out-of-towners who hadn't got the message, but the only person around, other than Rose and Co., was the tourist Evie had mentioned on the phone; the one who claimed her friend had gone missing.

Rose had set the tourist up in a camp chair and a blanket just outside the perimeter of the police tape, and she was huddled up, staring vacantly into space and clutching a bright green bit of fabric to her chest. Evie, Aveda, Lucy, and I were standing just far enough away that Rose could brief us out of the tourist's earshot.

"She refused to talk to anyone except Evie and Aveda,"

Rose said, nodding toward the tourist. "And she refused to leave until she got to talk to them. I could have arrested her for interfering with a police scene, but . . ." Rose let out a small sigh—a rare crack in her stoic façade.

"Are you tired, darling?" Lucy said, concern creasing her forehead. "You've been on shift since the wee hours, plus you had that very early morning mission with Aveda and Bea. Isn't there someone who can relieve you?"

"Yes, soon," Rose said, reaching over and giving Lucy a reassuring shoulder pat. "Thanks, babe. We got the twenty-four hour watch schedule fully set up for my team this after-noon, but I wanted to stay until I was absolutely certain everything was under control." She turned to me, flashing an exhausted half-smile. "Oh, and Bea—I have a little present for you, related to some of the things we discussed this morning."

She reached into a large bag at her feet and pulled out a battered gray metal box. I recognized it as one of the traps her team used to contain certain kinds of demons. The traps were part of the same array of demon tech as the old-ass scanners and, like the scanners, they were in desperate need of modern improvements. I'd actually tinkered with one of the traps a few years ago when we'd been chasing a particu-larly elusive—and invisible—demon pest. I had figured out how to use a certain kind of metal to reinforce the trap and keep the demon good and locked in. It had been so success-ful, Rose's team had added the upgrade to all of their traps.

"Oooh!" I said. "You're giving this to me? I get to play with it?"

"I checked in with Nate earlier today," Rose said. "He's still analyzing our scans from Pussy Queen, and we're going to try to get that funding for tech development as soon as possible. But in the meantime, I thought it might be best to at least try to prepare for whatever this latest menace is. You were so successful in your last experiment with these, I thought you could take an initial look for me?"

"I'd love to!" I said, taking the trap and cradling it against me reverently. Out of the corner of my eye, I spied Evie studying me. Oh, crap, I was getting distracted by shiny things again, wasn't I? Best to let her know I was totally dedicated to my new chosen profession. "Um. In between all of my super-important new superhero duties of course," I added.

"Of course," Rose said, nodding at me.

"So what exactly is the tourist saying?" Aveda said, all business as usual. She nodded toward the woman huddled in the camp chair. "Because all of the civilians trapped on top of those monsters yesterday were accounted for, every single one. So if she's trying to say someone's missing . . ." She let out a long huff. The very idea that Aveda had done less than her absolute best on a superheroing mission was more offensive to her than anything.

"That's just it," Rose said. "The way she tells it, her friend didn't go missing during the battle yesterday. She went missing *before* that."

"What?" Evie shook her head in disbelief. "Is this even related to the Wave Organ attack?"

"That's all she would say before she insisted on talking to you," Rose said with a weary shrug. "Her name is Tori, and the friend who went missing is Carmen. With that, I'll leave you to it. I'm completing the final stages of a thorough scan, just to see if we can pick up anything else. Luce, can you help me canvass that last corner over there by the graffiti?"

"I can," Lucy said. "But after that, you're coming home with me, no arguments."

"All right," Aveda said, as Lucy and Rose headed off. She rolled her shoulders and focused her laser-sharp gaze on the tourist. "Let's see what you can tell us, Miss Tori. If that's even your real name."

"Annie," Evie admonished, nudging her in the ribs. "We're not interrogating her. She may have lost a friend!"

"Or she may be trying to stir up trouble and gain attention while diverting important resources from an actual supernatural investigation," Aveda said, her eyes narrowing. "In which case, I should definitely be Bad Cop."

"You're always Bad Cop," Evie said, giggling.

I tuned out their strategizing and studied the tourist, Tori, for a moment. She really did seem distraught. And as I continued to study her, I realized she looked familiar.

"I saw her yesterday!" I blurted out.

Evie and Aveda stopped talking and stared at me quizzically.

"I mean. While I was running to meet you guys—she was one of the tourists in the group Lucy was evacuating," I continued. "I think she actually mentioned her friend was missing. Anyway, we should talk to her. Um, I can be another cop. Good Cop Two. Or Bad Cop Two? Whatever you guys need."

"You should observe, feel it out," Aveda said, nodding at me. "Don't jump in unless you feel you have something absolutely vital to add. It's still your first day on the job, and I haven't had a chance to share all of my important lessons with you. But here's another one for future reference: You might want to wear something a little more . . . sedate when talking to civilians. It makes them more comfortable." She gave my iridescent superhero outfit an unimpressed once-over, then turned on her heel and headed toward Tori.

"Really?" I muttered to Evie. "Aveda Jupiter is telling me to wear something *sedate*?"

"Give her a break, I think she's actually trying to help—in her own way," Evie said, laughing a little.

"She was just telling Maisy this morning not to judge my outfits," I said peevishly. "Why does she get to do it?"

"I'm sure she would tell you she's not *judging*, she's *advising*," Evie said. "She was so excited this morning about becoming your mentor. And she's learned a lot over the years about when to turn the diva up and down. You just kind of have to interpret her lessons through the Aveda filter."

"Or I could forego her 'lessons' and be my own damn self," I grumbled, but Evie was already walking toward Tori. I scurried after her, self-consciously smoothing the skirt of my costume. Yeah, so I did look a little out of place. Evie was dressed in her usual jeans/hoodie non-fashion, and Aveda was clad in her version of casual: black leather pants and a fitted black tank top. In contrast, I looked like I was ready to take on Roller Disco Bootie Mashup Night. The shine off my costume was probably semi-blinding to anyone who dared look directly at me.

Well, what was so wrong with that? I was a superhero now, after all, and I was proud of that. Why not show it off?

Once we all reached Tori, I felt ridiculous looming over her, so I settled myself on the ground, tucking my legs under me. Evie followed suit—sort of—kneeling down and supporting herself by holding on to the back of Tori's chair. Aveda, never one to give up ground, stayed standing, arms crossed over her chest.

"Hello," Aveda said, officious tone fully deployed. "I am Aveda Jupiter and this is—"

"Evie Tanaka, I know, I'm a big fan," Tori said. Her grip tightened around the green fabric she was still clutching to her chest, and she worried the material through her fingers. She turned to me. "And who are you?"

"Bea Tanaka," I said. And because that sounded sort of vague and lonely by itself, I added, "Um, superhero-in-training."

"Tell us what happened to your friend," Aveda coaxed.

"And take your time," Evie said, laying a comforting hand on Tori's arm. "We know this must be very difficult for you."

I wasn't sure what to do—I didn't exactly have a role here, they really did have both Good and Bad Cop covered. I shifted and then winced as the heavy material of my costume rustled loudly. Team Tanaka/Jupiter was a well-oiled machine, and I was a squeaky third wheel in search of a purpose. I settled for putting a hand on Tori's other arm, offering some additional comfort. Good Cop 2, indeed.

"We were down here exploring yesterday when Carmen lost her wallet," Tori said slowly. "We looked for hours, but we couldn't find it. I told her it was probably long gone, but she wouldn't listen to me. She's very stubborn." Tori shook her head, momentarily annoyed at the missing Carmen. "And beyond having all her IDs and stuff, I guess the wallet has sentimental value. She's been schlepping that thing around since college."

"Did you find it before the Organ attacked?" Aveda said, her voice growing impatient as she tried to keep Tori on track.

"Not exactly," Tori said. "We retraced our steps along the water. Then I got the bright idea of going and checking with the folks in the Yacht Club." She gestured to a small, squat building located a little ways down the shore. "I mean, I figured it was within the realm of possibility that some Good Samaritan found it and turned it in, right? Because there are still some decent, honest people in this world, not everyone would see a wallet lying on the ground and snatch it without trying to return it to its proper owner—"

"Indeed," Aveda said, through gritted teeth.

I couldn't help but empathize with her a little bit. I mean, this wasn't exactly what I'd imagined when I'd fantasized about being a superhero. This step-by-step questioning was actually kind of . . . boring. Just like staring at the Pussy Queen portal had been boring this morning.

My mind wandered back to all the weirdness with the bathroom wall and my mom's handwriting. What the frak was happening there, anyway? Or was my overactive imagination acting up even more? Was this "mystery" just another shiny thing I was allowing myself to be distracted by? And on my first day on the superheroing job, no less. Then again, Leah and Sam had seen it too and they'd agreed—

"Did the Yacht Club have your friend's wallet?" Evie's voice snapped me back to reality. She gave Tori's arm a reassuring squeeze.

"No," Tori said, shaking her head back and forth vigorously as her eyes filled with tears. "And when I came back out, Carmen had vanished. I found her scarf on the path." Tori held up the green piece of fabric she'd been clutching like a life preserver. "I started looking for her, but then the

Organ attacked, and we had to evacuate. I never found her. I came back, and I've looked all over, combed every inch of this place. I've texted, I've called. She's gone." Her voice cracked on the last word, and she buried her face in the scarf and let loose with some truly heart-wrenching sobs.

"Oh, no . . . it'll be okay," Evie soothed, putting an arm around Tori and giving her an awkward half-hug. "I promise you, we'll do everything we can to find your friend. This area is currently undergoing a thorough supernatural scan and our resident mage has been working on a pretty powerful locator spell. I'm sure we'll track her down."

Evie's brow creased with genuine worry as she comforted the woman. My sister's heart is butter soft—she's truly one of the most empathic people I know. Aveda, meanwhile, shifted from foot to foot, looking uncomfortable at such a loud, sweeping display of emotion. It isn't that Aveda doesn't feel for people; she's just dedicated to getting shit done above all else. She wanted to find Carmen, to help Tori by accomplishing this mission. But Tori's extended crying jag was keeping us from doing that. Meanwhile, I was sitting here, neither comforting nor getting impatient. Just kind of bored. Truly extraneous. Good Cop (or Bad Cop?) 2 felt more like Okay Cop No One Actually Needs.

"I wish she'd come baaaaaaack!" Tori wailed. "I wish I could calm down and approach this logically—"

"That would be helpful," Aveda muttered under her breath.

"But I'm so worried, I just caaaaaaan't!" Tori cried, then buried her face in the scarf again, sobbing away. "I wish I didn't feel this way, but . . . but . . ."

I wish I didn't feel this way.

Tori's words played back in my head, over and over.

I mean, that was within my power to change, wasn't it? It might be too casual of a power usage for Evie's liking. But wouldn't it help with this investigation? Move things along and get us back on track so we could possibly save the missing Carmen from whatever evil had befallen her? And with the added bonus of making Tori feel momentarily better, which she'd just expressed a desire for anyway. This definitely fell into the greater good category. And that was part of my code.

I breathed deeply and focused on Tori, who was still sobbing into her scarf. Then I concentrated on a feeling of calm. A sensation of sunlight washing over your arm, a breeze ruffling your hair, chocolate melting on your tongue. I focused on that until it was thrumming through my entire being. Then I sent it spinning in her direction. I turned it up so it was stronger than the usual initial projection I might send toward someone—Tori needed more than a freaking aromatherapy candle to calm her down, that was for sure. I kept it thrumming in her direction for a good, long moment. And slowly, her sobs subsided, and she looked up from the scarf.

"I'm sorry," she said, her voice quavery but more assured. She sat up straight, brushing away the last of her tears. "I'm so worried Carmen got eaten by one of those giant stone monsters. And I wish I could provide more information to help, but that's all I've got: she was here, and then she was gone."

"What you've told us is totally helpful," Evie said encouragingly. She looked surprised at Tori's sudden emotional about-face, but she was obviously pleased and wasn't going to question it. "Why don't we go through it again from the beginning? There may be some detail in there, something that seems innocuous, that's actually a clue. Maybe go back even farther if you can—how did you and Carmen find your way here yesterday?"

"Yes," Tori nodded, her expression turning placid and focused. "Yes, I can do that. Carmen and I were having a girls' reunion weekend. We hadn't seen each other in five years, and we thought, why not do something to get away from it all? Now, San Francisco wasn't my first choice, it's much too expensive, don't you think? I mean, the hotels in our budget were pretty much all glorified rat holes, but Carmen is so stubborn—have I mentioned that yet? And she had her heart absolutely set on San Francisco."

I groaned inwardly as she yammered on. How much more of this useless minutiae were we going to be subjected to? I snuck a glance at Evie and Aveda. Evie was rubbing Tori's back and nodding attentively while Aveda regarded her with razor sharp focus, clearly doing her best not to let any possible clue escape her.

Well. Since they were doing such a good job listening, they didn't need me. I pumped a last blast of extra calm feelings in Tori's direction, then got to my feet.

"I'm gonna go, uh, check out the area where Carmen was last seen," I murmured.

No one responded. I gathered up the trap Rose had given me and slipped off.

I walked the short distance to the edge of the waterfront, searching the area, trying to take everything in. It looked . . . normal. Who was I kidding? There was nothing. Tori was probably the exaggerating attention hound Aveda suspected her of being. Maybe Carmen had just wanted some quiet time away from her friend's detail-obsessed chattering. And if she *had* disappeared, Evie and Aveda would figure it out. They always did.

"What's that?"

The question startled me out of my reverie, and I turned to see a teenage girl with stringy brown hair and tiny round glasses staring at me inquisitively. She was clutching a sketch-book and a pen and—oh. It was the same girl I'd thrown myself in front of the day before, the one who'd cried out for help. Odd that she and Tori were both so eager to return to the scene of a giant monster attack, but I imagined that if I were a civilian, the thrill-seeker in me would've prompted me to do the same thing.

"Sorry, what?" I said.

"That—the thing in your hand," she said, gesturing to the trap with her pen. "What is that?"

"It's a supernatural trap," I said, trying to sound as officious as Aveda. "It contains certain kinds of demons."

"Huh." The girl cocked her head to the side, sizing me up. "Are you trying to trap something around here?"

"Um, that's classified," I said, straightening my spine. Hmm. I actually did sound a bit like Aveda. It was fun.

The girl nodded, looking like she was pleased to be let in on this bit of non-information. "Gotcha." She turned and faced the water, her gaze going contemplative. "It's nice out here tonight. Quiet."

"Yeah," I said. "But you know, you probably shouldn't hang out for too long. We don't know yet if this area is stable. It's supposed to be off-limits to the public for now."

She shrugged, still staring out at the water. "I'll wait for someone to officially kick me out. The quiet really helps with my inspiration." She gestured to her sketchbook.

"Are you an artist?" I didn't know what was compelling me to keep talking to her. Maybe it was the simple fact that this was marginally more interesting than our talk with Tori the blabbermouth. Or maybe it was because talking to her kept me from doing what I really wanted to do, which was emotionally project onto her to stop getting in Rose's way and get the hell out of here. But that definitely wasn't for the greater good.

"I am an artist," she said, giving me a small smile and flipping her sketchbook open. "And a poet. Wanna see?"

I leaned in gamely and perused her sketches; soft, intricate pencil scratchings on paper. "These are super good," I said, meaning it. Her sketches had a general theme— sequential drawings that seemed to tell loosely connected stories of ordinary-looking women morphing into various kinds of monsters. One became a giant squid with an elaborate web of tentacles. Another grew a lion's head next to her own, turning into a two-headed beast that roared in fury. But the soft, fluid lines kept all of these creatures very human, hinting at warm empathy from the artist. It reminded me a bit of Leah's work—offbeat interpretations of fantastical creatures. Leah would totally dig what this girl was all about. The sketches were surrounded by poems rendered in big, loose script—they seemed to mostly address the idea of hidden monsters and finding the power within.

"Thank you," the girl said. "I dunno. No one else seems to think so. Mr. Frankel—that's my art teacher—says I'm wasting my time on cartoony junk. And the other kids at school think I'm a fantasy-obsessed freakazoid."

"Wow, so freakazoid is an en vogue insult again," I said. "Didn't realize that one had come back around."

"Uh-huh," the girl said, giving me a quizzical look that seemed to say: *Are you really trying to relate to me here, Old Lady?*

I answered with an encouraging smile. Even though I wasn't that much older than her—maybe five or six years?—she saw me in that adult box, someone who couldn't possibly understand her day-to-day experience. But I understood what she was feeling more than she could know.

"Things will get better," I said, trying to sound encouraging. "Eventually you'll find people who recognize how cool your stuff is. How cool *you* are." But even as I spouted these PSA-ready aphorisms, I couldn't help but feel a twinge of . . . something. I mean, did I really believe that crap?

I'd actually been *super* popular in my tween years, poised to become one of the fabulous queen bees of my eventual high school class. Nicole and I had plotted our reign as co-prom queens, how we'd rule the roost with perfectly manicured iron fists.

Then Mom died and I'd kind of gone off the rails. I'd started wearing all black and doing my goth-y makeup thing. I'd stopped wanting to talk to anyone or hang out or do much of anything, really. I'd been in so much pain, I felt like my heart was being shoved through a cheese grater. And that pain hadn't left room for anything else. I'll admit I'd pushed Nicole away pretty hard. I'd started answering any query from her—whether it was about crushes or a cute new skirt or whatever we used to talk about—with a noncommittal shrug. I'd declined every social invitation she extended, and

I hadn't even tried to come up with good excuses. I'd just kept saying, "I don't want to."

Everything had come to a head one day when I'd told her no, I did *not* want to go to the mall after school, and she was overcome with frustration.

"Why *not?*" she'd demanded, putting her hands on her hips. We were outside in the quad, where we usually ate lunch.

"I don't want to," I'd said, for what seemed like the millionth time.

"What *do* you want to do?" she'd said. Her mom had just given her the okay to try a little makeup, and she was wearing this terrible sickly green eyeshadow that somehow made her look even more indignant. And also a little bit like she had some kind of plague.

"I just want my mom back," I'd muttered, pulling my too big cardigan around me like a cocoon.

"Bea." She blew out a long, exasperated breath. "I've . . . I've been trying so hard to make you feel better. But you don't want to do anything. You're so . . . *sad* all the time."

I'd shrugged, pulling my cardigan more tightly around me.

"You have to get over this," she'd said, frowning.

"This isn't something you just get over, Nicole."

"Well . . . then at least stop being such a *freak* about it," she'd exploded, storming off.

We'd stopped talking after that. She'd confided in all our friends that I was an irredeemable weirdo, and they'd stopped talking to me too. But I guess you could say things had got a little better since then.

I'd started to come out of my metaphorical and literal cardigan cocoon when I'd begun lending a hand at Tanaka/Jupiter HQ, assisting Nate with his research and updating Aveda's social media. I'd felt like I had a purpose again. And now I was a full-blown superheroine . . . who was currently feeling simultaneously weirded out and kind of bored by her first day on the job. Did that qualify as "getting better"? I didn't know that I could answer with any sort of clarity.

"Thank you, Bug."

My head snapped up, my jaunt down memory lane obliterated. Had the little artist-poet standing in front of me really just said . . . but, no. No way. Surely I must have misheard.

"Um, what?" I said, trying to ignore my quickening heart rate.

The girl tilted her head to the side and gave me a smile so peaceful, it seemed eerie. "I said, thank you, Bug."

I let go of the girl's sketchbook and took an inadvertent step back, all the blood draining from my face. There were only three people in the world who called me that: Scott, Dad, and my dead mother.

"Wh-who are you?" I managed. "What . . . how do you know that . . . ?" My brain was short-circuiting and I couldn't seem to think of what the right question was. Beyond, you know, *what the actual fuck.*

"I'm with you. Still," she said, continuing to give me that eerie smile. "And I need you to look for answers. Please, Bug."

"Answers to what?" I gasped, tears filling my eyes. Seriously, had Mom moved on from leaving me stalker messages on bathroom walls to, like, possessing some random person and using her to talk to me?

"Find me," she said.

"I . . ." I stepped forward, closing the gap between me and the girl. I dropped the trap on the ground and grabbed her by the shoulders. "How?" I said, shaking her a little. "Mom, are you still alive? I don't understand . . ."

A shadow passed over the girl's face, and she shook her head, as if trying to shoo away unwelcome thoughts. Then her eyes focused on me, and she looked totally confused.

"What are you doing?" she said, frowning at me and trying to pull away. "Let go!"

"What was that?" I said, tightening my grip. "What were you just saying? Please, I need you to talk to me!"

"Get off me, you *freakazoid*!" she shrieked, wrenching herself away from me. Clutching her sketchbook to her chest, she ran.

"Wait!" I yelped, taking off after her.

But she had a head start and was way faster than me. I could only watch her get farther and farther away, casting a last, fearful glance over her shoulder.

Dammit. I stopped, breathing hard, watching with mounting frustration as she got smaller on the horizon. Maybe I should take up running. Or . . . wait a minute.

I could project onto her, convince her that she wanted to stay and tell me everything about how she'd just channeled the spirit of my mom. True, I usually couldn't get people to do the total opposite of what they actually wanted, but maybe if I made the feelings way stronger, turned my aromatherapy candle way up, I could—

"Bea!" Evie's hand clamped on my shoulder. I whirled around. She and Aveda stood next to me, regarding me with concern. "Why are you chasing that girl? Does she know something about Carmen?"

"I . . ." I cast one last look at the girl, now a tiny dot way off in the distance. "I'm not sure," I said, a feeling of helplessness rising in my chest. "I'm not sure of anything right now."

CHAPTER NINE

I'D HAD ONE hell of a first day as a full-fledged superhero. And I was all-too-ready to recap when Sam opened the door to his apartment.

"Soooooo," I said, before he could get a word in. "My dead mom tried to talk to me again at the Wave Organ. Only she was, like, talking through this girl. Maybe she was possessing her? I don't know. Between that and the bathroom wall, I feel like she's trying to get a message to me. But I have no idea what it is. And . . . wait, you know what? I am totally just having this realization right now, but there was also this weird-ass voice in my head at the Grand Lake Market. Remember how I said I was feeling wonky? There was actually a voice in my head telling me not to buy a pretzel. Even though I totally wanted one. Maybe it's all connected. Maybe my mom is trying to reach me in, like, all the ways. What if she's still alive? I mean, I don't know how that would even be possible, but we live in a world where the impossible happens all the time, right? With the demons and the superpowers and—oh! Maybe she's a ghost? *Ghost Mom?* That could be cool. Holy crap." My eyes widened, my excitement ratcheting upward. "This is my first mission as a legit superheroine, Sam! I have to totally freakin' *find Ghost Mom!*"

"What did Evie say about . . . any of this?" he managed to get in, once I'd stopped to take a breath. Pancake, who was hoisted under his arm, snuffled inquisitively.

"I didn't tell her," I said, breezing inside and dumping my bag on the floor. "She and Aveda are looking for this tourist that went missing by the Organ and that seemed more important in the moment? Plus, they're still monitoring the Organ to make sure it doesn't rise up and try to kill us all again, so you know. Priorities." I paused. "Also, I figure I can take some decompression time tonight and put my encounters with this mysterious Mom Voice in some kind of coherent order to present to them, so they don't think I'm just getting distracted by shiny things."

"Posterboard time?" Sam said, closing the door behind me.

"Posterboard time," I confirmed. "But first: eating time. Something smells amazing." I inhaled deeply, taking in the delectable scents of curry and frying panko. That comforting aura of spice soothed my jangled nerves, made my shoulders relax. It's weird how something as simple as the promise of beloved foodstuffs can make you feel like everything's gonna be okay. "Do you have something I can change into? Maybe something one of your latest Not-Girlfriends left behind? This outfit is great for superheroing, not so great for slobbing around and pigging out, which is my whole plan for tonight."

"Nah, I have a very strict policy when it comes to leaving shit behind," Sam said, setting Pancake down on the floor. He scampered off in the direction of the curry smell. "You take whatever you brought in with you. That way, no easy excuse for 'just popping by' and turning our perfectly wholesome few hours of fun into something messy, complicated, and *not* fun."

"Did you really just confess that 'a few hours' is the longest you can manage to pleasure someone?" I said, cocking an eyebrow. "Don't let that get out. It will ruin your reputation."

"My reputation is well-earned, well-maintained, and needs no defending." He flashed me that *beaucoup fromage* smile. "But as far as clothes, you can pull stuff from my workout pile. It's in the bin next to my bed."

"Mmm, workout clothes," I said, wrinkling my nose at the thought of scratchy basketball shorts rife with old sweat stains. "Do you have anything in, I don't know, the pajama category?"

"I don't wear pajamas to bed." He shrugged, his grin turning extra cheesy. "I don't wear *anything* to bed."

"Guh." I made a gagging face. "Cut that out, please. Turn Calendar Sam off. I came here for Curry-Making Supportive Friend Sam."

"Anyway, you're asking for a lot from free clothes that you're probably going to wear home and never return to me, don't you think?" he said.

"I'll make do with your disgusting workout gear," I said, letting out an over-dramatic sigh. "Where's Leah? Did she have to close today? Damn, it's been hours since I checked my texts." I fumbled around in my pocket for my phone.

"No, she had to go help her mom with something—"

"Ah, something involving her mom's seven lizards?" I guessed. "Which is why Pancake is hanging out here solo." Leah's mom was a reptile enthusiast—and her menagerie did *not* get along with Pancake. I pulled up our group chain in my texts and saw the Pancake-relevant exchange between Sam and Leah. "I should go help her. Or I should've been around when she needed help. Or something." I usually accompanied Leah when she had to help her mom out with the lizards. If one (or more) of them escaped, it was useful to have both of us there so one person could hunt down the wily reptile and the other could comfort Leah's mom. Teamwork in action. I rubbed my eyes and texted a message of encouragement and an offer to help if Leah needed it. Yes, I'd just had a long day, but I'd totally down some caffeine and Uber it over if she needed me.

"She's got it under control, I'm sure," Sam said, just as Leah texted me back that she was handling things fine solo. "Stick with me and Pancake, we're having a slumber party."

"Then you better invest in some pajamas," I called out, stuffing my phone back in my pocket as I headed down the hall and into his bedroom. "Because Pancake won't stand for any of that human nudity nonsense. He needs a nice, soft fabric to cuddle against—consider flannel."

I found the bin of workout clothes next to Sam's bed and was pleased to see everything was neatly folded and appeared to be clean. I plucked out a long, worn tank top with a faded boxing gym logo and a pair of striped boxer shorts—really? He had special workout boxer shorts?—and quickly changed out of my sweaty superhero costume. It wilted into a limp pile of glittery material as I dropped it to the floor.

Hmm. Would I need to get my costume cleaned every day? Would I have to invest in *multiple* costumes? That was what Aveda had done, but she'd been a few months in before she'd gone all-out with wardrobe.

I rolled the top of the boxers over so they would stay put and headed out of the bedroom and into the kitchen, where Sam was whistling and drinking a glass of red wine as he fried up katsu cutlets. Pancake was on the floor, eagerly snarfing up a plate of bacon set in front of him.

"Did you cook him his own special dinner?" I said to Sam, inclining my head toward the bacon-crazed pup.

Sam shrugged, looking moderately embarrassed. "Leah said he can't have the breading on the cutlets. And he definitely can't have curry, it's too spicy. So. . ."

"Most spoiled puppy ever," I said, nudging Pancake with my foot. He ignored me in favor of continuing his love-fest with the bacon. I padded over to the fridge and opened it, scoping the interior for potential katsu beverage pairings.

"Oooh," I said, spying a bottle of something pink and bubbly, "what's *this*?"

"Some kind of grapefruit-flavored prosecco something-or-other that's probably mostly sugar," Sam said. "I got it for you and Leah."

"Because heaven knows your palate can only take the most refined, expensive, altogether snooty pinot type things. That's okay, more girly trash for me." I liberated the beautiful pink bottle from the fridge, twisted off the top (because of course it had a twist-off top), and took a big swig. The bubbles went immediately to my head, making me feel weightless and wobbly, and I remembered I hadn't eaten anything since the elephant ear-pretzel combo at the Grand Lake Market. "Whoa," I said, my knees buckling a little.

"Bea!" Sam looked up from plating his katsu masterpiece and crossed the room in a few steps, grabbing my elbow. "Can you maybe not chug that garbage before you've cushioned your stomach with actual food?"

"Unhand me, good sir," I said, affecting a terrible British accent. I shook him off and took another swig. "I've had a long fucking day, and I need to unwind."

I settled in at the table with a heavy *thump* and waited patiently as Sam brought the food over, taking more ladylike sips of my bubbly pink drink.

I really should save some of this for Leah, I thought, as my head became even lighter and fizzier. Eh. She'd understand. I'd buy her a bottle of her very own and we'd toast tomorrow— to triumphing over evil and jerky lizards. It would be magical.

"Here we are," Sam said, placing a heaping plate of food in front of me. He set his own plate in front of the chair next to me, then grabbed his glass of (snooty, pretentious) wine from the stovetop and sat down.

I took a deep inhale of the deliciousness in front of me. The rich smell settled over me like a fuzzy blanket, and the sight of that big, oozy curry pool soaking into fluffy rice was so welcome, I nearly teared up.

"Yesssssss," I whispered, letting out a sigh that bordered on orgasmic. I took another swig of pink drink, then picked up my chopsticks and started shoveling food in my face with gusto. Pancake, having finished his bacon feast, figured out there was something new and exciting happening at the kitchen table, so he trotted over and bumped his head against my leg. "Oh, I am for sure not dropping any of this," I said, pointing my chopsticks at him. "Your mom will murder me if I let you eat something that's been specifically designated as off limits. Also, it's just too good."

"You're welcome," Sam said, cocking an eyebrow at me and raising his wine glass.

"Thank you." I lifted my pink drink bottle in a toast. "And thank you for driving me to the East Bay today. And then back to the bookstore. And for this incredibly fashionable ensemble." I gestured to the clothes I'd snagged from him. (And that I probably wasn't giving back. They were so comfortable.) And then, because I was feeling generous, I added: "Bea: 1275, Sam: 1164."

"So I'm catching up to you," he said, cocking an eyebrow.

"I'm just letting you think that. All part of my grand plan."

"Oh, like losing to me at the Great Calculus Bee of Sophomore Year was part of your grand plan?"

"By one point!" I protested, poking him with my chopsticks. The alcohol was fizzing around my brain in earnest now, making my voice louder and my gestures more expansive. "One. Tiny. *Point*."

"One *very important* tiny point," Sam countered, batting my chopsticks away.

"I'm still ahead in the grand scheme of things by *double digit* points," I said. "And that's, like, in the game of life."

We stared at each other, that familiar competitive flame sparking and transporting us back to that seminal moment of our shared teenagedom. The Great Calculus Bee of Sophomore Year stood tall as one of the main incidents that had solidified our ongoing competition. Our calc teacher, Mr. Palmer, set up a friendly afterschool competition for our class, wherein we had to take turns solving increasingly complicated equations. And, as in a spelling bee, we were eliminated whenever we got a question wrong.

"Remember, kids, this is all in good fun!" he'd said, beaming at us as he crossed his arms over his festive holiday sweater vest. (Mr. Palmer had a sweater vest for every occasion, even Groundhog Day.) "Let's enjoy ourselves while we get our integrals on, eh?"

Slowly, the whiteboard at the front of the classroom had exploded in a rainbow of equations, solved with lightning speed by the best and brightest our high school had to offer. But none were quite as bright as Sam and I, who picked off every so-called competitor one by one, taking them down with lightning-fast mathing. Until we were the only two left standing.

We faced off across the whiteboard, markers in hand. Ready and waiting. I could still remember the way he'd smirked at me, the way he *always* smirked at me—like he knew everything about me, all my vulnerabilities. That smirk should have gotten under my skin, but in a weird way, I found it comforting. Even if he did know everything about me, he never judged me for any of it. He never whispered behind my back like Nicole and so many of the other kids did—about how weird I'd gotten after Mom died, about how I'd started wearing too much eyeliner and stopped hanging out with my queen bee crowd and isolated myself in a permanent sulk because I thought I was "too good" for the rest of the student body. I never thought that. I just couldn't bear to be around anyone who looked at me with pity.

Sam was the only person who never did. He never looked at me like I was a sad puppy in need of rescuing. Sure, perhaps this spoke to his deeply ingrained shallowness and the fact that he never wanted to deal with anything as complicated and messy as, you know, death. But it also meant he always treated me as an equal when we went head-to-head in any kind of academic battle. I never had to worry about him letting me win because he felt sorry for me. Whenever I beat him, I knew it was fair and square.

"Shout out to my esteemed opponent," he'd said, giving a little bow and gesturing to me with his marker. "Let's fight this shit out to the death."

"Language, Sam," Mr. Palmer said wearily.

I think Mr. Palmer expected the entire competition to last about an hour. Instead, Sam and I kept going back and forth, back and forth, neither of us willing to give up ground. The whiteboard got so covered, it looked like it was bleeding rainbows. Sweat beaded my brow, and my hand cramped up as I scrawled out answer after answer. I waited in heady anticipation for each new problem, my brain latching on to numbers and how they fit together to produce the correct solutions. It was as if the world narrowed to include only me and Sam, the whiteboard, and our endless series of equations.

The competition ended up lasting well into the night, Mr. Palmer growing more aggrieved the later it got and making a big show of clearing his throat and checking his watch. But Sam and I were oblivious. We were lost in Fight It Out to the Death Calculus World. And as Mr. Palmer delivered the equation that would be my undoing, I realized I'd gotten so lost in this world, in this narrow plane of focus, that I felt euphoric. My face was flushed, and the fact that Sam refused to go even a little easy on me goosed my competition-loving adrenaline. Our tiny world, our back-and-forth, made me feel *alive*. And I hadn't felt like that—not really—since Mom died.

To be honest, it had been so much fun, I hadn't even cared that much when I lost. Sam, however, had been so gleeful over his win that he still had the "prize" Mr. Palmer rustled up out of his desk drawer—a novelty eraser shaped like a trophy with a big, cheesy "#1!" emblazoned on it. It was proudly displayed on his TV stand, and I threatened to steal it pretty much every time I came over. Since I was currently the real #1 and all.

"So do you want help with your posterboard?" Sam said, snapping me out of my trip down memory lane. "Or I could coach you on the presentation part. You know, help you find that essential charm that really makes it sing."

"I think I've got this," I said, rolling my eyes. Pancake head-butted me again. "Really, there's no one better than me to chronicle the dead mom conversations."

"Right," he said slowly. He set his chopsticks down. "So. Are you, like, okay with all this?"

"What do you mean?"

"Well, like you said when you got here. You've had quite a day. And actually, the one before that had a ton of shit going on too." He regarded me keenly, his gaze sweeping over my face. His expression had gone all serious again, his eyes intense, and I squirmed uncomfortably.

"Oh, no, don't try to hug me or give me Calendar Sam again," I said, taking another swig of pink drink. "I'm here for Supportive Friend Sam, remember? Supportive Friend Sam makes me curry and loans me his ugly sportsball clothes and buys me shitty pink alcohol. That is all I require from him."

"Don't forget the part where he also gives you rides everywhere," he said, raising an eyebrow. "I've already done all that, so what can I do for you now? Since you won't let me make your posterboard as definitively awesome as we both know it could be."

"Ooh!" I said, perking up as I drained my pink drink bottle. I waved it around in his face. "You got any more of this? Because it's de . . . delishussssss."

"Yes, lush, I have more," he said, downing his own glass of wine.

"Then I have something fun for us to do," I said, clapping my hands together. "Everyone's favorite sergeant, Rose Rorick, gave me a very special gift today: one of the old-school demon traps to tinker with. Maybe make better. And I thought you might have some ideas for that as well."

He shook his head, trying to fully wrap his brain around what I'd just said. "You got the head of the Demon Unit to give you official tech to *tinker with*? Only you, Beatrice."

"She's my frieeeeeeendddd," I protested, poking him in his arm. Whew. I probably shouldn't have chugged the last of the pink drink quite so fast.

"Rose is a kind, decent person with many friends," Sam said, standing and walking over to the fridge. "I don't think most of them are getting traps to tinker with."

"Come on, then!" I yelped, leaping to my feet and clearing the dishes with much fanfare. "Let's tinker. Let's tinker our collective ass off."

"Aw, shit." Sam pulled something out of the fridge and made a face. "I'm out of real wine. Looks like I'll be indulging in this sugar slop with you." He waved around an un-opened bottle of pink drink, then unscrewed the top and took a long gulp. "Gah. It's like fucking Kool-Aid."

"Hey, don't hog it all," I protested, dumping the dishes in the sink and crossing the room. "Leave it for the people who can actually enjoy its fine fizzy charms." I snatched the bottle from him and headed for the living room, chugging all the way. I felt loopy and light, like any worries I'd accumulated over the course of the past two days were evaporating in a cloud of pink bubbles.

I pulled the trap Rose had given me from my bag and settled on the couch, placing it in front of me reverently. Pancake shuffled after me, depositing himself at my feet and giving me a vaguely accusing look. He still hadn't forgiven me for not sharing my curry. Sam sat down next to me and took the pink drink bottle, eyeing the trap. I could practically see the gears in his brain shifting, cataloguing its boxy shape, its plain gray exterior.

"It's so basic," he said.

"I know, right?" I ran a finger along the top, where the mechanism opened. "Consider when they were invented: nobody knew what we were dealing with as far as our demon-y little friends went. I think they for real just looked to *Ghostbusters* for inspiration."

"It kinda worked," Sam said. "What do you think Rose wants out of this tinkering?"

"She wants us to see what kind of upgrades we can make. How we can make it more powerful," I said, steepling my fingers and letting out a supervillain cackle.

We both stared at the trap for a moment, passing the pink drink bottle back and forth and taking long, contemplative sips. I let my mind wander over its gray surfaces, the little dip of the panel that popped open and shut, the gentle protrusion of the button on the side. I imagined the series of wires and gears beneath its blah exterior that connected button to panel, the mechanism that made it pop open and shut on command. I stared at it hard, wishing I had x-ray vision, that

I could actually *see* the way it all worked. I flashed back to being in my dad's study, staring at his radio receiver.

I looked up to see Sam studying the trap as intently as I was. He met my eyes.

"We should take it apart!" we exclaimed in unison.

"Is that okay?" Sam said, his gaze going back to the trap. I could tell his mind was working overtime, strategizing the best way to detach all the pieces from each other. "Will Rose murder us?"

"Rose will *not* murder us." I defiantly raised my index finger in the air as I took another gulp of pink drink. "Rose will welcome our technical innovation when we present her with the best trap of all time ever, which we will only be able to achieve if we *take this thing apart!*"

"Yes!" Sam pumped a fist in the air and snagged the pink drink bottle from me. "Let's do it!"

He took a drink, then passed the bottle back to me and hopped up from the couch, hustling into his bedroom. I sipped from the bottle as Pancake stared at me inquisitively.

"We're gonna blow this thing wide open, Pancake," I said, my words slurring. "Wiiiiiide opeeeeeeeen." Pancake blinked at me then set his head on his paws and shut his eye. Clearly, Pancake was not as excited about this as Sam and I were.

Sam returned with a small toolkit—a pouch about the size of a paperback book containing various screwdrivers—and sat back down on the couch.

"This is delicate work requiring delicate tools," Sam said, carefully laying the kit out between us. He ran a finger along the trap's top panel, his brow furrowing. "So I'm thinking we should start by detaching the panel, since that and the button are probably the most detachable—"

"No way," I interrupted, batting his hand away. I flipped the trap over and pointed to one of the tiny screws holding the bottom part in place. "We should start *here* so we can see how everything's working before we completely disassemble it."

"That would be the pedestrian approach," Sam said,

putting his hand over mine. "But if we're going to innovate
this design, we have to innovate how we're going about it."

"Did you just call me pedestrian?" I growled, tightening
my grip on the trap.

"No, I said your *approach* is pedestrian," he said, tightening his hand around mine.

I met his eyes and felt that competitive spark humming
between us again, bright and sharp enough to pierce my
drunken haze. Or maybe it was *enhanced* by my drunken
haze? I wasn't sure. All I knew was I was suddenly hyper-
aware of the heat of his hand on mine, of our warring grips,
of how my blood was racing through my veins and that feeling of being totally *alive* was swelling in my chest. It felt like
the Calculus Bee all over again.

"You're flushed," Sam said, his dark eyes holding mine.
"Why are you flushed?" His breathing sounded heavy, un-
even. Maybe we were both a little more drunk than we'd
realized.

"You're flushed, too," I countered, refusing to relinquish
my grip on the trap. His hand stayed on top of mine, neither
of us willing to give in. "We both have the Asian Flush from
drinking, *duh*."

He leaned in closer and looked like he was about to retort
when a strange expression passed over his face. It was there
and gone so quickly I wondered if I'd imagined it—the whole
drunken haze thing again. And I couldn't parse it exactly,
but if pressed, I'd maybe say he looked . . . confused? Sort
of? Before I had a chance to analyze further, he abruptly
pulled his hand away.

"In the name of speeding things up, we'll try your way,"
he said, rolling his eyes and leaning back on the couch. "But
let the record show I firmly believe that the most obvious
route is not always the correct route."

"Whatever," I said, but I was already reaching for one of
the tiny screwdrivers that would allow me to unlock all the
trap's deepest secrets. One by one, I carefully removed the

screws holding the bottom panel in place. Sam watched, sipping the remainder of the pink drink. I lifted the bottom panel reverently, as if whatever we were about to see would reveal the fate of the universe. And then we both leaned in to better scrutinize the maze of wires and gears, the stuff that made it work.

Man, I *love* seeing what makes stuff work.

"Okay," Sam said, his breath warm against my ear. "So we can obviously give this thing an initial upgrade by replacing some of these basic parts. This all looks fucking ancient."

"Now who's being pedestrian?" I turned to face him. "Is that really how you'd approach making it better? If you replace all this stuff with new versions of what's already there, you're only going to get something that works as well as it did when it was first invented. Which was like thirteen years ago—"

"Did I say that was the only step?" he said, giving me an exasperated look. "That's just the first step. So we can get a baseline—"

"Uggggh, you and your baseline," I said, rolling my eyes in the most exaggerated way possible.

"Baselines are *important*!"

"Baselines are *boring*!"

That competitive spark that had been percolating all night felt like it was blazing now, a fierce heat rushing through my bloodstream and roaring in my ears and making me realize that we'd been moving closer and closer as we'd been fighting and now we were *so close* and his lips were inches from mine and his hand was on my shoulder and I felt that heat again . . .

The alcohol swirled through my brain, making me forget everything but that heat, and our competitive spark that always made me feel alive, so fucking *alive*, and how I was craving more of that, wanting to feel it in my whole body, my whole soul, my whole . . . everything.

I closed the tiny bit of distance between us and pressed my lips against his.

He made a surprised sound in the back of his throat, but

then he was kissing me just as fiercely, his hands sliding up my shoulders, his tongue parting my lips so we could taste each other.

I sighed into the kiss, thrilling in the way his tongue stroked against mine, the way he caught my lower lip between his teeth. His hands tangled in my hair and he pulled me even closer, then allowed his fingertips to drift down and feather over my collarbone and . . . oh, *god*. Why did that feel so fucking *good*? My sigh turned into a gasp, goosebumps pebbling my skin. His touch was the perfect mix of firm and gentle, aggressive yet coaxing, and I desperately wanted him to touch me *everywhere*.

Then he made that *sound* in the back of his throat again— a growl that made my nipples tighten and my blood fizz with pleasure. My hands went to his chest and my fingertips skated over that hard wall of muscle, reveling in the heat of his skin through the thin cotton of his t-shirt.

We kept kissing even as I pushed him back against the couch so I could straddle his body—I needed to feel every single inch of him against me. His hands slid down my back and underneath my shirt, his palms warm against my bare skin. They slid higher to cup my breasts, his thumbs stroking my nipples, sending delicious little shivers up my spine. I shuddered, throwing my head back and losing myself in this feeling of being surrounded by pure sensation, of the chills racing through my entire body.

I went back to kissing him and pressed my hands more firmly against his chest muscles—even though they were still covered by his t-shirt, I could tell the calendar hadn't done them justice. And he was a *really* excellent kisser, which I knew he was always bragging about, but—

Something pierced my brain at that moment, some kind of weird realization. I mean, of course I knew I was kissing Sam. But the fleeting thoughts of the calendar made me realize I was kissing, you know, *Sam*. My friend, my rival, somebody I maybe, probably . . . no, *definitely* shouldn't be kissing.

I pulled away, gasping for breath. "Sam," I said out loud, as if reminding myself it was really him.

"Bea," he said, in pretty much exactly the same tone.

"I . . ." I tried to start. "We . . ."

"We . . . have definitely had too much to drink," he said.

"Yes." I grabbed on to this explanation like a drowning woman grasping a life preserver. *"Yes."*

He gently moved me to the side, setting me next to him on the couch. Luckily I remembered to remove my hands from his chest.

"Let's pick this up in the morning," he said lightly. "Um, the trap. I mean the trap."

"Of course you mean the trap," I said, way too loudly. "Of course."

"You can have the bed," he said, standing and making an exaggerated "after you" gesture toward the bedroom. "I'll take the couch. Unless you want an Uber or something?"

"Oh, um. No, that's okay," I said, getting to my feet. Pancake stirred and stood up, blinking his one eye suspiciously. "The bed is . . . is great."

I winced at how fumbling and awkward we sounded. And I probably should've just taken an Uber back to HQ, but I couldn't process the full act of going outside and getting in the car and going home and . . .

"Great," he said. And now *his* voice was too loud.

He put a hand on my back and steered me toward his bedroom. Pancake followed, looking like he was trying to figure out what we were up to. Oh, Pancake. If only you knew. The tiny dog trotted into the bedroom with me, and I closed door behind us before Sam could even say goodnight.

I sat down on the bed with a heavy *thump*. Pancake whined and batted my foot with his paw. I picked him up and cuddled him to my chest.

I'd had one hell of a first day as a full-fledged superhero-ine. And I thought it had been over.

I had been so, so wrong.

CHAPTER TEN

REMARKABLY, I DIDN'T have a hangover. My first instinct was to send Sam a smug text, noting the apparent hangover-proof qualities of sugary pink drinks with twist-off tops. My next instinct was to remember that I was passed out *in Sam's bed* after trying to eat his face off the night before. All right, so yay pink drink for being hangover-proof, boo for increasing the likelihood of making out with totally inappropriate people.

Also, I'd gotten so wrapped up in Sam and the trap and drinking too much that I'd completely failed to make a poster-board documenting my Ghost Mom interactions. I'd totally gotten distracted by something shiny. Well, muscle-y. I could practically hear Evie tsk-ing in my head.

I wanted to text Leah, but I didn't even know where to begin. Best to save it for an in person catch-up. So I got up, made the bed, gathered my stuff, and borrowed a hoodie from Sam's workout clothes basket to throw over my make-shift pjs. Then I prepared to slip out—stopping to serve Pancake a bit of leftover katsu with the breading picked off. The poor pup deserved a treat after being forced to watch his mom's two best friends paw all over each other the night before.

Sam was passed out on the couch, one arm thrown over his face, a blanket wrapped around his lower half. His upper half was not wearing a shirt, which was a factoid I would not have considered notable before last night, but now my eyes couldn't help but linger, taking in the hard ridges of muscle, those beautiful abs—

Ugh. WTF.

I scrubbed a hand over my face. Maybe I had a hangover after all. I contemplated his sleeping form for a moment more. *You could make it go away*, a little voice piped up in my head. *Just, like, project a feeling of total non-awkwardness onto all your interactions with him until this blows over.* I shook my head. No. No fucking way. How could I say I had a code if I used my powers for something like *that*? I mean, I guess one could argue it was for the greater good— but really only *my* greater good.

It was tempting, though, especially when I imagined the levels of awkward our next interaction had the potential to reach. I cringed at the very thought. Then I pulled myself together, sent Sam a bland *thanks, see you later* text, and caught the bus home.

It was still early and things were quiet when I reached HQ. I headed to the kitchen to get myself some cereal and found Evie and Aveda huddled at the table, talking in low, hushed tones. Aveda was dressed for a workout: tank top and span-dex pants, hair pulled into her sleek, superheroine perfect ponytail. Evie, on the other hand, was still slobbing around in her bathrobe.

"Interesting contrast between you two," I said, grabbing cereal and milk and plopping myself into a chair next to them. They both jumped, startled, like they hadn't realized I was there.

"Bea," Evie said, turning to study me. "Annie and I were just discussing the missing tourist."

"Er, yes," Aveda said, her gaze shifting to the side a bit. "That is correct. We were *only* discussing the missing tourist."

"Ohhhkaaay," I said, drenching my cereal in milk. I liked to drown all cereal-type foodstuffs until they formed a mushy, goo-like paste—something that always totally dis-gusted Evie. Evie was too busy giving Aveda a warning look to take notice of my balanced breakfast, though. I imagined they'd probably been talking about me right before I walked in, maybe evaluating my superheroing performance from the day before.

"Try as we might, we could not find hide nor hair of this Carmen, and our supernatural scans were inconclusive," Aveda continued, smoothing over the awkwardness. "Which is my least favorite thing ever."

"Nate is going to do a deeper analysis of the scans using his power," Evie said.

Nate had a demon superpower: he could see things in what Evie called "4D." That meant he had an extra level of observation most people didn't, and could do things like tell you the exact makeup and fiber count of the shirt you were wearing. Sometimes, it allowed him to see extra stuff on supernatural scans, too, which came in handy when the scanners failed us. "In the meantime," Evie continued, "the Wave Organ's completely off limits to the public." She hesitated, studying my face. "Bea, are you okay? I know you stayed over at Sam's last night, but—"

"How do you know that?" I blurted out, my defenses going up. Jeez, was my sister spying on me? Did she have a hidden camera implanted in my phone? Was Pancake her man on the inside? And, uh . . . did that mean she'd seen what went down between Sam and me the night before? I *was* still wearing his clothes . . .

"You *told* me you were going over there," Evie said, tilting her head at me quizzically. "I assumed you'd decided to crash there after working on your trap experiment all night. Plus, Nate is obsessive about the 'find this person's phone' function when it comes to pretty much everyone in this household. He always lets me know you're somewhere safe if you haven't checked in. Otherwise I . . . I have a hard time sleeping. I know. Momming it up." She raised her hands in mock surrender. I noticed then that she looked tired: there were dark circles under her eyes and her smile was wan.

"Sorry," I said, tamping down on my usual instinct to snap at her for babying me. "I should've checked in, but . . . well.

Lots of weirdness took place. So much weirdness. Actually, I need to talk to you about some of it."

No, I didn't have my Ghost Mom posterboard ready, but hey, I could wing it.

"Yes," Aveda said, stabbing the air with her index finger. "I had a whole superheroine mentor lesson planned regarding honing your observational skills when it comes to all things weird, and I'm so happy to see that you're already on that, Bea." She rested her elbows on the table and leaned forward, eyes gleaming with anticipation. "So?"

"Oh, um . . ." How could I explain that this was something I wanted to talk about with just Evie, at least initially? The Mom piece of it felt intimate, something only Evie could truly understand. But I couldn't deny that I still wanted to superheroine-bond with Aveda, even though her "lesson" about wardrobe yesterday had kind of annoyed me and—

"Wait," Aveda said, interrupting my runaway train of thought. She held up her hands. "I feel like we're having a moderately tense silence here. Are we having a moderately tense silence? This is a social cue I should be picking up on, yes?" Without waiting for a response, she rose from the table and flipped her ponytail over her shoulder. "I'll leave you two alone," she said. "Social cue *understood*."

"Aw, look at you, picking up on this stuff," Evie said, patting her arm. "You've grown so much."

"I'm also late for the first of my daily workouts," Aveda sniffed, sticking her tongue out at Evie. "I need to meet Scott for our kickboxing session."

Evie's brow crinkled. "I thought Scott didn't know how to kickbox."

"Oh, he doesn't," Aveda said, breezing out of the kitchen with something that definitely sounded like an Evil Supervillain Cackle.

"There are so many ways that could be interpreted, and I'm not going to ask about any of them," Evie said, chuckling as she turned back to me. "All right, Bea. Let's hear about the weirdness."

"I guess it started when I went to get Mom's stuff," I said, thinking back to the day before, "which you still haven't seen, but don't worry, I brought it back with me. Or actually, I guess it was before that. The bathroom wall." I shook my head, trying to get the order of events straight, then spewed it all out at her. The message on the bathroom wall, the voice in my head at the Market, the strange interaction with the artist-poet girl at the Wave Organ.

"Okay," Evie said slowly. "So what you're saying is: you think our dead mother has been trying to contact you through various channels, and her messages are things like 'good job' and 'I'm still out there' and 'maybe chill with the junk food'?"

"Yeah, pretty much." My cheeks heated as I realized how ridiculous it all sounded.

"All right, so we need a plan," Evie said, nodding. "The team should do a full scan of It's Lit for sure. Unless something else happens, though, why don't we wait on that until you and Leah have had a chance to look through the bookstore security videos—see if you find anything that might help us direct our energy. Rose and her team are still monitoring the Wave Organ, but we can tell them about this new wrinkle, see if they notice anything down there. And we need to find this mysterious artist-poet girl, even though she may just be a vessel for whatever happened yesterday. Did she reveal anything about herself that might be helpful?"

"Not really." I replayed the moment in my head. "She said she was an outcast at school, but that's a lot of kids." I scrutinized Evie's face. "Are you saying . . . I mean, you believe me?"

Evie studied me. "Bea. We've fought off demon princesses and demon bloggers and evil bridezillas and . . . and *evil cupcakes*. The most logical explanation for anything happening in this city is that there's some truly fucked up supernatural shit going down. Of course I believe you."

"True," I said, grinning. "But I know you think I'm very distractible and sometimes I exaggerate a lot because I'm trying to get attention. Maybe because in the past I've exaggerated a lot. To get attention."

"Well, yeah," Evie said, giving me an indulgent smile. "But like I said the other night, I *am* trying to see you as the adult you are. I'm trying to grow as well—you know, tamping down on the Momming instincts."

"Wow," I said, grinning at her. "Are we actually getting along and shit?"

"We are," she said, her smile widening. "Kind of cool, huh?"

"Doesn't it make you wish you'd promoted me to full superhero a lot earlier?"

She cocked an eyebrow at me. "I wouldn't go that far."

🔥

"Is this the same person we saw three minutes ago?" Leah said, tapping on her laptop screen. Some of her glittery nail polish flaked off, giving the latest unremarkable person entering the It's Lit bathroom a sparkly halo. "Are they leaving you messages or do they just have a frighteningly small bladder?" She furrowed her brow, making a note on the spreadsheet we'd started. We'd spent most of our shift thus far going through the security camera videos to see if they provided any further clues about the bathroom writing.

I'll admit I kept irrationally hoping to catch a glimpse of Mom—or maybe her ghostly form. But so far it had been an endless parade of regulars, randos, and people who worked here.

"I'd guess bladder," I said, tapping my foot impatiently. Something sharp poked at my heel and I winced. I had once again donned my hole-y ankle boots without thinking, and I definitely had a new little rock friend rattling around in there. The hole just kept getting bigger and bigger. Pretty soon I was going to have a whole-ass boulder in my shoe. "I gotta admit, I thought investigative superheroing would be more exciting than this." Pancake, who was lounging on his special pillow, made a whuffle-y sound of agreement.

"We're sorting minutiae. Which I thought you enjoyed?" Leah said, cocking an eyebrow at me.

"I do when it's data on action-packed demon attacks," I said. "Not so much when it's an endless parade of people who have to pee."

"Hopefully there's some bit of information in here that will help," Leah said. I marveled at her ability to remain determined—and awake—after hours of going through footage. I stifled a yawn as we watched the millionth nondescript customer enter the bathroom. I was having the same feeling I'd had yesterday while I was checking out the Pussy Queen portal with Aveda and interviewing the distraught tourist. Like what we were doing should have felt way more exciting than it actually was. I mean, at the very least, shouldn't a superheroic investigation be more exciting than serving—

"Coffee?" My head snapped up to see Nemesis Nicole rattling her stupid empty cup at me. "The café section of your establishment appears to be unstaffed. Again."

"It's closed right now," Leah said, her eyes not leaving the laptop screen.

"How can it be closed when there are customers?" Nicole huffed.

"The only customer in the café is you, and you've been sitting there for three hours reading a bunch of books you're not going to buy," I said.

"Yeah," Leah said. "Purchase something and we'll talk."

Nicole glared at us. "I don't see a posted *policy* about that."

"So put that fancy paralegal training to good use and sue us," I said.

Nicole looked like she was winding up to say something else, then settled for turning on her heel and stalking back to the café area.

"I should probably go in there and make sure she doesn't take her rage out on anything expensive," I said, yawning again. I rubbed my eyes. "But I don't want to break from watching the footage, because that will just make it go on longer."

"You look extra tired, Bebe," Leah said, leaning her head against my shoulder. "Sam came by to drop Pancake off and said you guys took apart one of those trap things. Now *that's* the kind of minutiae you enjoy, right? Breaking electronics into tiny pieces to look at their guts?"

"Um, yes." I flashed back to the other things Sam and I had done last night. And I wondered if Sam had told Leah anything about it. Although, if he had, surely she would have greeted me with some kind of shriek or demand to tell her more. As if reading my mind, Pancake raised his head and gave me an accusing stare.

"Bebe." Leah lifted her head from my shoulder and turned to face me. "What's up? You went all stiff. Did you see something on the footage?"

"No," I said, feeling a flash of guilt as I realized I hadn't even been looking at the laptop screen for the last five minutes. What if I'd missed the one crucial moment of importance lurking in the vast sea of boring? Ugh. This was so frustrating. I'd thought my new superheroing life would have me experiencing a multitude of thrills by the minute, but instead I was doing the same thing I'd done every day for the past four years: slogging my way through boredom with Leah and Pancake and fending off annoying customers. I'd tried to liven things up earlier by mind-mojo-ing a cute guy who'd come in to ask for directions—you know, to set Leah up with. But she'd nixed my efforts yet again.

Well, if we were going to be stuck looking at this stupid video footage for hours on end, I might as well introduce some scandalous discussion into the proceedings. I hit pause on the laptop and turned to face Leah. "Sam and I made out last night."

The shocked face she gave me was the most excited either of us had looked all day.

"Whaaaaaaat!" she cried. "Oh my god, Bebe!" Then she shook her head and dissolved into giggles.

"Excuse me," I said, my boredom/irritation cocktail swiftly replaced with indignation. "Why is that funny?"

"Because the two of you are so ridiculous!" Leah exclaimed, whacking me on the arm. "You both need so much drama in your lives. And if it's not happening, you'll go out of your way to *create* drama."

"That is *not* true," I said, crossing my arms over my chest. "It's not like we planned it, we were both drinking and then we started talking about rebuilding the trap, and then we just got caught up in the moment and—"

"—and you're both phenomenally bad at impulse control so you decided to smash tongues," Leah said. "Makes perfect sense. I love that it was all that tech-y talk that turned you on. Let me guess: you weren't just *talking* about rebuilding the trap, you were *fighting* over who had the best approach to rebuilding the trap."

"I can't believe you're reducing us to horny teenagers," I said, my face flushing. No way was I gonna tell her she was right. "If we're so bad at impulse control, how have we avoided tongue-smashing shenanigans all these years?"

"Pancake and I are always around, for one thing," Leah said, poking her pup affectionately. He flicked an ear at her. "Y'all never had the magic cocktail of too much alcohol, arguing over nerdy shit, and being alone together."

"That is . . . that is *not* . . ." I sputtered, reluctant to cede ground.

"So how was it?" Leah said, linking her arm through mine and putting her head on my shoulder again. "How far did you get? Was there any nudity happening?"

"Kissing. And some touching . . ." My face flushed again, but for different reasons. "He's a *really* good kisser, Lee."

"Not that you'll ever admit that in his presence," Leah said.

"Never," I agreed. "We don't need his head getting any more massive than it already is. But what do I do now? I'm already dreading the awkwardness of our next interaction."

"I'd guess that the one interaction will be awkward, and then you guys will decide it was a fun mistake and move on to whatever your next exciting drama is," Leah said with a shrug. "Easy."

"Really? That's it?"

"Bebe." Leah gave me an appraising gaze. "The two of you are always chasing whatever the next thrill is. And making out with your previously platonic best friend is only thrilling and naughty and weird the first couple times. After that . . ." She shrugged. "You'll both get bored."

"I . . . I guess." Why was this making me feel so deflated?

"What else do you want it to be?" Leah pressed. "Do you want to *date* Sam?"

"Ew, no." I gave a little shudder.

"Exactly," Leah said. "So skip the 'oh gawd this changes our friendship *forever*' agonizing. In this case, I don't think it does."

I was nodding, but something was still bothering me, making me feel deflated and restless. Had last night's make-out session really only happened because I was so desperate for excitement? And if so, why was that bothering me? Shouldn't I want things to be simple, want my relationship with Sam to be as easy as it usually was? Shouldn't I feel *relieved*?

"Bea!" Leah and I swiveled to the bookstore's entrance, where Evie was bustling in, waving at me enthusiastically. Aveda, Scott, Nate, and Lucy trailed in behind her. Aveda was toting one of the scanners, and Lucy was carrying a large, domed Tupperware.

"Hey, guys. Luce, is that . . . did you bring a cake?" I said warily.

Lucy was a notoriously terrible baker, but she was so enthusiastic about her creations, nobody had the heart to tell her. Also, she was good at everything else, so it didn't really matter.

"Indeed I did!" she enthused, setting the Tupperware down on the counter. "I thought we should have something to celebrate your first official mission as a full-fledged superheroine. Well, really it's more like your third mission, but who's counting?" With great flourish, she lifted the dome off the Tupperware. "Ta-da!" she said, revealing a . . . umm "blob" was probably the best description for it. It was a sickly off-white color and oozing all over the serving tray so that it had no discernable shape. The texture looked somewhere in the realm of extra lumpy split pea soup. YAY, BEA! was spelled out on top in bright purple icing.

"Don't worry," Evie whispered in my ear. "We got you an actual cake from Cake My Day. We'll have that later as a second celebration. But she was super excited to make you something."

"It looks so good, Luce," I said, feeling genuinely touched. "Is it, ahhh, vanilla?"

"I think so," she said, her brow furrowing. "You know, I just kind of made it up as I went along."

Pancake sniffed the cake and recoiled, scampering to the other end of the counter. He side-eyed the blob cake disdainfully.

"I'm sure we all can't wait to try it," I said. "But what do you mean, mission? And what are you guys doing here? I thought you were gonna wait for me and Leah to submit our findings before doing any kind of scan."

"There are no new disturbances by the Wave Organ, and we haven't been able to track down the missing tourist and your mysterious teenage poet," Aveda said, shaking her head in frustration. "It felt like a dead-end morning, so—"

"Not *all* dead ends," Nate said, giving her a disapproving look. "I finished my analysis of the scans Rose took of the Pussy Queen portal yesterday."

"The ones with the weird gibberish," I remembered. Damn. Yesterday morning seemed like it had happened *centuries* ago.

"Correct," Nate said. "The results were fascinating. It appears that the 'gibberish' was signaling something—the atmosphere around the supernatural energy from the portal was heavier, somehow. More concentrated than usual."

"But the energy is still dormant because it's from the portal, right?" Aveda said, rolling her eyes. "Booooring."

"Not boring at all," Nate said, stiffening. "It is, in fact, quite intriguing, and I would like to conduct further research—"

"Yes, yes, we know," Aveda said, waving a hand at him. "But in the meantime, we thought the best use of our time might be expediting the scan of the bookstore."

"'We'?" I muttered under my breath.

"She was going stir crazy at home," Evie murmured in my ear. She gave me a conspiratorial grin. "Sometimes part of being a superhero team means knowing how to really listen to your partner and meet their needs."

"Sounds like being married," I said, raising a skeptical eyebrow.

"Kind of the same thing," she said with a laugh.

We shared a smile, and I felt a surge of easy warmth between us, the same easy warmth I'd felt in the kitchen that morning. I wasn't accustomed to that, I realized. Evie's and my relationship had always been mercurial, marked by big, loud bursts of feeling rather than even keel companionship. And they weren't all bad feelings: I loved her more fiercely than I could imagine loving anyone. But this everyday sisterhood thing was new to me. It was nice.

"I also have a spell I'd like to try on the bathroom wall writing," Scott said. "I'm going to try sending a mental connector out and see if there's anything on the other end to—for lack of a better word—catch it."

"Like you could maybe *communicate* with the writing on the wall?" I asked.

"That's the basic idea," he said, grinning at me.

"Way cool," I said, giving him finger guns. "Let's do it."

"So that means we can pause this thrilling video surveillance?" Leah said, gesturing to her laptop. "I guess I could go see if Her Highness Nicole wants more coffee."

"No!" I said, holding up a hand. "Not unless she buys something. We just made that rule, now we have to abide by it."

"Then I should go make sure she hasn't *broken* anything,"

Leah said with a laugh. "Take Pancake with you to the bathroom—you know animals have a sixth sense when it comes to creepy shit. And Pancake is extra intuitive."

"That he is," I said, scooping up Pancake. "Come on, team." I beckoned everyone to follow me to the bathroom.

"Yes, Bea, lead the way," Aveda said, giving me an approving nod. "This is the perfect opportunity for another important superheroing lesson: When you're the team member who's most familiar with an investigation site, take charge and do so with confidence. Confidence always wins the day."

"We like her," I whispered in Pancake's ear. "And I think she and I could form a meaningful superheroine bond. But she's a little much sometimes."

I entered the bathroom first and flicked on the light. The craft wall looked as cool as ever. Other than that, it looked like . . . you know, an adorable bathroom in an adorable Bay Area bookstore. Nothing weird happening.

"Wow," Evie said, zeroing in on the message I'd been obsessing over. "It really does look like Mom's writing." She ran her fingers over it and swallowed hard. I knew she was feeling what I had felt when I'd made the connection between the writing and the letters: that bizarre emotional gut punch. We'd gone through Mom's letters together before I'd departed HQ for my bookstore shift—another nice moment of sisterly bonding. I shifted Pancake to one arm and reached over to squeeze her hand. She squeezed back, then briskly scrubbed a hand over her eyes. "Let's try scanning first."

It felt like we were collectively holding our breaths as Aveda stepped forward, flicked the scanner on, and waved it over the bathroom wall. Nothing happened. No beep, and the read-out area remained blank. We all let out a long sigh.

"That doesn't necessarily mean there's nothing here," Aveda said, glaring at the scanner. "I really can't wait for these things to get an upgrade."

"Let me try the spell," Scott said. He flashed Aveda a teasing grin. "Though remember, it has the potential to be as unreliable as the scanner."

"So much nicer to look at, though," Aveda said, arching an eyebrow.

Scott smiled at her again, then turned to the wall and placed his hand on top of the writing. He closed his eyes, took a few deep breaths, and concentrated.

And once again, it felt like we all stopped breathing for a moment. The air in the room became weighted, quiet except for the sounds of everyone shifting apprehensively from foot to foot, waiting to see what would happen. I felt like the heavy silence was pressing against my skin, making me itchy and uncomfortable. Pancake let out a tiny whine.

Then, just when it seemed like we'd been living in that silence forever, just when I was certain Scott was going to drop his hand and step back from the wall and be all like, "Sorry, nothing here" and give Aveda another flirty grin . . . it happened.

Scott's head snapped up, his eyes went wide, and he jumped back from the wall.

"What?" Aveda demanded. "What is it? Is there something here?"

He didn't answer, just started shaking his head back and forth. "It's . . . ." he said, then whipped around and flung an arm out, like he was trying to throw something off of him. "It wants . . ."

He turned further. And looked straight at me.

"What—?" I started to say, but then—

WHOOM

The sound blasted through my head, like a massive gust of wind whooshing in one ear and out the other. My vision went black, and I had the sensation of falling, but not landing anywhere. It was like I was suddenly floating through an expanse of starless night. I thought I could hear Pancake barking faintly in the background, but I couldn't tell if it was real or all in my head. He definitely wasn't in my arms anymore, though.

"*Wha—what!*" I gasped, my hands flailing, clawing the air around me. But there was nothing there. Nothing for me to grab on to, nothing for me to see, nothing for me to do except scream into the void, hoping someone would hear. Panic seized my heart in its icy grip and I swallowed hard, trying to keep the fear at bay. I still couldn't see anything except an oppressive veil of complete darkness. "Where am I, what's happening?! Evie . . . anyone, can you hear me?"

Bug.

The voice echoed through my head, silencing me. Gentle, musical, so familiar. And even as I kept thrashing around, trying to find something to anchor me in the empty air, my eyes filled with tears.

"Mom?" I cried out, my voice sounding strangled. "Is that you? Is that—"

Please, my darling. I'm trapped here. I need you.

"Trapped?" I squeaked. "Where? What is this place?"

I need you to look for answers.

"Answers to what?" I managed. I stopped flailing for a moment and allowed myself to float. It was such a weird sensation. There was nothing supporting me, nothing holding me in place. Yet I didn't fall. It was like being suspended in one of those weird oxygen tanks.

The evil that took me. It's back.

"I need . . . more than that," I said, frustration welling in my chest. "Please, Mom, tell me what's going on."

It will take more of us. We will all be trapped in this demon dimension if you don't act.

Tears filled my eyes. What was she saying? I wanted to talk to her, dammit, to have an actual conversation, to be able to touch her and ask her questions and—

WHOOM

That same whooshing blasted in my ears again, and then the floor materialized beneath me, and my eyes were blinking open, and I was gasping like I'd just been held underwater for a very long time.

"Bea!" Evie shook my shoulders, her face pale. "Are you okay?"

"We were just about to call 911," Nate said, leaning over to inspect me, his brow creasing with concern.

"What happened?" I croaked. I sat up slowly, feeling lightheaded. "I mean, what did you guys see happening just now?"

"After Scott turned to you, your eyes got really big and you collapsed," Lucy said. "It was very dramatic, darling, and I planned on commending your swooning once we determined you were okay."

"I think I'm fine," I said, taking stock of the various parts of my body. Nothing felt broken, altered, or like it was cause for distress. "I think I went somewhere else. In my mind. Obviously not physically, since my body was still here—oh, Pancake! Did I drop him?" I looked around wildly. Leah would straight up murder me if anything happened to that dog.

"He jumped to the ground when you started freaking out," Aveda said.

As if on cue, Pancake trotted up and started licking my thumb.

"It was almost like I got transported to another plane of existence," I said, turning the experience over in my mind. "Scott, what did you feel right before? I mean, clearly there is or was some kind of supernatural energy here, right?"

"That would be a logical hypothesis," Nate murmured.

"It was so strange," Scott said. "At first, there was nothing there—it was like looking at this big, blank canvas. And then all of a sudden, I felt it—something reaching out, trying to make contact. But it wasn't interested in communicating with me. It was like it was trying to lunge past, trying to get to you, Bea."

"It was my mom," I blurted out. "Our mom," I amended, reaching over to squeeze Evie's hand. Tears pricked my eyes again as I remembered her voice, echoing through my head. "She spoke to me. She told me . . . she's trapped. And whatever trapped her is back. That it will take more people . . ." I shook my head, trying to make sense of the scraps of information Mom had been trying to give me.

"Where is she trapped?" Aveda asked.

My brow furrowed. "She said . . . a demon dimension."

"We only know of one of those, right?" Lucy said, raising an eyebrow.

"Wait." Evie held up a hand. "Bea, are you saying . . ." Her eyes widened as she tried to wrap her head around the idea. "Is our mother—who we've thought was dead for a decade— *trapped in the freaking Otherworld*?"

The most bizarre feeling was building in my chest. It was a combination of two completely opposite emotions and I wasn't sure if I wanted to cheer or burst into tears or somehow do both at once.

"It sure looks that way," I said.

Chapter Eleven

MY MOTHER IS alive.

My mother is dead.

My mother is being impersonated by a bunch of demons who have somehow learned my childhood nickname.

My mind was whirling, and I couldn't contain it. We were back in the common area of It's Lit, and I was sitting on a stool by the register, downing water. Nate had insisted that even though I seemed to feel okay, I should hydrate. Pancake had forgiven me for nearly dropping him on his ass, and was sprawled in my lap, allowing me to pet him.

"Has there ever been a case involving a human getting trapped in the Otherworld?" Evie asked Nate. "Did Shasta ever mention anything?"

"No," he said, his brow furrowing. "I can honestly say I've never heard of anything like this. The way she talked, the demons in the Otherworld thought of humans as vastly inferior beings. Their goals were more along the lines of enslavement and taking control of the human world. Not holding them prisoner in an alternate dimension for no apparent reason."

"How would our mom have even gotten to that alternate dimension?" Evie said. "She died years ago."

"She died after the first demon portal opened up, though," I said. "Maybe something weird happened to her, something we had no clue about at the time—"

"Bea, we need to keep in mind that this could very well be some kind of Otherworld trick. I watched her waste away," Evie said, her voice gentle. "From the cancer. There was nothing supernatural about it. You might not remember—"

"I remember," I snapped, my voice harsher than I intended. "I wasn't a total child."

Admittedly, most of what I remembered was Evie shuttling me out of the room whenever things got really bad, when Mom was throwing up from chemo or too tired to lift her head. I remembered Evie shielding me at every turn. I knew I should appreciate that, but all I felt when I revisited those memories was resentment that I had been denied those last moments with my mother, traumatic as they might have been.

The worst had been the day she died. She'd been in the hospital for weeks at that point, but was having a particularly bad time of it that day. Evie had situated me in the waiting area and kept bringing me random treats from the vending machine while she and Dad tended to Mom. I sat there for hours, getting increasingly frustrated and hopped up on sugar. A landfill of candy wrappers sprung up around me. Finally, Evie had come hustling back one last time in the late afternoon. I sprang to my feet, my face red, my blood racing, and demanded she take me to Mom. She'd grabbed my hand and pulled me back down on the couch. And looking into her eyes, leached of hope . . . I'd known. She hadn't even had to say the words.

"Anyway," I said, trying to get my temper under control, "it's not that I think she didn't have cancer, but what if something else was going on, too? What if her body died, but her mind, her spirit, went elsewhere?" I stroked Pancake's fur, replaying what Mom's voice had said to me when I was in the freaky spacescape. Had that been part of the Otherworld? Had my consciousness *visited* the Otherworld? Holy shit.

"She told me whatever took her is back," I said. "That it's going to take others, that everyone will be trapped like she is . . ." I shivered.

"So where do we start?" Aveda said, leaning against the

front counter. "We need more information on . . . well, oh so many things."

"We should do a thorough scan of the bookstore," Nate said. "See if we can pick up any additional readings or data points. Perhaps Leah and Bea can complete their review of the security camera video. And . . ." He hesitated, cast a sidelong look at Evie, and put an arm around her shoulders. "I believe we should look more closely into the circumstances of your mother's death. Bea is right: I don't know everything Shasta was up to back when she was plotting to take over the city. Perhaps one of her schemes had consequences unknown to us until now."

"True," Aveda said. "But Evie is also right: this could be a prime example of Otherworld trickery. Using the idea of your mother to get to you is very potent, Bea, and could be the work of a particularly nefarious demon. This is another good superheroing lesson for you: always stay on your guard, because supernatural forces will try to take advantage of any perceived vulnerabilities you might have."

"I know that," I muttered, picking at an invisible bit of lint on my sleeve.

The thing was, I was absolutely certain this force, this voice, this being—whatever you wanted to call it—was my mother. My science brain longed for more concrete proof. My gut told me this was the only possible explanation, and it didn't matter if anyone else believed me. Maybe it had something to do with the special connection Mom and I had shared, but I just *knew*. I'd felt that fierce, undeniable bond when she'd spoken to me just now, in the weird spacescape. This was no Otherworld trick. Mom was trapped somehow, and I had to help her.

"So we'll pursue several avenues of investigation at once," Scott said, trying to smooth things over.

"Agreed. For instance, we really need to track down the little seaside poet Bea was chatting with yesterday," Lucy said. "Maybe she experienced a weird connection similar to the one Bea experienced in the bathroom."

"Oh! I have an idea for that," Leah said, raising her hand. She'd been quiet up 'til this point, listening to Team Tanaka/Jupiter strategize.

"You can just talk, Lee," I said encouragingly. "You don't have to raise your hand."

"I've been planning on hosting this big art jam here at the store," Leah said. "We'll provide basic supplies and people can also bring their own and it'll be a whole night of people painting and reading and writing and crafting and sharing their art with each other. That sounds like something our little poet girl would be into, yes?"

"Very much so," I said. "Good thinking, Lee. Let's make sure we get the word out to all the local high schools." I turned to Scott. "Do you think your spell had something to do with Mom connecting to me so directly this time? In a way that transported my consciousness somewhere else?"

"I'm not sure, Bug," Scott said. He gave me a patient smile. "That's the first time I've attempted that spell, and I don't know what, exactly, happened back there."

"Can we try it again?" I set Pancake down next to the register—earning me an indignant look—and got to my feet. "Maybe I can go back to wherever I was and get more information. I can go in with actual questions now that I know what's happening. I can—" I probably would have kept going in this vein for quite some time, but I was swiftly drowned out by a chorus of *No*.

"It's too dangerous," Scott said.

"We don't have enough data about how this affected you physically," Nate said.

"No," Evie said. "Full stop."

"But—" I said.

"No!" everyone else said, in near unison. Even Leah. I shot her a look, and she gave me an apologetic shrug.

"I don't want you mind-transporting into freaky space-scapes until you know more about what you're dealing with, Bebe," she said.

"Fine," I said, slumping back on the stool in a sulk. "So

Nate said we should look more closely into Mom's death—how do we do that?"

"I can gather up whatever records I have from that time," Evie said slowly.

"A good place to start," Aveda said, nodding. "And maybe you and Bea could do a more thorough read-through of those letters in the box Kathy gave you, maybe they can give us some clues—you said they were written close to your mother's death?"

Evie nodded, but looked reluctant. Delving into the details around Mom's death was something she generally avoided.

"We should probably visit the hospital. Where she died," I said. "I can take that on."

"Oh, Bea—you don't have to," Evie said quickly. "Not by yourself."

"I won't be by myself, I'll take Sam." I heard both Leah and Pancake snort behind me, like they were trying to keep from laughing. I ignored them. "He's off shift for the afternoon. And he has a car." And I could rip off the potential-awkwardness band-aid. Might as well get that out of the way as soon as possible.

"All right," Evie said. "In that case, I'll email Dad, see what he remembers from that time period. That way we're splitting up the potentially emotionally taxing tasks."

"Yay, sister teamwork," I said, giving a little fist-pump.

"This is so touching!" Lucy said. "And it reminds me, we still haven't eaten any of my cake. Seems like a very appropriate moment to do so, does it not?"

"Oh, absolutely, Luce," Evie said weakly.

"I can't wait for this deliciousness," I said, plastering on a big grin.

"Yummmmmm," Aveda said, sounding the least convincing of all of us.

We all turned back to the counter—just as Pancake trotted over and sat his ass down right in the middle of Lucy's oozy blob cake.

"Oh, what a shame," Leah said, not looking the least bit sad at all. She patted Pancake on the head. "Bad dog."

🔥

"I need you to drive me to the hospital."

I hadn't rehearsed what I was going to say to Sam—I had quite a few things to cover, after all—so when he answered the door to his apartment, I blurted out the first thing that came to mind.

"What?!" he exclaimed, shaking his head. He put his hands on my shoulders and gently guided me inside, looking alarmed as he scanned my face. "What's wrong? Are you hurt?"

"What—no!" I said, belatedly realizing what my breezy proclamation had sounded like. "Sorry. Let me back up." I took a deep breath and tried to put all of my disparate thoughts in order. "I need you to drive me to the hospital where my mom died so we can learn more about the exact circumstances of her death. Scott did this spell in the It's Lit bathroom that somehow ended with me talking to Mom, and she's maybe trapped in the Otherworld and is currently worried other people are gonna get trapped too. I volunteered to do this hospital part because I think it will be less emotionally taxing for me than Evie and also probably way more exciting than all of the superheroic investigating I've been doing so far, which really isn't very exciting at all. Also, Leah thinks you and I kissed last night because we were bored and trying to create drama, which is kind of insulting, but also maybe makes things easier because we can just sort of agree that's what happened and move on. Right?"

I paused my motormouthing, slightly out of breath, and cocked my head at him. I don't know what I was expecting—that he'd laugh and agree, and we could speed off on our hospital mission, and it would be as easy as Leah had claimed, I guess? Instead he studied me, his gaze a mix of surprise and befuddlement. His hands were still on my shoulders, I realized, and I was suddenly very aware of their

weight, their warmth, the way that simple touch made me
flash back to those same hands pressing against the small of
my back the night before, urging me closer—

Argh. What was I *doing*? Why did my brain choose *now*
to replay that moment in graphic detail?

"You're flushed," Sam said, putting a hand on my forehead. "Are you sure you don't need to go to the hospital?
Maybe you're running a fever."

"I'm fine," I sputtered. "And did you hear anything I just
said? Because it's pretty freaking important, and if you're
going to make me repeat it all, well, I really do not have the
time for that, I need to get to—"

"I heard you," he said, giving me an exasperated look and
dropping his hand from my forehead. I had a sudden, irrational wish for him to put it back. "I'm processing. You talk
faster than any normal human being should."

"Can't keep up with me?" I said, attempting to kickstart
our usual competitive sniping. "What a shame."

"I'm keeping up just fine," he said, rolling his eyes at me.
"So to start with the last thing: Leah thinks I kissed you to
start drama? Do *you* think that?"

"Excuse me." I crossed my arms over my chest and drew
myself up tall. "You did *not* kiss me. I kissed you."

"I know when I kiss someone, Beatrice," he said, giving
me an especially smug version of his self-satisfied smirk.
"Believe me."

"I kissed you first—you kissed me *back*," I protested. My
flush had escalated to the face-on-fire level and irritation
crawled under my skin. I poked my index finger into his
chest. "I remember because you made this sort of growling
sound in the back of your throat, like you were surprised,
and then you . . ." I trailed off and swallowed hard. My mouth
was totally dry, my face was flaming hot, and I couldn't seem
to remove my finger from his chest. I was picturing everything that had come after he'd made that sound . . . Goddammit, that *sound*. Just thinking about that husky growl spilling

out of him, that sound that had to mean he was turned on, that sound that reverberated through my entire body—

"And then I what?" he said, covering my hand with his. His voice had the challenging tone it always got when we were trying to one-up each other. And just a hint of that same growl. I shivered.

"You . . ." I tried to force my brain to spit out a coherent thought. Just *one* coherent thought, that's all I was asking for. But my brain was super not into cooperating, and his hand was pressing mine against his chest, and I could feel his heart beating against my palm. That little rush I always got from challenging him, from him challenging me, from our all too familiar pattern of trying like mad to get the other person to concede, was racing through my bloodstream. It felt amplified, exaggerated. Like someone had turned the volume way up.

This time, he definitely kissed me first. I'll give him that. Bea: 1275, Sam: 1165.

His arms went around my waist to pull me closer, his hands sliding under my shirt. Blood roared in my ears as his tongue parted my lips and I gasped against his mouth and pressed myself more firmly against him, craving more.

Why does this feel so fucking good?

Because it's giving you that drama you need so badly, a little voice in my head piped up helpfully. *Remember what Leah said—*

Shit. Right.

I pushed away from him and took two big steps backward, putting a decent amount of space between us.

"Hey," I said, giving him a stern look. "We're supposed to be agreeing that we don't need to be doing any of *that—*" I made a broad gesture at the space between us. "—and moving on to what's actually important here. Which is going to the hospital and doing some hardcore supernatural investigating."

Sam gave me a look. "You know that agreeing on something requires input from two people, right?"

I put my hands on my hips. "You do agree with me, though, right?"

"Am I agreeing with you or with Leah? Because you've told me what she thinks, but not what *you* think—"

"I think what she thinks," I said stubbornly. "Leah and I have the same opinion about a lot of things."

"Fine. But I don't think something Leah said should dictate whether or not we kiss again."

"Do you want to kiss me again?"

He stared at me for a moment, silence building until it felt like an oppressive force taking up the whole room. Then he stepped forward, closing the space I'd put between us. His expression shifted ever so subtly—like the smug heartthrob Calendar Sam mask fell away, leaving Supportive Friend Sam in its place. He reached over and brushed my hair off of my face, and I found myself leaning into his touch. I desperately wanted to look down, to alleviate the intensity humming between us, but I couldn't break eye contact. That would've felt like losing. Like conceding an especially precious point.

"Yes," he finally said. "I do want to kiss you again. But I don't think I should."

I shook my head. "What?"

"I don't totally agree with Leah," he said, still playing with my hair. Which was making it extra hard to focus on what he was saying. "I don't think we were trying to create drama. But I do think we know how to make things fun. Exciting. Kissing you is both of those things." His hand stopped messing with my hair and cupped my face. "And usually I think we both know how to make sure things stay in that place and don't get messy."

"You with your 'no article of clothing left behind' rule," I said, and was dismayed to hear my voice coming out all thin and breathy.

"You with your 'no one interests me for more than five seconds' thing," he said. "Normally I'd trust both of us to keep things there with this, too—we could have fun—"

"—until we don't," I said. "And then we just reset to being friends who don't kiss. No harm—"

"No foul. But right now, you've got a ton going on, Bea. You're dealing with some serious emotional shit. I don't want to get us all tangled up in a way that's going to hurt you."

He was looking at me so earnestly, his thumb stroking my cheek. Like Supportive Friend Sam, but Supportive Friend Sam who was definitely maybe about to kiss me again, and that combination was so intoxicating, it took me a few moments to fully process the utter load of shit that had just come out of his mouth.

"Hold. *Up*," I said, taking a big step back, out of cheek-stroking, hair-playing distance. "Are you seriously saying we can't kiss again because I won't be able to stop myself from *falling in love with you*?"

I burst into uncontrollable giggles.

"Oh my *god*," I gasped, leaning back against the wall. "Oh, mercy." I doubled over, clutching my stomach. The giggles just kept pouring out of me. The release felt good after the past couple days of superheroing boredom and Ghost Mom weirdness, and I kept giggling until my sides hurt and tears streamed down my face.

"Why is that funny?" Sam said, his voice peevish. "It's not that far out of the realm of possibility."

"I assure you it is." I stood up straight and wiped tears from my eyes. "You are astonishing levels of full of yourself, Samuel." I closed the distance between us yet again and put a hand on his shoulder. "You know what? I think kissing someone who's not all gaga over Calendar Sam would be good for you. It will knock your sense of self down to an acceptable, normal person level. So let's kiss. Let's kiss up a storm. As long as it's fun and exciting, we'll keep kissing. And I one-hundred-percent promise to never fall in love with you."

"You sure about that?" His expression had shifted from sulky to amused to something more familiar. Now it almost looked like he was challenging me. How quickly he forgot how far ahead I was in our point competition.

"Oh, yeah," I said, leaning in closer so my lips nearly brushed his. "Count on it." I was pleased to hear his breath quicken, to see his gaze lock on my mouth. To see that I could distract him as well as he could distract me. I pulled away and was even more pleased to hear him let out a groan of disappointment. I turned toward the door. "Now. Let's get the non-kissing part of this show on the road."

🔥

San Francisco General Hospital had once been modern and state of the art—at least that's how I remembered it from ten years ago, when I'd been a wide-eyed, impressionable twelve year old. The hospital I saw now, though, had definitely seen better days. Everything about it was chipped and peeling and relentlessly beige. And the unimpressed woman who greeted Sam and me from behind the front desk had a flat, beige quality about her as well.

"Visiting hours ended fifteen minutes ago," she droned, not looking up from her computer screen.

"Oh, we're not here to visit anyone," I said.

"The entrance to Urgent Care is around back," she said.

"Not here for that, either—"

"We as a facility are satisfied with our current roster of representatives from pharmaceutical companies—"

"And also not that," I said, my frustration rising. "If you could give me a moment to explain: my name is Beatrice Tanaka and my mother passed away in this hospital—"

"I'm sorry for your loss," she said, still looking at her computer screen, monotone unchanged. "If you'll wait here, the doctor will be right out to guide you through—"

"She didn't die *today*," I snapped, my irritation boiling over. Honestly. I should've donned my superhero costume for this outing. Maybe then she'd take me more seriously and stop interrupting me at every turn. Unfortunately, my costume was at the dry cleaner. "She passed away ten years ago. I was wondering if I could look at any of her records you might have from that time period. Maybe even the room whcrc shc, um, died." I felt that lump rise in my throat again, that weird little gut punch that always came out of nowhere. Sam's hand brushed against my back. I shook him off and cleared my throat.

"I do not have the authority to release medical records. You will need to submit your request in writing," she said. "And I can't allow you into the patient rooms area of the facility unless you're an approved visitor during visiting hours or a patient yourself."

"It's part of an important supernatural investigation," I pressed. "An official case being pursued by Jupiter/Tanaka, Inc. and—"

"If it's official, then you obviously have some kind of written authorization co-signed by the San Francisco police department." Monotone Lady peered up from her computer screen for the first time. She regarded me over the tiny half-lens glasses perched on the tip of her nose. She totally had the air of that stereotypical humorless librarian who's always shushing everyone. "I am a big fan of everything Evie and Aveda do for our city, of course. But protocol must be adhered to. I'm sure they understand that."

"Of course," I said through gritted tccth.

Frak. Evie had warned me this might be a problem, had suggested I just find out what we needed to get the records, and we'd come back, but . . . but . . . I didn't want to wait. I wanted to actually *do* something, something beyond the mind-numbing minutiae that'd been occupying my superheroing thus far. I wanted to make meaningful progress in figuring out what was going on. I wanted to save Mom.

Maybe I could fake an injury and become a patient myself, if that's what it took?

"Listen. Edna," Sam said, smiling warmly at Monotone Lady. What? How did he know her name?! Had he just guessed? Oh—I saw now that she was wearing a nametag. Though "Edna" would've been a pretty good guess, it was *such* a Humorless Librarian name. "Obviously we don't want to get you in any kind of trouble." I suppressed my eye-roll.

He was using his heartthrob voice. "But it would mean so much to our investigation if—"

"Sorry." Edna cut him off and turned back to her computer. "Rules are rules."

"She must not have seen your calendar," I murmured, nudging him in the ribs.

Don't give up. The voice popped into my head. I'd been so wrapped up in Edna and Sam and my roiling frustration, I nearly jumped.

Don't give up, it repeated. *Convince her.*

Mom? I thought at the voice. It didn't sound quite like her, though. It didn't have the familiar musical quality of the voice that had communicated with me back in the It's Lit bathroom. And it was more urgent, more demanding. Maybe she'd gotten more desperate in the hours since she'd last talked to me. *How?* I thought. *'Cause Edna here made it pretty clear—*

You know how, the voice said.

I did?

I glanced back at Edna. She was staring at her computer screen with renewed ferocity, as if concentrating extra hard would force us to leave. How could I get her to change her mind? How could I take this person who obviously felt very strongly about not giving us any further information and make her feel the exact opposite way—

Oh. Of course.

I mean, we were investigating a case, weren't we? This was clearly a Greater Good situation. But what kind of emotion could I hit ol' Edna here with? She was so dedicated to her monotone, I couldn't tell if she possessed any emotions at all. I glanced around her desk, looking for some kind of hint of a personal life. But her desk was pretty bare, Spartan—and neat as a pin. Nothing there except—wait. I squinted, zeroing in on a photo of a tiny Pomeranian wearing about a million pink bows tucked next to the phone on her desk. *Bingo.*

I took a deep breath and focused, calling up a feeling of

warm sympathy. I mixed in a dash of pity—sadness for this poor girl standing in front of Edna, looking for answers about her dead mother. I didn't bother with the gentle aromatherapy approach. I projected that feeling at Edna full blast, a powerful fastball from an ace pitcher. I saw it hit, saw her shake her head in confusion.

"Bea," Sam said. "Should we go or—"

"Shh," I hissed, focusing with all my might on Edna. I plastered a sad look on my face and kept pushing my feelings cocktail at her. "Edna," I said, "please. I really need to get this information today. It's super important. See, it's Pancake's birthday—that was Mom's prized Pomeranian puppy." I said a silent apology to the real Pancake for twisting his identity in this manner.

"Your mother's dog is still alive ten years later?" Edna said, her brow furrowing suspiciously. "Poms have very delicate health."

"It's a small miracle," I said, really going all in on the lie. "We got him right before Mom died. As a therapy animal." I could feel Sam staring at me, probably in bewilderment. I just bulldozed on and kept not looking at him. "He's getting pretty old now, the poor dear. And it would mean so much to him if I could show him a photo of the room where Mom passed. To remind him of the last time they were together." God, this lie was atrocious. I wiped a fake tear from my eye and projected even harder. I saw her eyes soften, saw her look at me with more care than she had since we'd arrived.

"Your dog came with your mother to the hospital? We don't allow animals in here," she said, but her voice sounded a bit unsure now. I saw her gaze wander to the dog photo on her desk.

"Oh, I know," I said quickly. "We had to smuggle Pancake in. That really is kind of an unfair rule, don't you think? I mean, pets are technically part of the family, aren't they? Seems very discriminatory."

"That it does," she said, her eyes still on her desk photo. I could see her love of rules warring with her love of her own dog. She met my gaze again. "That was nice of you to do for your mom."

"Mmm," I said, nodding, like it was hard for me to even talk about. "I think if Pancake could experience one memory of her on his birthday, it would mean so much."

"Weeellll . . ." Edna said, and I could tell she was wavering.

So close. I was *so close* to getting her to relent, I could feel it.

"I thought you said it was part of a supernatural investigation," Edna said, her brows drawing together. "What does getting a photo for Pancake have to do with that?"

"Um . . ." Dammit. She'd tripped me up. "That was . . . not exactly true," I said, making my face extra regretful. "I told a bit of a white lie. I'm *so* sorry. I would do anything for Pancake. Anything. Do you know what that feels like, to love something so much?"

Her gaze went to her dog photo again, and I could see the internal struggle playing out on her face. She *wanted* to say yes to me. But her ingrained love of doing things properly (and, let's face it, the tiny bit of power she was able to wield over people while she was sitting behind that desk) held her back.

I reached deep inside of myself and projected my feelings cocktail at her, pushed it with all my might, imagined myself burrowing inside her brain and taking hold and refusing to let go.

You want to help Pancake, I thought at her fiercely. *I know you want to, somewhere deep inside. Just say yes. Say, 'I'll get you the records.' Say—*

"I'll get you the records."

"What?" I shook my head, unsure I'd heard right.

Edna stared back at me, her expression suddenly very mild. Her eyes were glazed and she wore the oddest little half-smile—a complete change from the stern enforcer she'd been just moments ago.

"I'll get you the records," she repeated, tapping away at her computer. "What was your mother's name?"

"Uh, Vivian. Vivian Tanaka," I said, still trying to process Edna's abrupt change in demeanor. Sure, I was used to shifting people's moods gently, gradually. But I'd never implanted a direct thought and had them spit it back at me word for word. And . . . was that even what had happened just now? If not, it seemed like a pretty big coincidence.

Well, now wasn't the time for pondering. I'd take the win and dissect it later.

"Ah, yes," Edna said, tapping on her computer monitor. "I'm afraid those records—which should have a note of which room your mother was in—aren't located here. They're too old to have been digitized, though we're slowly getting up to speed on that. Any charts of deceased patients that are ten years or older are kept in our archive in the basement."

"And we can go down there?" I asked.

Edna gave me that bland smile again. "Of course, dear. Bernard should be working. Tell him I sent you. Tell him it's a code six-two-nine."

"Thank you so much, Edna!" I said, grabbing Sam's hand and pulling him toward the elevator. Best to get down there before the mental whammy wore off.

"Poor Pancake," I heard her murmur as we hustled into the elevator.

I pressed the button for the basement level and the doors closed and we were on our way.

"Holy shit," I said, turning to Sam. "I think I just implanted a whole actual thought in that lady's brain."

"And you've never done that before?" he said.

"No. Usually it's just a big emotion. An emotional state. A mood. Not a whole word-for-word thought!" I shook my head in wonder. The whole thing was stoking my adrenaline, making me giddy.

"So you extra mind-mojo-ed her," he said. "New power development?"

"Maybe. There was this voice, talking to me and . . ." I frowned, trailing off. Where had that voice come from?

"Your mother again?" Sam said.

"Maybe," I said. "I definitely need to experiment with this."

The elevator dinged and the doors slid open, revealing a dimly lit corridor. If I hadn't been riding the high of what I'd just accomplished, I probably would've been totally creeped out. The floorboard creaked under our feet, and a couple of naked lightbulbs swung above our heads. It looked like the set of a haunted hospital horror movie where the ghosts of former patients are about to rise up and murder whoever comes along.

We made our way down the creepy corridor and pushed through the double doors at the end. A sad-looking sign that said ARCHIVE was posted next to them.

If the reception level of the hospital looked dated, this basement records room looked positively archaic. Rows and rows of metal shelving housed box after box of papers sporting various complicated labels. The whole thing was presided over by a short, round man with a truly impressive combover and a tie with a soup stain on it. In contrast to Edna's desk, his was a total mess: papers, folders, and the occasional frozen burrito wrapper jostled for space, but the most prominent feature was his collection of pens. Pens of all kinds were jammed into a haphazard array of cups and coffee mugs. Every shade, tone, and hue of every color of the rainbow was represented.

"Hello," he said, blinking at us in surprise. "Are you lost? If you're trying to check in, everything has to go through Edna upstairs—"

"We've already seen Edna," I said, giving him what I hoped was a winning smile. "She actually sent us to you."

"She did?" He frowned, looking instantly suspicious. "Are you sure?"

"Yes," I pressed on. "You're Bernard?"

"I am." The cloud of suspicion hadn't left his face. He

reached over and fiddled with one of his mugs of pens, as if to soothe himself.

"We're looking for information on a patient who passed away here ten years ago," I said. "Vivian Tanaka. Edna said you could pull her file for us?"

"I can," he said, his eyes narrowing. "As long as you're *sure* you have permission."

"We do," I said. "Edna said to tell you we have a code six-two-nine."

"Well, then," he huffed. "All right. This will take a moment, though."

He tapped a few keys on his computer, muttering under his breath, then rose from his chair and stalked toward the back of the room, wending his way through the maze of shelves.

"Interesting system they've got here," Sam said.

"I think that's an insult to the word 'system,'" I said. "I would classify this as a 'big ol' mess.'"

After a moment, Bernard shuffled his way back to us, brandishing a fat file folder.

"The record you requested," he said, sounding extremely put out.

I practically snatched it from him and started rifling through the mess of medication records, chemo reports, and other paperwork that made up the end of Mom's life.

"Excuse me," I said, as I got to the end of the file. "There's no death certificate here. Or any record of her death. This file ends three days before she actually died."

Bernard shrugged. "Whatever we have is in there."

"But . . . but . . ." Frustration welled in my chest. Frak, *no*. My mission could *not* end this way.

"Perhaps your mother was transferred somewhere else before she died," Bernard continued.

"She wasn't," I said, trying to get control of the hurricane of feelings coursing through me. "She was too weak, I was *there* . . . I mean, I wasn't there in the room, but I know we didn't move her anywhere else. I *know* . . ." My voice cracked and I swallowed hard. "I need to take this with me," I said abruptly.

"That is completely against policy," Bernard said, then lowered his voice and whispered: "Edna will *murder* you— and me—if you try to remove a file from the premises."

"Oh, I don't think she will," I murmured under my breath.

Sam cast a sidelong glance at me. "Bea," he hissed. "What are you . . ."

But I was already winding up my mental fastball, projecting a direct, word-for-word thought at Bernard. Telling him exactly what he needed to say to us.

You can take the file and leave. Have a nice day.

Bernard's eyes got that same glazed look as Edna's. "You can take the file and leave," he said. "Have a nice day."

So we did. And Edna, contrary to that naysayer Bernard, did *not* murder us. Because I told her exactly what to think, too.

CHAPTER TWELVE

"I NEED TO go back to the Otherworld."

Predictably, my assertion—spat out as I paced the length of our kitchen over and over again—was met with yet another chorus of *No* from everyone on Team Tanaka/Jupiter. I stopped pacing and faced them, hands on my hips.

"You guys can keep *no*-ing me until you're blue in the face, but the fact remains: the best way to get direct answers is for me to talk to Mom again."

"Slow down, Bea," Evie said, her voice tired.

"And *sit* down, while you're at it," Aveda said, giving me a stern look. "You're giving me whiplash."

"Plus we have tacos," Scott said, holding up a messy shell stuffed with carnitas. "From La Taqueria, even."

"I will sit down for La Taqueria," I relented. I crossed the room, plopped down next to Nate, and swept three tacos onto a plate. "God, I'm starving."

"So let's go back to this whole thing with the hospital records," Evie said. "First of all: they really didn't need some sort of written request or authorization to release Mom's file to you?"

"Nope," I said, my mouth full of delicious carnitas. "That hospital has gone way downhill. I think their policies are more lax all around." Okay, that was only half of the truth. But I didn't feel like getting into the specifics of how I'd finagled things. I didn't want to distract us from the key mission at hand, which was figuring out what had happened to Mom, and me bringing up a possible new development in my powers would definitely send us down the path of Let's Lecture Bea For Hours On End. I was just gonna direct us right around that little traffic jam, thank you very much. I had told them that a voice that was maybe Mom or maybe connected to Mom had communicated with me on the brain plane again, but I'd kept the details of our communication vague. This had still been enough to prompt Aveda to ask if there was any possibility I was possessed and/or being influenced by these mysterious voices, because we'd had our fair share of issues with that sort of thing before. I'd assured the team that I wasn't, but had agreed to submit to supernatural and magical scanning to double check.

"There's a point where the paperwork just stops—right before Mom died," I continued. "There's no discharge record, nothing. It's like she disappeared."

"Surely there would be a note, a full investigation, if that happened," Nate said. "Hospitals don't tend to just shrug if a patient vanishes into thin air."

"Right, no matter what happened to Mom: some records have disappeared," I said. "We don't know what they say. Which is frustrating. Which is why I want to try talking to her again in the Otherworld."

"What about your mother's doctor?" Aveda said. "Could they shed some light on this?"

"The doctor mentioned in her chart retired and moved to Kansas eight years ago," I said. "Sam and I Google-stalked her—she passed away last year."

"I haven't heard back from Dad yet," Evie said. "But . . ." She hesitated and frowned down at the half-eaten taco on her plate.

"But what?" Aveda prodded.

Evie sighed and looked up. "But I do remember this: None of us were in the room when she passed. I'd gone to get something from the vending machine. Dad had gone for a walk down the hall. And Bea was . . ."

Parked in the waiting room because you wouldn't let me see Mom, I thought.

"God." Evie rubbed her temple with her fingertips, her face going a little green.

"Evie," Nate murmured. "Are you feeling . . ."

"I'm fine," she said, pushing her plate away. "Just done with dinner."

"I'll take that," I said, swiping her unfinished taco.

"What happened in those few minutes?" she said, her eyes going to the ceiling. "Did she really get somehow taken to the Otherworld? Her spirit, anyway?"

"Did you . . ." Nate hesitated. "I'm sorry, I know this is sensitive . . ."

"We didn't bury a body," I supplied. "She was cremated and we scattered her ashes in the ocean. Although . . ." My brow furrowed. "How do we know that the remains we got were actually, um, hers? It's not like we were there for the process. Anyway. I can find out more. If you guys would just let me—"

"Bug," Scott said gently. "We still don't know exactly what happened in the bookstore bathroom."

"But we could find out. We could experiment with different methods. I mean, what I'd do first is recreate the circumstances: go back to the It's Lit bathroom, have you do the same spell—"

"It's too dangerous," Evie said. "And if humans are getting trapped in the Otherworld, we can't risk you getting trapped too."

"I'm working on a few different spells," Scott said. "Remember, I wasn't actually *trying* to connect you to the Otherworld—whatever supernatural energy was present in the room reached out for you through my spell. If we're going to try again, we need to make sure you're safe and secure." He hesitated. "If I can develop a protection spell—like a supernatural spacesuit, of sorts, to encase you in—maybe we could try it. In an extremely controlled environment, of course."

"I am going to spend most of tonight analyzing the scans we took at the bookstore after the incident in the bathroom—as well as the most recent scans Rose's team took at the Wave Organ," Nate said. "Leah and I completed the review of the video footage from the It's Lit bathroom—there was nothing there. But I'm hoping the scans will provide us with further data we can use."

"I guess," I crabbed. But I was already thinking of other ways I could try to connect with Mom again. Maybe I could leave her another message in the bathroom? Or go back to the hospital or Market and see if voices appeared in my head again?

"Back to this missing paperwork," Nate said. "Did someone take it? If so, what are they trying to hide?"

"Do you want to take a closer look at your mother's letters, like we talked about earlier?" Lucy said, nodding at Evie and me. "There could be a clue in there somewhere."

"Oh, um, sure," Evie said. "Bea, do you have time tomorrow before your bookstore shift?"

"Well, yeah," I said, polishing off the last of my taco. "But we could also get to it tonight. It's barely eight."

"Right, yes," Evie said, shaking her head. "Sorry, I didn't realize it was still early. I just got hit by a big ol' wave of tired."

"Let me take a shower, and we can convene in my room so we're not getting in Nate's way," I said, rising from the table and gathering my dirty dishes. "Meet me in twenty minutes?"

"You got it." She smiled at me, and I warmed at that nice wave of sisterly togetherness—despite the annoyance I'd felt moments earlier when she'd insisted me going to the Otherworld was too dangerous. I'd just have to work harder to convince her.

You could plant that thought in her brain, a little voice in my head noted. *Just like you did with Edna and Bernard.*

No. I couldn't do that. Even though I was desperate to experiment with this possible new power level-up, I would *not* use it to make my sister give me whatever I wanted. The one time I'd mind-mojo-ed Evie had actually led to the formulation of my code. Right before Evie's wedding, Aveda had talked me into using my emotional projection to soothe Evie's stressed-out mood. We'd proceeded with this little experiment without telling Evie and the end result was her and Aveda having one of their most explosive fights ever, in front of all of their friends and family, on a karaoke stage littered with sex toys.

Those two never did anything halfway—I'd give them that.

Since then, I'd decided: I could only use my powers for the greater good, to make the world a better place. To be a hero, like my sister.

But as I turned the memory over in my brain, I realized I'd never thought about how that moment had been so important to my general state of being . . . but to everyone else, I was a footnote in this story. Because that whole incident hadn't nearly destroyed my and Evie's sisterhood—it had nearly destroyed Evie and Aveda's friendship.

I mulled it over as I crossed the kitchen and dumped my plate in the sink, rinsing off taco detritus. I barely noticed when Nate sidled up next to me.

"Bea," he said. "I know you and Evie are about to embark on a full evening of important research, but I was wondering if I could bother you about something else." He held up a thumb drive. "Kai, my colleague in Maui, had the opportunity to re-interview the two people she saved from drowning. I was wondering if you could look through the transcripts, see if you notice anything that stands out, anything that might lead us down some new investigative paths." He hesitated, studying me. "I know you no longer wish to assist me in this type of work, but I thought perhaps since you have reintegrated yourself into Team Tanaka/Jupiter—"

"I'll do it, bro-in-law," I said, giving him a reassuring smile. Nate had been extra respectful of the boundaries I'd drawn when I started working at the bookstore. I'd always figured, given his stoic, extreme introvert ways, he'd probably been secretly relieved not to have my loud-ass presence taking up space in his lab anymore. "But don't you have a bunch of fellow fancy pants demonologists looking at all this stuff?"

"Yes," he said, giving me a half-smile. "Although I think most of them wear pants you would categorize as fairly dull. In any case, I've always found your perspective to be—shall we say—fresher."

"Thank you," I said, feeling touched. "Can I also get—"

"I left a paper copy outside your door," he said.

"You're the best," I said, holding up my fist for a fist-bump.

"Oh . . . ah . . ." He held up his own fist and gave mine an awkward little tap.

"I'll try to get to it tomorrow," I called over my shoulder as I raced up the stairs to my room. I snagged the folder placed outside my door—glittery purple cover, I noticed. *Aw, Nate.* I breezed into my room, dumped the folder on my bed, and shed my clothes for the much anticipated shower.

The bathroom attached to my room was miniscule, but I considered it the height of luxury since not all the bedrooms in HQ had them. Some people had to *share.* Leah and I had fixed up the bath/shower combo last year with the lovely holiday bonus I'd gotten from Charlotte. It had colorful mismatched tiles I'd collected from various Bay Area flea markets, a detachable showerhead with adjustable water pressure, and a sliding glass door instead of a claustrophobia-inducing curtain. It was my little haven, my oasis, a place where I cleared my mind.

I tied my hair up in a topknot, stepped under the water, and let out a long sigh of relief. This entire day had been packed with so many frustrations, it felt like I had an ever-present hum in my ear, an army of tiny bugs crawling under my skin. I had the burning need to know what was happening with Mom, how I could free her . . . and no concrete way of figuring it out. I knew we were taking all the logical, sensible steps we could. But it felt so *plodding.* I replayed my day in my head, trying to recall if there was anything that would lead us to more decisive action.

The water sluiced down my back, and my shoulders

relaxed, the army of bugs crawling under my skin dissipating. My brain paused at one particular, not-exactly-irritating moment from the day—pressing myself against Sam, brushing my lips against his, coaxing that irresistible growl from his throat.

Despite the heat of the shower, I shivered. I couldn't explain what that growl did to me, how it made longing coil low in my belly, how it made me want to wrap all my limbs around someone I'd been perfectly happy having a pleasantly contentious friendship with for years.

After we were done with this whole kissing thing, we'd still have that friendship. But thinking about it sure was fun in the meantime, a nice little getaway from freaking out about my dead mother being trapped in the Otherworld. In fact . . .

I eyed my detachable showerhead. I hadn't chosen it *just* for the water pressure.

I took it down, leaned back against the misty tiles, and pressed the showerhead against that crucial spot between my legs. The images from the day embroidered themselves into something more elaborate as I gave in to the delicious pressure, the rhythm. Sam kissing me, his big, gorgeous hands sliding against the bare skin of my back. Sam all dirty and sweaty from working on cars all day, his mechanic's overalls half-shucked off, like they were in the calendar. Sam kneeling in front of me—hands digging into my hips, his clever tongue showing me just how clever it could be—

I came so hard I nearly dropped the showerhead.

I stayed leaning against the tiles, steam still rising in clouds around me, allowing my breathing to slow.

Wow, this was *definitely* fun. And I felt way more relaxed now, totally ready for my and Evie's research session.

I turned off the shower, wrapped myself in a fluffy towel, and exited back into my bedroom. I flopped on the bed for a moment, allowing my heated skin to cool down. I grabbed my phone and paged through my texts, leaving hearts on all of Leah's photos documenting Pancake's trip to the groomers.

Then I got a little idea. I pulled up my phone camera and scrutinized my appearance. My hair was still mostly in its topknot, but a few damp, wispy blue pieces had gotten free and were floating around my face. My skin was flushed and speckled with water droplets. And I still looked kind of . . . aroused. All glowy and shit. I made what I hoped was a sultry face and snapped a picture, making sure to frame it so you could see my bare shoulders, but nothing below.

Then I sent it to Sam with a note: *Thinking of you.*

Feeling smug, I set my phone down and went to scare up some pajamas. I already felt confident in amending our current score.

Bea: 1276, Sam: 1165.

"Wake up, Big Sis." I nudged Evie's shoulder. She had propped herself up in a mostly sitting position with a couple of pillows stacked against the headboard of my bed, but she kept nodding off. I couldn't blame her. We'd read through nearly all of the letters, trading them back and forth so both of us could hunt for clues. The words were starting to blur together and—much as I hated to admit it—lose a bit of their poignant *oomph* the longer we stared at them. I'd set up a spreadsheet to document our findings, but so far all we'd managed to glean was:

Mom had a lot of cool ideas for crafts she never got to make. (There was one involving decoupage and antique spoons that sounded particularly intriguing.)

Mom had a lot of high hopes for Evie and me, that we'd grow into strong-willed women who traveled the world, would find great love, and live life to its fullest. (Resounding "yes" on the strong-willed part. Go, Evie, on the finding great love part. Big, fat zero for both of us on the world travelers part. But you couldn't have everything.)

Mom's handwriting got more cramped and spiky the sicker she got. Which was super sad if you thought about it too much, but on a purely practical level, also made things hard to read.

"Sorry," Evie said, rubbing her eyes and sitting up straighter. "Man, I swear there was some kind of secret sleepy ingredient in those tacos." She picked up the letter she'd been studying and frowned at it. "I know this sounds awful, but the longer I stare at these, the more I'm getting desensitized to Mom's moving messages to us. They're starting to look like a bunch of scribbles that aren't really telling us anything."

"No, same," I said, my brow furrowing as I stared hard at the letter I'd already read three times.

"We might have to call it a night," Evie said, letting out a monster yawn.

"No!" I said quickly, even though I was yawning too and it came out more like "Nyaaaahhh!" I shook my head, trying to chase away the cloud cover that had descended over my brain. "We have to keep going. There must be something in here." I stared at the paper so hard the words blurred before my eyes.

"Bea," Evie said, her voice hesitant. "You know this might still end with us not finding Mom, right? All we have right now are . . . well. As Nate would say, unsupported suppositions. Fuzzy hypotheses. Or if we do find her . . . I mean, we don't actually know how to free her from the Otherworld."

"Not yet," I said fiercely. I recognized that stubborn note creeping into my voice, the one that always seemed to rise up especially hard whenever it seemed like Evie was going to stop me from doing something. I set the letter to the side and glared at her. "How can you give up that easily?"

"I'm not giving up," she said, her tone mild. This was one of our familiar patterns: the more upset I got, the calmer she got. It always made me want to scream. "I just want to make sure you're mentally prepared for the possibility that whatever's going on isn't guaranteed to end with us all being reunited as one big happy family."

"I know that," I said, flopping onto my back. "I thought you wanted me to keep finding hope in stuff, though. That's what I'm doing here: hoping."

My voice was peevish, but the one tiny shred of practicality I possessed recognized what she was trying to communicate to me and why she was doing it. She didn't want me to be crushed, like I had been with Dad. Like I had been every time he'd left or missed a birthday or made me believe he possessed any kind of parenting skills whatsoever. That's what having hope did sometimes: set you up for extra big disappointments.

Evie flopped onto her side next to me. I didn't look at her. "I do want you to hope," she said. She slung an arm around my waist and leaned her head against my shoulder. "But I also don't want you to be sad. Which I know is a mixed message. I'm sorry if this is coming out all wrong. I'm tired, and my eyelids feel like they have tiny weights attached to them. I love you."

"I love you too," I muttered, sounding every inch the surly teenager who I kept trying to leave behind.

We lay there for a moment in silence, her breathing soft in my ear.

"Evie," I said hesitantly. "Do you ever wonder what things would be like if Mom was still here? I mean. Not that I wish anything was different, necessarily, we seem to have done okay constructing a weird but really pretty entertaining life for ourselves. But . . ."

But would I feel less like a piece of me is always missing?

Would I feel less like I'm always searching for something I can never find?

Would I understand who I am and actually feel . . . whole?

"Of course I wonder about that," she said.

I rolled on my side to face her. Did she understand? Was she about to vocalize what I'd always been afraid to? But she just smiled affectionately and smoothed my hair off my face. "But I wouldn't trade what we have now for anything."

I managed to smile back, but I still felt unsettled.

"Let's try one last thing," I said, sitting up. "And then we'll call it a night, I promise. It's a very basic data collection technique Nate taught me. Like, when you're not getting *anything,* and you want to look at things on the simplest possible level. Sometimes doing that actually produces the most informative results."

I'd unconsciously started mimicking Nate's know-it-all, science-y tone while I'd been talking, and now Evie was smiling at me with amusement. I cleared my throat and held up one of Mom's letters. "Go through the letters and make a note of words that seem to be appearing frequently—but not like 'the' and other stupid connector words. Count how many times each of these stand-out words appear. Then look at them and see if they tell you something."

"Sounds like one of those word puzzles we used to do when we were kids," Evie said. "I'm game. New spreadsheets for these, I assume?"

"Yes," I said, pleased that I didn't have to instruct her on this point. "Here, you use the iPad. I'll use my phone."

I tapped in a new spreadsheet doc on my phone and picked up my stack of letters with renewed vigor. Then I started to read again, looking for words that appeared a lot.

Decoupage

Ice cream

Love

I tapped them in dutifully, my brain hooking eagerly into the task. I was so absorbed in searching through the letters, I nearly fell off the bed when my phone let out a loud *ding!,* indicating I had a new text.

"Oops!" I exclaimed. "Sorry." But Evie was wrapped up in her own word search and didn't even look at me. I swiped over from my spreadsheet to my texts and found a new message from Sam.

Are you trying to distract me?

I flushed, remembering the photo I'd sent him earlier.

Are you looking to be distracted? I responded.

The three little dots appeared immediately, indicating he

was writing back. I cast a surreptitious look at Evie, but she was still engrossed in studying the letters. I tried to appear casual as I looked at the phone screen and hoped my face wasn't too red. I didn't really want to explain what was going on with Sam and—okay, I'll admit it—giving whatever we were doing a slightly illicit cast somehow made it even more fun.

I was just at my parents' for dinner/tech support, so yes, he wrote back.

I smiled. Sam was his parents' not-so-secret favorite, and that meant they occasionally smothered him. He was the baby of the family, the one who'd stayed behind while his siblings went out into the world. And that also made him the one who took care of his parents and made sure their various electronics were in working order. Even though his siblings were off doing more traditional, Asian-approved occupations, Sam's parents loved him the most—which grated on his siblings and gave them further cause to treat him like shit.

You're welcome, I wrote back.

His reply text appeared almost immediately. *Think it's only fair that I distract you right back.*

Wait . . . what?

The screen flashed: dot, dot, dot. I leaned in close and nearly banged my nose against my phone. And then a photo appeared. Sam. Lying on his bed, grinning his best *beaucoup fromage* grin. Totally naked.

Okay, okay—so he'd cropped things at the exact right spot (or exact *wrong* spot, depending on how you wanted to look at it) to keep the photo from being X-rated. But I could certainly still see enough. All of that broad, beautiful chest. Those ridiculous abs, with their lickable ripples of muscle. And that spot where things narrowed into a perfect vee, leading into . . . well. That was where he'd cropped it. I held the phone closer to my face and scrutinized it extra hard just to be sure.

"Bea?" Evie's voice jolted into my thoughts, and I yelped and nearly dropped the phone. "I'm done," she said, holding up the iPad. "Are you?"

"Um, one second," I said, my voice coming out all squeaky.

I pretended to consult one of the letters again, then turned back to my screen, making sure it was facing completely away from her.

Did you just sext me? I wrote back. *Are we sexting now?* No way was I letting him know how much that photo had affected me.

You started it, he wrote back. *And we're too far away for the real thing.*

Dot, dot, dot.

I pulled the phone closer to my face.

But we can change that. Tomorrow.

Jesus Christ. At this rate, I'd need to visit my showerhead again before bed.

I swiped back to my spreadsheet. I'd leave him hanging on that note. That would really drive him crazy.

"I think I'm ready," I said briskly. "What did you find?"

Evie tapped on the iPad screen, her brow furrowing. "Lots of mentions of things to do with crafting. Travel."

"Regrets," I said, tapping on my own spreadsheet. "As in, she didn't want to have any before she died."

"Yes," Evie said. "And . . . huh. That's interesting."

"What?"

"There's a name that keeps coming up. I mean, besides yours, mine, and Dad's," she said, frowning.

"Hmm." I scrolled through. "Yeah, on mine, too."

"And . . . actually. Wow. This name is the fifth most mentioned word in my stack of letters."

"And there are multiple references in what appears to be the last letter she wrote before she died."

"Which is not necessarily totally suspicious, but . . . huh. This way of cataloging does put things in perspective," Evie said. "Wait, are we talking about the same name? Is it—"

I landed on the name in yet another letter, just as she was about to say it out loud. And so we said it together: "Kathy Kooper."

TRANSCRIPT

Interview with Janine Jacobsen
Conducted by: Dr. Kai Alana

This interview is part of an investigative study of the recent near-drownings in Makena Beach State Park. Ms. Jacobsen is the second individual to report an incident of this kind. She was rescued by the interviewer, Dr. Alana, while Dr. Alana was out for her usual morning walk.

DR. KAI ALANA: Can you tell me what happened?

JANINE JACOBSEN: Do I have to? I've already told this story like forty-seven times.

KA: I understand it might be difficult to revisit—

JJ: Who said anything about difficult? I don't find it *difficult*. I just hate repeating myself.

KA: I understand completely. Just, please, it would be a great help to me. I'm trying to understand why this happened, why you went out into the surf when you can't swim—

JJ: Who said I can't swim?

KA: . . . you did. Was that incorrect? Can you swim?

JJ: No.

KA: Maybe start at the beginning. What were you doing that morning?

JJ: Well, my whole family's on vacation here in Maui. I'm the youngest of five adult siblings, and we rotate who gets to pick the vacation spot, but somehow the rotation *never* lands on me.

KA: So Maui wasn't your choice.

JJ: Too many lizards. Too much sun.

KA: Where would *you* go?

JJ: It doesn't matter, does it? The rotation will *never* land on me.

KA: But if it did?

JJ: I'd go to Burlingame, California.

KA: Oh, what an interesting choice! That's near the Bay Area, no? You know, I did my graduate degree there. So many wonderful places to eat—

JJ: Burlingame, California is the home of the Burlingame Museum of Pez Memorabilia.

KA: Oh . . . how . . . that's so interesting . . .

JJ: I *really* love Pez.

KA: Well . . . who doesn't! Okay, so you're here with your family. What led you to the beach?

JJ: I was trying to get *away* from my family.

KA: And what do you remember before you ended up in the water?

JJ: Not much. It's like one minute I was on the shore, the next I was calling for help. But I guess you could say . . . while I was on the shore, I felt like something was . . . calling me. Telling me if I just got in the water, well . . . I'd be happy. It was like this force was pressing down on me, all heavy, pulling me toward the water. And I hate the water. Almost as much as I hate sun and lizards.

But this force, it, like . . . convinced me. That if I just went into the water, I'd get that feeling I get whenever I think of Burlingame, California.

KA: And the Pez Museum?

JJ: And the Pez Museum.

CHAPTER THIRTEEN

"SO KATHY KOOPER visited Mom a bunch in the hospital—which Evie vaguely remembers, but obviously she was kind of preoccupied with other things. And which isn't necessarily suspicious since Kathy and Mom were close and all, but since Kathy is mentioned so much in Mom's last letter, I mean, it's possible she was the last person to see Mom alive, so obviously I need to talk to her again. To see if she can shed some light on the circumstances around Mom's death. So Evie, Aveda, and I are going to adventure to the East Bay this afternoon to talk to her. Finally, a superheroic task worthy of their beloved Heroic Trio! And hopefully this will help us free Mom from the Otherworld once and for all!"

I finished my latest bout of motormouthing and struck a pose in front of the Cozy Mysteries section of It's Lit. Pancake stared back at me with his one eye, unimpressed. Then he flopped on the ground and started chewing enthusiastically on his foot.

"You are a terrible audience, Pancake," I said, deflating. "You're supposed to give me the doggie equivalent of 'Yasssss, get it, girl!'"

"Yasssss! Get it, girl!" Leah yelped, running up to me. "Sorry, Bebe, I had to deal with a scone emergency in the café. But it's under control now. Pancake, paws do *not* go in your mouth." She scooped the pup into her arms, making tsk-ing sounds.

"Look at you," I said admiringly. "Dealing with scone emergencies and your mom's lizard-herding emergencies and book-selling emergencies all in one go. Is there anything you can't do?"

"I'm a real wonder woman," Leah said, moving behind the counter and setting Pancake on his special pillow. "And I love that you're wearing your costume again." She nodded at my ensemble.

"Got it back from the dry cleaner," I said, preening. "And just in time for me to go on a real mission type thing." I struck another pose, then winced as some unattended bit of shrapnel on the floor poked my foot—I'd once again donned my hole-y purple ankle boots. The original hole just kept getting bigger and had been joined by an additional hole closer to the toe area. But I'd discovered they were the only shoes I owned that really went with my costume, so I'd resigned myself to sucking it up until I could get them fixed or replaced.

"Awesome blossom," Leah said, opening her laptop and tapping away. "In the meantime, check out the flyer I designed for the Art Jam. Think it will get your little artist-poet friend out?"

"Ooh, I love it," I said, draping myself over the counter to look at her screen. "This would totes get me in here if I was a disaffected teen ostracized by my peers and channeling all my feelings into outsider art."

"Let's hope it does exactly that!" Leah said, tapping on her keyboard with flourish.

Someone cleared their throat, and our heads snapped up in unison. We'd been so engrossed in admiring Leah's flyer, we hadn't noticed when Nicole sauntered up to the counter.

"Hey," she said, regarding us with her usual disdain.

"Charlotte's working the café side," Leah said, cocking an eyebrow. "She can see to all your coffee refill needs."

"Um, no, it's not that," Nicole said, shifting awkwardly from foot to foot. "Bea, what is this . . . outfit?" Her nose wrinkled ever so slightly as she looked me up and down.

"None of your business," I said. "But if you really want to know, you can read all about my new adventures on Buzz by the Bay—Maisy Kane's blog?"

I hadn't checked Maisy's blog in a couple days, but I was guessing she'd posted some breathless, gossipy bit about me officially joining the team. And yeah, it maybe wasn't going to present me in the most flattering light, but Nemesis Nicole sure wasn't getting mentioned in Buzz by the Bay *at all*, so. I won.

"I read Maisy's blog every day," Nicole said, raising an eyebrow. "Today's posts were mostly in-depth reviews of the comic books starring Evie and Aveda and some galleries documenting how you can get 'fashion inspo' from their latest outfits. Nothing about you."

Huh. Really? Maisy had been so excited the other day about fully exploring my problem-child state of being. Maybe she was taking her time, doing a more extensive write-up?

"You probably missed it," I said.

"Anyway." Nicole rolled her eyes at me. "I, was, uh, looking for some book recommendations."

"What, so you can pull them off the shelves, drag them over to the café, drip coffee on their beautiful pages, and then leave them out for me to put back?" I tried to match her disdain with my own. "I don't think so."

"I don't drip coffee on them," she said, her expression ratcheting up from disdainful to haughty. "I'm very careful."

"Not my main point, but okay," I said.

"Listen," she said, looking down her nose at us. "I'm a customer, and I'm asking you to do your job. Don't you think it's in your best interests to do it?"

Our eyes met and we stared each other down. I sure as hell wasn't answering that question, and she sure as hell wasn't repeating it, so whoever said something next lost this little competition.

Ugh. I didn't want to deal with Nicole today. I just didn't.

I was feeling confident in my official superhero costume, I was excited about going on a real mission and hopefully getting some meaningful clues about how to help Mom, and I got a tingle whenever I thought about the delicious little game of sext Sam and I had been playing last night. Also, I'd spent the morning poring over the transcripts Nate had given me from his friend, Kai, and sent her a few notes. She'd responded right away, thanking me for my "unique insights." And right before I'd left for work, I'd gotten supernaturally and magically scanned by Nate and Scott, who had concluded I was definitely not possessed (which I already knew, but whatever). Things were *good*. So why was I letting Nicole ruin it?

I intensified my stare and projected a single thought in her direction:

I will go now. And leave you guys alone for the rest of the day.

I saw it hit. Saw her look momentarily confused. Then her eyes took on that blank, glazed look, like Edna's and Bernard's had the day before.

"I can rec some books if you like," Leah said, looking up from her computer. "Are you looking for something historical and murder-y or do you generally prefer, like, sexy vampires, or—"

"I will go now," Nicole said, looking like her mind was about a million miles away. "And leave you guys alone for the rest of the day."

Then she turned and headed toward the door.

"Uh, did you get your purse?" Leah called after her, her brow furrowing.

I need to get my purse, I thought at Nicole.

"I need to get my purse," she said out loud, abruptly shifting course to the café.

And leave Charlotte a really big tip for my endless refills, I couldn't resist adding.

"And leave Charlotte a really big tip for my endless refills," she said, nodding to herself.

"Wow," Leah said, frowning at Nicole's retreating form. "That was bizarre. Almost like she . . ." She turned to me, her frown deepening. "Bebe. Did you mind-mojo her? So she would go away?!"

"Maybe, kind of, sort of?" I said, examining my nails. "Okay, yes. I did this thing yesterday where I think I actually implanted a specific thought in someone's brain. I've never been able to do that before. Or maybe I just never tried? Anyway. It was way cool."

"Hmm." Leah regarded me keenly. "That doesn't seem totally in line with your code. I mean. Implanting whole, entire thoughts in people? It's a slippery slope, is it not? Like, we've talked about you trying to set me up and how much care you put into that thought process. How even if you could make someone do something they didn't want to— which it sounds like you might be gaining the capability to actually do—you wouldn't. Isn't suppressing someone's free will veering into the bad guy side of things?"

"I can handle it," I said. "And it's still for the greater good. In this case, the greater good of Nicole leaving us alone and not ruining the really good mood I'm in."

"Okay," Leah said, her brow furrowing. "But—"

"I'm pretty sure she actually wanted to leave anyway," I said. "She was fed up with me, too."

Leah's brow furrowed further. "Buuuuut—"

She was interrupted by the door chime and Sam loping in. He'd clearly just gotten off work—still in his mechanic's coveralls, a swipe of grease on his neck. In short, he looked just as mussed and dirty-hot as he had in my fantasy the night before, and I surreptitiously brushed a hand against my mouth to make sure I wasn't drooling. I leaned against the counter, trying to look casual.

"Visiting us right after work?" Leah said to him. "What gives? Usually you like to go home and wash all that engine grease off first."

"Usually, yes," he said, giving us an easy grin as he strolled up to the counter and scratched Pancake behind the ears.

"But I got off a little early and thought I'd pop in, make sure you guys are doing okay. I didn't see the usual onslaught of texts this morning, so I got concerned."

"Hmm, our group chain has been a bit sparse," Leah said, glancing at her phone.

My face flushed. I had a feeling he didn't mean our group text chain.

"That it has," he said. He leaned against the counter and shifted to the side a bit so that our elbows brushed. I did my best to remain perfectly still; I wasn't about to move and let him win this round. But *goddamn*, he smelled good. And it was igniting my imagination all over again. Had he purposefully showed up in his calendar outfit because he somehow knew what it did to me? I shuffled to the side a fraction of an inch, so our entire arms were brushing each other now.

"We're fine, Sammy," Leah said. "Just busy bookstoring. And Bebe has to go to Oakland later for a bona fide superhero mission."

"As long as I don't have to drive her again," Sam said. "I'm gonna have to start charging you for gas money, Beatrice."

"You should consider it an honor to assist in official superheroing business," I said, giving him an imperious look that would have made Aveda proud. "But no, I don't need you and your car today. Evie, Aveda, and I are going together. It's a pretty big deal mission."

"Sounds like it," he said, giving me an amused smile. "You'll have to tell me all about it later."

And then he shifted just a little bit closer and now our arms were basically pressed up against each other and he smelled *so good*—

"Oh, god." We both turned to see Leah frowning at us. Weirdly enough, Pancake seemed to be frowning at us as well, his one tiny eye narrowed. "I can't believe this," Leah continued, rolling her eyes skyward. "I mean, I guess I *can*, I just didn't realize we'd already gotten here. You guys are totally fucking."

"What!" I screeched, just as Sam yelped, "Not *yet*!"

Leah burst out laughing, then pointed an accusatory finger at us, jabbing the air with every syllable. "Ri. Dic. U. Lous."

"We are *not*," I said, indignant. "I mean, we're just . . . just . . ."

"Flirting? Sexting?" Leah arched an eyebrow. "Guys, I don't care. I just need you to understand that I will make fun of you for however long this lasts. Mercilessly." Pancake snorted in agreement.

I opened my mouth to retort, but was interrupted by my phone buzzing against my hip. I whipped it out and looked at the screen. Nate.

"What's up, bro-in-law?" I chirped, pressing the phone to my ear. "I cc-ed you on the notes I sent Kai, did you get them? I may have time later to discuss in-depth if you need, but I have an important official superheroing mission this afternoon and that has to be my top priority—"

"I got the email, Bea," Nate said. I could hear a hint of a smile in his voice. "Thank you, that was great work. And I am aware of your mission later. But I was actually calling to see if you could meet me down at Pussy Queen for a couple of hours. I have done some deep analysis of the scans from It's Lit and the Wave Organ and I believe Scott and I have devised a method for you to attempt to connect with the Otherworld again. In a safe and secure way."

"Really?!" I had *so* many questions. But of course the most pressing was, "Is this okay with Evie?"

"Do you think I would be speaking to you if it wasn't?"

I laughed. "Point."

"So are you able to meet me?" Nate said. "I do not want to interfere with your bookstore duties, and I want to make sure I am being respectful of your boundaries—"

"You're doing great," I said. "You're *always* super respectful. I'll see you down at the PQP in fifteen?"

I grinned to myself as we hung up, giddiness bubbling

through my heart. Two official superheroing missions in less than twenty-four hours?

This day just kept getting better.

♨

"Beatrice Tanaka." The Maisy Kane who greeted me today was much different than the chattery gossip who'd welcomed Aveda and me into her store a couple days ago. Now she was subdued, her eyes cast downward, and referring to me in an uncharacteristically formal manner rather than trying to be all chummy.

"Hi, Maisy," I said, cocking an eyebrow as I entered Pussy Queen. "Are you feeling all right?"

"Delightful as always," she said, but her withdrawn expression seemed to indicate the opposite.

"Bea!" Shruti bustled up to me, beaming. Her long, glorious hair was done up in a complicated braided formation and she was wearing a silky pink sheath with rosettes along the neckline. She tucked her arm through mine and ushered me toward the portal, where I saw Nate and Scott already conferring.

"What's with her?" I murmured, nodding toward Maisy. She was already shuffling across the room, away from us.

"Ah." A slight smile played over Shruti's lips. "I believe she's trying to avoid interacting with you. Aveda gave her an earful about leaving you out of her, hmm, how did she put it? 'Scandal-mongering internet trash'? Something along those lines."

"*Another* earful? 'Cause she already ranted at Maisy about that—you know, when we were visiting the other day?"

"Yes, there was definitely an additional phone call involved," Shruti said, squeezing my arm. "Maisy's been sulking about it ever since, because Aveda told her she could not, under any circumstances, mention you *at all*. I heard she was quite formidable—she can go a little Darth Vader, no? She doesn't even need the mask."

"That's why we love her," I agreed. "Though I don't know that she needed to turn all that Dark Side mojo on Maisy. I guess that's why Maisy hasn't written anything about me joining the team?"

"You sound disappointed," Shruti said. "Do you *want* to be on Maisy's blog?" She gave me a sly smile. "Because I think Evie and Aveda would be perfectly happy if that little piece of the internet disappeared forever."

Hmm. I couldn't deny the disappointment stabbing at me. Why was I so twitchy and out of sorts about *not* having my photo and some kind of insulting "problem child" headline plastered all over the blog that had caused my superheroing cohorts so much grief?

Maybe because that kind of attention would mean I was a *real* superhero, not some irritating pretender? Or because it would get Nemesis Nicole to shut up and stop looking at me with her special brand of complete disdain? Or because I just needed attention, period? (That probably would have been Evie's guess.)

"Shruti," I said, "you don't get as much play on Maisy's blog, either—I mean, except when you join Team Tanaka/Jupiter on a mission, she pretty much leaves you out of it. Does that ever bother you?"

"No," she said, giving me her brilliant smile. "I don't need Maisy's assessment of my skills in that arena—and anyway, I adore being a part-time superheroine, at least for now. I don't want to dedicate my whole life to it, like Evie and Aveda do. I'd miss scouring estate sales and flea markets for my vintage babies and matching them up with my wonderfully fashionable customers—that's my true passion. But I love helping the girls out whenever they need me." She studied me as we came to a stop near the portal. "There's more than one way to make use of your gifts, Bea, remember that. You have to find what makes you happy."

"Right. Well. Luckily I know what that is already." I gestured to my sparkly costume. "I *do* want to be a full-time superheroine." And hopefully I'd eventually get recognized for it—even if it came with an unflattering Maisy blog headline.

"Then you're already well on your way," Shruti said giving me another arm squeeze coupled with a brilliant smile. I flushed. Okay, so maybe I *still* had a little crush on her.

"Bug," Scott said, beckoning me closer to the portal. "So glad you could join us."

"Yeah, what's the deal?" I clapped my hands together, giddiness welling in my chest again. "I get to visit the Otherworld?"

"Oh my goodness, Bea," Shruti murmured. "The boys filled me in and this sounds like transporting to another planet! Very *Star Trek*."

"We are going to try something," Nate said. "First, let me bring you up to speed on my research. I have completed my in-depth analyses of the scan data from the bookstore and the Wave Organ. The bookstore scans we did after the incident in the bathroom did not pick up any supernatural energy—but it seems obvious that something was present, at least for a moment. The energy at the Organ, meanwhile, still appears to be from a different source than the portal here. But my further analysis revealed . . ." He hesitated, frowning at the portal as if willing it to give up its secrets. ". . . the atmosphere around the energy at the Organ has that same heaviness around it as the energy here at Pussy Queen. I found traces of the same gibberish code, lurking just beneath our initial readings."

"Whoa," I said. "So the recent supernatural happenings have something in common with the portal, even if they didn't originate here?"

"That seems logical," Scott said. "And that got me and Nate thinking: what if I used the spell I did in the bathroom yesterday to try to access the energy here at Pussy Queen? Even if it's not from the same source, that heaviness we're picking up might be able to tell us something about the recent incidents."

"Right," I said, turning the idea over in my mind. "Unlike at the bookstore, we know this energy will be present—because thanks to the portal, it's *always* present. And unlike the Wave Organ, we know it's dormant—no chance of giant stone monsters coming to life and stomping us to death."

"That's the hope," Nate said, nodding.

"When I do the spell, I'm going to try to actually direct the energy to you this time," Scott said. "If it connects to you—"

"Then I'll be back in the Otherworld!" I marveled. "And I can find Mom again. Awesome."

"Scott has also worked out a spell that will provide you with protection," Nate said. "An invisible force that will wrap around your body—"

"The supernatural spacesuit!" I exclaimed.

"So *Star Trek*!" Shruti crowed, doing a fist-pump.

"Are you sure this part is Evie-approved?" I said.

"It is," Scott said, grinning at me. "I don't want to get murdered."

"None of us do," Nate said, his mouth quirking into a half-smile. "Part of Scott's spell involves him remaining connected to you at all times—if anything goes wrong, he'll pull you out immediately. I will use my enhanced vision to keep track of your vital signs. And Shruti is going to assist us as well."

"I'm going to use my hair to hold both you and Scott in place," Shruti said, beaming. "To anchor you here. True, it sounds like your consciousness did the traveling to the Otherworld, not your physical body—but we believe extra grounding of your physical body will bolster the effects of Scott's supernatural spacesuit."

This was all so cool, I could barely stand it.

"I'm so ready," I said. "Spacesuit me up, Scott!"

"Take my hand," Scott said, reaching out to me. "You should feel a slight tingle. Then Shruti will use her hair to secure us. Finally, I'll reach out to the energy and see if I can direct it your way."

I nodded, took his hand, and held tight. Then I closed my eyes. I don't know why; it just felt like the right thing to do.

The tingle came first—a light touch, like feathers brushing against my skin. I felt Shruti's hair wrapping around my torso and legs, another layer on top of the feathers, cocooning me. My head got light, and I swayed to the side a bit, vertigo overtaking me. But Shruti's hair kept me upright and in place. Scott's palm pressed against mine: a grounding force, keeping me tethered to the world.

I braced myself for the *WHOOM*, for the gust of wind blasting through my ears, but it didn't come. Instead, I suddenly felt weightless. Floaty. The ground underneath my feet disappeared, and I couldn't sense Shruti's hair pressing against me anymore. All I felt was Scott's hand, still firmly clasping mine.

I opened my eyes.

I expected the starless expanse again, but that wasn't what I saw at all. Actually, it looked like I was still in Pussy Queen. I saw Nate standing over the glittery black portal, studying me intently, trying to hide his worry. I saw Shruti off to my left-hand side, her beautiful hair flowing outward to wrap around me. Out of the corner of my eye, I saw Maisy, fussing with one of her colorful underwear displays.

For a moment, disappointment roiled through me—was nothing happening? Were we just standing here in this extremely elaborate supernatural set-up, looking like fools?

But . . . no. Something was different.

For one thing, the room was eerily silent. I couldn't *hear* Maisy's fussing or any of the other little sounds that are the basic fabric of everyday life. For another . . . I squinted. There was a weird veil over my vision, casting a gray-ish shadow on my surroundings. It looked like a classic Bay Area fog had somehow descended over Pussy Queen.

I reached out with my free hand to see if I could touch this mysterious veil. My fingertips brushed against a surface that was soft, velvety. I tried tapping my foot and that same velvet texture poked through the hole in my shoe, brushing against my exposed skin. I opened my mouth and tried calling for Mom. But nothing came out. I tried again.

Mom? Mom?! Are you there?

Still no sound. It was extremely disconcerting—trying to scream, feeling the exertion in my chest, but hearing *nothing*.

My heart rate ratcheted upward and panic skittered through my gut as I doubled down on my efforts, trying to scream with all my might. The creepy silence felt like it was wrapping around me, muzzling me somehow.

I tried reaching out with my mind, tried to call out for her in my head, but all I got back was silence.

Why couldn't she hear me? She *had* to hear me. This was my chance and I had to find her, I had to *save* her, I had to . . . had to . . .

"Bea!"

It all happened so fast. Scott's voice was in my ear, breaking the silence. Then everything went black, and I blinked once, twice. When I opened my eyes again, the veil had dissolved and I was back in regular ol' Pussy Queen, Nate and Shruti and Scott clustered around me. Shruti's hair was back to its normal length, no longer holding me in place.

"Why did you pull me out?" I protested, dropping Scott's hand. I frowned at him. "I was getting somewhere—I think maybe I was in the Otherworld again, but it was different somehow. I was trying to find her, I know I could have found her, but . . ."

"Your heart rate was elevated. Dangerously so," Nate said, resting his hands on my shoulders. "And some of your other vitals were cause for alarm. We couldn't risk it."

"We can't lose you on one of your first away missions," Shruti said, patting my arm. She smiled, but her eyes were lit with concern. "You're no redshirt."

"What did you see?" Scott asked.

I managed to push aside my irritation long enough to describe my brief adventure. But my mind was still on Mom.

"So you reached out and touched things this time instead of floating in the air," Nate mused. "But your physical body

was still here in Pussy Queen—did you feel like you did in
the bookstore, like it was merely your consciousness that
traveled to the Otherworld?"

"Actually . . ." I forced myself to stop dwelling on my failure to find my mother and focused on his query. "It did feel
like I was actually *there*, body and all. It was like I was between worlds, in a way. Like I'd jumped sideways into the top
layer of another world, and I could still *see* this one . . . Does
this make any sense at all?" I shook my head and tapped my
foot on the ground, trying to put the right words together.
The cold tile of Pussy Queen brushed against the ball of
my foot, that spot on my shoe with the stupid hole, the hole
that just kept getting bigger and bigger and bringing friends
with it—

Wait.

Sometimes I have these weird moments where a bunch of
random factoids connect in my brain and everything lights
up. It's like those times when I finally get a gadget I'm tinkering with to work perfectly.

"Guys," I said, the realization forming slowly but surely.
"I've got a theory. This is just like my shoe."

"What?" three voices said at once.

I slipped my boot off and held it up, brandishing the hole-y
sole.

"Over the years, we've hypothesized that the Pussy Queen
portal is causing supernatural energies to leak through," I
said. "A steady little trickle of energy, all coming through the
same spot." I tapped the original hole in my shoe. "But if you
keep putting pressure on that one spot—which I've been doing by continuing to walk around in these broke-down
shoes—the hole gets bigger and increases the likelihood of
other holes forming." I tapped the new hole forming mere
centimeters from the first one. "And more stuff just keeps
getting inside your shoes, period."

"Take it out of the metaphor for us," Nate said—something
he used to say to me all the time when I was assisting him
and would try to explain things via metaphors involving ice

cream, nail polish, or, in one particularly dramatic case, the treacherous mechanics of high school social circles.

"I think the presence of the Pussy Queen portal has caused the walls between our world and the Otherworld to rub thin in spots—to make way for more holes and allow more stuff to get through," I said. "So the source of the energy in certain spots, like the Wave Organ, might be different because it's a new hole in the wall. Maybe that's what's happening in Maui, too. But it all leads back to the same place." I paused, thinking it over. "Just now, it felt like I could actually see that fabric separating our worlds—and it was extremely thin. Like a gauzy curtain or a light fog."

"And maybe that's why you're picking up that heavy atmosphere around these latest supernatural energy readings," Shruti mused. "Because the energy is now pressing more heavily against the places where the walls are thin."

"Yes, exactly," I said, holding up my hand for a high-five. She grinned and slapped my palm. "And maybe that's why Mom is able to reach me *now*. Maybe she's been trapped all these years, and it's only just now that she's been able to get through. Because she's found a spot where the walls between our worlds are especially thin." A lump formed in my throat, thinking about Mom being trapped and helpless for so long.

"This is a lot to think about," Nate said slowly.

My phone buzzed before I could respond. I looked at the screen: Evie.

"Hey, Big Sis," I said, answering. "Oh my god, things are so exciting over here. I can't wait to tell you all about it. Actually, why aren't you and Aveda here? You are missing out on some primo supernatural fun times. Anyway, I'll fill you in during our mission. Which is happening in, like, half an hour, right? I was thinking: we should go through the letters on the way there again, maybe pick out a couple of specific memories to grill Kathy on. Aveda can drive Lucy's car, right? Or is Lucy coming, too? You know what, I could read the letters out loud while we're on our way over—"

"Bea," Evie cut me off. She sounded rushed, harried. "Annie and I actually have something else we need to take care of. Lucy, too—"

"Oh, okay," I said, switching gears with ease. "Is it an emergency? Should I meet you . . . wherever you're going?"

"No, we've got this," Evie said. "I'll fill you in later. We were thinking it'd be a better use of time if you could still go over to the Market to talk to Kathy? Could Sam drive you again?"

"Of course," I said, trying not to let my deflated state come through. I knew it was silly to be deflated, but I'd been so excited about the prospect of going on a real mission with them, the three of us finally working together as a team to do some real superheroing. And I'd been extra excited to share my new findings and tell them about my second Otherworld adventure.

I hung up and glanced over at Nate, Scott, and Shruti. They were all conferring over the portal.

I suppressed a long sigh, plastered a bright smile on my face, and pulled up FaceTime on my phone.

"Hi," I said brightly, when Sam answered. "Guess who gets to drive me to Oakland again?"

CHAPTER FOURTEEN

I'D MEANDERED THROUGH the Grand Lake Market the first time, but today I was determined to march through with purpose—I had a mission, after all. And even if it wasn't the mission I'd originally envisioned, I was still determined to accomplish it with gusto. I tried to mimic Aveda's purposeful stride, my head held high, and not get distracted by shiny things. (I did spy a table of sparkly notebooks filled with graph paper—I'd need to backtrack and check it out later—but I'm proud to say I stayed strong and kept walking.)

"Be cool, Samuel," I muttered to Sam, who was doing his best to keep up with my determined march. "Let me do the talking. You're just here—"

"—because you don't have a car?" Sam said, amused.

"And to soften Kathy up if she proves to be a tough customer," I said. "Deploy your manly charms."

"So I'm here to give you rides and be eye candy." He cocked an eyebrow.

"I love that you catch on so fast," I said, pretending to swoon. "Anyway, don't you enjoy being eye candy? Isn't that your whole thing?"

"I'm starting to doubt my abilities." He pulled a mock broody face. "Given that someone didn't respond to a certain text last night."

"Maybe someone was busy," I said, my face flushing.

"Too bad," he said. "I was hoping for more pictures."

"The one I sent didn't sufficiently distract you?"

"Oh, it did. It distracted me all night long." He waggled

his eyebrows at me, and I couldn't help it—I burst into giggles.

"Oh my god, you are so cheesy right now," I said. "Dial it back, dude."

"Always laughing at me," he said, shaking his head. "So what were you doing before you texted me that picture?"

I shrugged and picked up my pace toward Kathy's booth, trying to look nonchalant. "Taking a shower. And . . . thinking about some things."

He matched my stride and leaned in close, his breath tickling my ear. "Did these things involve your detachable showerhead?"

"What! How do you know about—"

"You *told* me about it, Beatrice. When you first got it put in."

Oh, right. My flush intensified. This was all so weird, us bouncing back and forth between our usual good-natured sniping and this more charged flirting. One moment he was Mr. Beaucoup Fromage, who I couldn't imagine taking seriously about anything, the next I wanted to shove him into one of the secluded corners between Market booths and kiss his face off.

But the back and forth also made me feel amped up, excited. Maybe Leah was right—I lived for the in-the-moment thrill. Well, so what? He and I had an agreement, and for now, this was just too much fun. My favorite dragon-shifter lady would totally approve.

"I did make excellent use of my showerhead," I said, arching an eyebrow at him. "Just indulging in a little harmless fantasizing."

"Tell me about it." His fingertips brushed the back of my neck, and I thrilled at that familiar coil of heat in my belly.

"You were in the shower, too—on your knees in front of me," I said, trying to keep my tone even, like this was the kind of thing I thought about every day. "Your hands were on my hips, holding me in place. And you were—"

"—showing you how good I am with my tongue?"

I swallowed hard and fought like mad to keep my tone even. "Yes."

"As it happens, I am *very* good at that."

"Duly noted," I said, and cursed my voice for coming out all thin and breathy. I cleared my throat, trying to get control. "But you know, I don't know if we can actually be naked together. I might be too overcome with giggles, like I am whenever you go into Calendar Sam mode."

"We'll see," he said.

We came to a stop in front of Kathy Kooper's booth—and I did a double take.

"Where are the pretzels?" I blurted out. The giant pretzel booth was empty—no pretzel-preparing staff, no pretzel-heating equipment, no guy dressed as a giant pretzel yelling at passers-by. The sign screaming "GIANT PRETZELS" was still up, but that was about it.

"That's weird," Sam said. "It seemed so popular."

"Bea!" Kathy called out, waving to me. "What are you doing on this side of the Bay? I thought you lived in the city."

"I do," I said, giving her a bright smile and moving toward her booth. "But I just . . ."

Hmm. I hadn't really thought about my in with her. I'd spent all my prep time poring over Mom's letters, trying to figure out what to ask Kathy.

". . . had the day off!" I improvised.

"And it's such a nice day," Sam said, deploying his heartthrob smile. "I hope it's been good for business?"

"Oh, indeed," Kathy said, fluttering her lashes. "I've had a steady stream of customers since opening. You've caught me in a rare lull."

"Evie and I wanted to thank you again for that box of Mom's stuff," I said, my brain clicking into gear. I silently blessed Sam's heartthrob powers—they were actually coming in handy. "It turned out to be a bunch of letters to us, and it was very special. I was wondering . . ." I paused, trying to craft the exact right bend of the truth. "She mentioned you a lot," I continued, deciding to start with something like the actual truth. "It sounded like you were visiting her quite a bit in the hospital?"

"Of course," Kathy said, looking pensive. "She was my best friend."

"I was so young," I said. "I visited her, of course, but I wasn't . . . around as much."

"Your sister tried to protect you from the worst of it," Kathy said, making a sympathetic clucking sound.

"I was wondering if you would mind sharing more from that time," I said. "If you had any, like, memories you could recall for me. To make me feel like I was there."

"Are you sure about that, dear?" Kathy said, reaching over to touch my arm. "I think that might be very difficult for you."

"I want to know what she was going through," I pressed. "From her letters, it sounds like things were really strange."

"She knew she was dying, hon," Kathy said, looking at me quizzically. "That definitely makcs things strange for a person."

Crap. I was striking out, here. I studied her, tried to pick up on some nuance that would give me a clue as to how to get her talking. I could try projecting, try something that would alter her mood . . . but I wanted to make sure what I was getting was total, unvarnished truth. I also wasn't sure what was going on with this whole implanting specific thoughts thing, and I didn't want to accidentally give her a thought that was going to muck things up.

Go to the Ferris wheel.

I nearly jumped out of my skin. There it was again, a random little voice in my head, a voice that was maybe Mom, maybe not. What did this one sound like? I tried to listen harder.

What? I thought back.

Go to the Ferris wheel.

I'm kind of in the middle of something important, here?

Go to the Ferris wheel. Now. Please.

It was the "please" that got me. If it was Mom, maybe she

was about to let me in on the secret to saving her. Which, for whatever reason, existed right in the middle of a bunch of janky carnival rides.

I focused back in on Kathy. Luckily, Sam had engaged her in a detailed conversation about her artistic process while I'd been talking to myself. Or to the voices in my head. Or to my possibly not-so-dead mother.

What an interesting array of possibilities.

"I, uh, need to use the restroom," I said.

"Okay," Sam said, looking at me quizzically. "Shall we take off or—"

"No!" I said, way too loudly. "I'll just be a sec. Don't let me interrupt your conversation."

I flashed him a quick smile that I hoped he knew meant *Just keep her talking 'til I get back* and took off toward the carnival section of the Market.

My eyes scanned the sky, the massive Ferris wheel looming in the distance. Weirdly, it didn't seem to be in motion today. In fact, it looked totally empty. Abandoned. It was a perfectly still bit of punctuation in the sky, the lack of movement giving it an eerie quality. I shivered.

I reached the arched entrance to the carnival, guarded by a solitary dude sitting on a stool. He was scrolling through his phone and looked like he was about to fall asleep.

"Hey there," I said. "One carnival admission, please."

"Sorry, we're closed today," he said, not looking up from his phone. He made a vague gesture toward the entrance— which I now saw was blocked off by a chain and a sign that proclaimed its closed status.

"Closed?" I said. "Aren't you guys open whenever the Market is? During the warmer months, that is?"

"Usually, but we're having technical difficulties," he said with a small shrug, like, "what can ya do?"

So that explained the unmoving Ferris wheel. Maybe if I just stared at it from here, that would be sufficient?

No! The voice was back in my head again, loud and insistent. *You have to go to the Ferris wheel. Go to it. Now.*

"Um," I said out loud to the carnival attendant. "Is there any way I could pop in real quick to look at the rides? I'm a huge fan of, like, ride architecture. I'm kind of *obsessed*." I made a goofy face, as if to insinuate that rides were my equivalent of boy bands. "I'm visiting from Oregon for just a few days and I came here specifically to see the rides. I've heard so much about them."

"You have?" The guy looked up from his phone, his brow crinkling in confusion. "Our rides? Because they're pretty much a bunch of rusty old junk."

"That's exactly why I'm such a fan!" I enthused. "They're classics." I gave him a hopeful smile and tried to widen my eyes in that extra innocent way so many guys are suckers for.

"Huh," he said, looking mildly intrigued by the idea that something in his tiny corner of the world had fans. "I can't do that, sorry. My crew's coming by later to work on the rides, but in the meantime, it's just too dangerous to let anyone in. Something might fall on you."

I gritted my teeth. Really? The rides were having technical difficulties and might fall on me, and this was happening on the one day when I actually needed to get inside? Or maybe that's *why* I needed to get inside? Maybe the technical difficulties were going to reveal something?

Go to the Ferris wheel, the voice said in my head.

Fuck, I'm working on it, I thought back.

I studied the guy. He was back to his phone, clearly hoping I'd give up. But I couldn't. Because for some reason it was imperative I look at this damn Ferris wheel, all up close and personal.

I want to let you in, I thought at him.

He looked up, his eyes getting that blank look.

"I want to let you in," he said.

"Oh, how nice!" I said, like it was a big fucking surprise.

I'm going to go get some food. At least twenty minutes away from here, I thought at him.

"I'm going to go get some food," he said, sliding off his stool and pocketing his phone. "At least twenty minutes away from here." He shook his head and made a face, as if clocking that that was a pretty weird thing to say out loud.

These aren't the droids you're looking for, I couldn't resist adding.

"These aren't the droids you're looking for," he called over his shoulder as he wandered off.

I slipped under the chain blocking the entrance, taking care not to disturb the CLOSED sign. Whatever communing I had to do with the Ferris wheel was best done alone.

As I strolled through the empty carnival, the noise from the rest of the Market faded to a distant burble and I half expected to see tumbleweeds rolling past my feet. It was creepy to wander around this giant, festive space, so obviously set up for lots of people, when there were no other people around. The Ferris wheel loomed at the very outer edge of the carnival area, so I had to walk through the entire thing to get there. My skin crawled as I wended my way through the maze of rides and games and booths, the air thick with the scent of stale popcorn and cotton candy. The whole affair was pretty shabby. Ticket taker guy wasn't wrong, it did look like a big ol' pile of rusty junk. I walked by a games booth featuring one of those simple set-ups where you have to throw ping-pong balls at moving cups. The prizes were rows and rows of stuffed animals strapped by their necks to the back wall of the booth. The effect was ghoulish in the harsh light of day, and I felt like they were all staring at me, a mosaic of beady little eyes following me as I moved.

I passed by a classic carnival ride—I think it was called the Octopus or the Spider or . . . some kind of animal with a lot of appendages, clearly. It was painted a shiny black and had a bunch of curved metal "legs" attached to a central base. Each leg had a bucket-like car that held two passengers, and the whole contraption spun around and lit up and made those with weaker stomachs generally sick. I remembered convincing Evie to go on that ride when we were younger and how she'd nearly barfed over the side. I, of course, had loved it. But now it was all still and silent and almost as menacing as the beady-eyed stuffed animals.

Finally, I arrived at the Ferris wheel. I stared up at it, craning my neck, trying to take in every bit of it. Up close, it was a strange mix of stately and shabby—an old soldier, just trying to stay upright. But the utter stillness totally creeped me out.

"Okay," I said out loud, feeling ridiculous. "I'm here. I made it to the Ferris wheel. What did you want to show me, pesky, mysterious voice that is possibly my mother?"

I stood there and stared. Seconds passed by. Then minutes. I started to get a cramp in my neck from staring up at the thing. But nothing happened.

I let out a long, gusty sigh.

"Feeling pretty awkward here!" I called out. "Can we get this going? Whatever this is supposed to be? Because otherwise, I'm outta here. I have to get back to the mission I was on, talking to Kathy Kooper."

Nothing. No response. Just that eerie silence that made my skin crawl.

"Fine," I said. "Thanks for the wild goose chase. I'm leaving."

I turned on my heel, trying to be extra dramatic about it, and started back toward—

Get on the Ferris wheel.

I stopped in my tracks.

Excuse me? I thought back. *I don't know if you heard, but all the rides are having technical difficulties right now. It could be dangerous.*

Get on the Ferris wheel.

The voice offered no further explanation, but there was a firmness to its tone this time. Like it wasn't about to take any back talk from me.

I'd come this far, hadn't I? Gone to the trouble of mind-mojo-ing the guy out front and left Sam to make endless small talk with Kathy about cat-hair knitting or whatever, right?

I strode over to the bottom car of the Ferris wheel. The

rusty metal bar made an ominous creaking sound as I un-latched it and climbed inside. And then I just sat there, once again feeling vaguely ridiculous. Was the thing going to start up all by itself? Was I about to be trapped on top of a Ferris wheel with no way of getting off and no one around and no people within screaming distance? I'd had a fantasy in my tween years about getting trapped at the top of the Ferris wheel with whatever dorky, floppy-haired boy or mysterious gothy girl I'd been crushing on at the time. It had seemed devastatingly romantic. Now it seemed like a really stupid way to die.

But the Ferris wheel wasn't starting. I was still just sitting, waiting for something to happen.

I slumped back in the seat, running my fingers along the multiple rips in the cheap vinyl lining of the car and wondered how long I should wait around before I declared this tangent to my mission a proper failure.

"This isn't the weirdest situation I've been in the past few days," I said out loud, "but it's certainly the most—"

WHOOM

The blast of sound whooshed through my ears, making me gasp. It was just like the sound in the It's Lit bathroom and was followed by the same sensation: falling and falling and falling, surrounded by a starless spacescape. I couldn't see . . . couldn't see . . .

SMACK

This time, I landed somewhere instead of being suspended in mid-air. I felt around—the surface I'd landed on was soft and cool and had a velvety texture. Just like the surface I'd reached out and touched earlier today at Pussy Queen.

I struggled to get to my feet, but attempting any kind of movement was slow going. The air was thicker, the gravity greater, weighing all of my limbs down. I managed to get myself upright, but I couldn't stand up totally straight. I was sort of stooped over, like the atmosphere was pressing down on my back. I tried to move forward and only managed the tiniest of steps.

Where the fuck am I?

I tried to look around, but all I could see was blackness. The starless spacescape again, but now I could walk through it, sort of. And I realized if I squinted really hard, I could make out vague, shadowy shapes here and there, but I had no clue what they were.

Beatrice.

A voice echoed in my head. I squinted with all my might— was it one of these vague shapes? Were they talking to me? It didn't sound like my mom . . .

Hello? I thought back. *Who are you? Am I in the Otherworld? Really, any direct answers would be—*

Don't trust Kathy Kooper.

Okay, so that was a direct answer to a question I hadn't actually asked.

"Why not?" I said out loud. My speech came out slow and watery, like it had been run through one of those distortion machines they use to disguise people's voices on reality TV shows.

"She has done unspeakable things," the voice said out loud, and I nearly jumped out of my skin—or I would have if I'd been able to move with any kind of ease. The voice was slow and distorted, like mine, but I could tell it was coming from somewhere on my right. With great effort, I turned in that direction. One of the shadowy shapes I'd made out earlier seemed to be coming into some kind of focus. Or I was delirious from being trapped in this freaky demon spacescape. You know, either/or.

"What kinds of things?" I said, trying to step toward the voice. It seemed like I was starting to move a little easier, but every motion I attempted still felt like pulling teeth. "Did she hurt my mom, somehow? Please, tell me the right questions to ask—"

"She banished me," the voice spat out. "She is hateful. She . . . she . . ." The voice sputtered, trying to compose itself. I was starting to make out its form, which seemed to be coalescing before my eyes, the shadowy blob turning solid and person-shaped. The voice was also starting to sound more familiar, but I couldn't place it.

"I'm sorry," I said. "I'm gonna need more than that." I realized that I had to raise my voice to be heard, that I was practically shouting. I shook my head, trying once again to find my bearings. There was a dull roar in my ears, like a plane trying to land. And getting closer and closer, louder and louder . . . "What's that sound?"

"Our time is drawing short," the shadowy figure said, nodding its blobby head sagely. "Don't trust her. And ask her about . . ."

The figure trailed off and the roaring got louder, making me want to put my hands over my ears. I tried to lift my arms, but my body was still weighed down by the heavy atmosphere of this strange place.

The roaring was so loud it drowned out everything, and I couldn't tell if the figure was still speaking, if I was missing some crucial piece of info. Frustration clawed at me, and I wanted to scream loud enough to drown out the overwhelming roar.

"What?" I yelled, desperation lacing through my voice. "Ask her about *what*?!"

"Pr . . . ellllsssss . . ." The shadowy figure was trying to yell over the roaring, but I still couldn't hear them.

"What?!" The roaring sounded like we were right under a freakin' plane now.

"PRETZELS!"

All of a sudden, the blobby figure came into focus, and I could see him clearly. It was none other than the guy in the big foam pretzel costume—the one Sam and I had seen on our last visit to the Market. He was still wearing that ridiculous costume, but now he looked haggard, distressed. There were dark circles under his eyes, and his mouth was open wide as he screamed that last word at me. His costume looked raggedy and frayed around the edges, like he'd been wearing it for a while.

"What—" I started to say.

WHOOM

There was that gust of wind crashing through my head again, and now I could move way more easily. I clapped my hands over my ears, and then my eyes flew open and I was back in the stupid Ferris wheel seat, the rest of my question dancing on the tip of my tongue.

That loud roaring was still overwhelming me, forcing me to keep my hands over my ears. I looked around wildly, trying to pinpoint its source. But something was wrong. The carnival looked like it had a weird film over it, like . . . oh, holy shit. It was a foggy veil, like the one I'd experienced earlier at Pussy Queen. Was I between worlds again?

Wherever I was, that loud sound was more distinctive and layered here. It had a metallic aspect to it, like gears grinding against each other or a squeaky wheel that needed a major dose of oil. It also sounded like . . . crashing. No, *stomping*. Like a dinosaur or some other gargantuan monster was bulldozing its way through the abandoned carnival.

I slid under the metal bar, wriggled my way out of the Ferris wheel car, and jumped to the ground. I looked around frantically, my heart racing, adrenaline spiking my blood. The sound was definitely getting louder . . . closer . . . *what the fuck . . .*

CRASSSSSSHHHHHHHHHHHHHH

Through the veil, I saw the games booth—the one with the freaky rows of beady-eyed stuffed animals—go down, crumpling like a used up tissue. And then I saw . . . *it*. Rising out from behind the wreckage.

It was the ride from before—the Spider, the Octopus, whatever animal you wanted to call it—and it was crashing its way through the carnival, stomping things to the ground with its thick metal legs.

CRASSSSHHHHH CRASSSSHHHH BOOOOM-MMMMM

A hot dog stand went down. Then a ticket booth. Then a kiddie ride with cars shaped like ladybugs.

I ran.

As if sensing my presence, the Spider turned and altered course, its metallic parts squeaking and creaking with the effort. And it started stomping and crashing and booming its way toward me.

Fuckfuckfuck

I tried to run faster, cursing my lack of athletic prowess and the fact that the fog-veil thing was impeding my ability to see very far. Occasionally, my hands brushed against something that felt like that odd velvety texture, but I barely registered that. My breath wheezed out in rapid gasps until I was practically hyperventilating, and my heart kept up its million-beats-a-minute pace. Sweat poured down my face, and I couldn't summon up a single coherent thought. Just, *Get out get out get out.*

I risked a quick glance over my shoulder and then was sorry I had, because the thing was gaining on me. Its black paint gleamed malevolently in the late afternoon sun, and I felt my terror intensify, consuming me, every pore of my body emanating fear.

Goddammit, I wish Evie and Aveda were here. I wish . . . I wish . . .

Wait.

Wasn't *I* the one who'd kicked ass at the Wave Organ? I had powers, too. I was strong, too.

I stopped in my tracks, whipped around, and let out the most ear-piercing scream I could muster. I had a fleeting moment of panic that it wouldn't be loud at all since I'd expended so much breath on running, but it was loud enough to claw my throat raw, to make my ears ring. And yes, to shatter the giant Spider monster in front of me, which made one last heaving step and then crumbled to dust at my feet.

I fell to my knees, breathing hard, nearly face-planting on the ground. Tears of relief and shock streamed down my cheeks. Holy shit. Holy *fuck*. I'd just been chased by a gigantic mecha carnival ride. Evie and Aveda would be disappointed to hear they'd missed out on so much excitement.

I'm not sure how long I stayed in that position, sprawled

out on the ground, trying to regain control of my breath. But when I finally looked up, I did a double take—the veil had cleared. It looked like I was back in the real world. There was no shiny black Spider detritus at my feet. No wrecked carnival in front of me. Everything was totally back to normal. I got to my feet slowly, and cautiously began to retrace my steps. The hot dog stand was back. Ditto the game booth with the creepy stuffed animals, who were back to staring at me with their creepy beady eyes. And the Spider? I turned around and saw it—back in its original spot. As if nothing had happened.

What. The. Hell.

Had everything I'd experienced after the Ferris wheel happened in that weird space between our world and the Otherworld? Was the carnival located in a spot where the walls were super thin? And if so, how had I managed to jump back to the real world myself, without any help from Scott's spells?

I made my way back to the carnival entrance, trying to remain hyper-vigilant and aware of my surroundings. But it didn't matter. The carnival was back to being its creepy, empty self. No mechas chasing me and destroying everything. I slipped under the chain at the entrance and saw the guy from before, who was back on his stool, scrolling through his phone.

"Hope you had fun, Miss!" he said, giving me a jovial smile.

"I guess that depends on your definition of fun," I muttered. But he was back to being engrossed in his phone and didn't hear me.

I stomped back toward Kathy's booth, my head swirling with everything that had just happened. Where did I even begin to try to make sense of all of this? I only had one clue: Kathy. And I needed to treat her as more of a hostile witness, because if anything Pretzel Guy had said was true . . .

What had he said, exactly? I shook my head, replaying our conversation. She couldn't be trusted. She'd banished him there.

Holy frakballs, Kathy, what have you been up to? And what does all of this have to do with Mom? What did you do to Mom?

I finally reached Kathy's booth and saw Sam leaning against one of the tables displaying her wares, looking bored. Kathy was helping a customer, showing them one of her cat-hair creations. I felt a wild, irrational stab of anger. How dare this woman act like everything was totally freaking normal, going on and on about her dumb crafts and looking pleased as punch about it, while I was getting my ass chased through a creepy carnival by a giant Spider mecha?

"Bea!" Sam spotted me and stood up straight, looking relieved that we could finally leave. I stomped past him and elbowed my way into the space between Kathy and her customer.

"Beatrice," Kathy said, looking appalled at my rudeness. "As you can see, I'm with a customer—"

"And they were just leaving," I said, my voice flat. I snatched the cat-hair craft out of her hands and passed it to the customer. "Here, you can have this. On the house."

"Excuse me," Kathy said, eyes wide with indignation. "It certainly is *not* free, that one-of-a-kind creation is three hundred and—"

"Free," I repeated loudly, grasping the customer by the shoulders and meeting their eyes.

I love it and I'm so grateful and I have to go now, I projected at them.

"Wow, I love it and I'm so grateful and I have to go now!" the customer sang out, waving and trotting off into the distance.

"I'm not sure what you think you're doing," Kathy said, her voice laced with quiet fury. "But—"

"Tell me," I said, whipping back around and glaring at her. "What did you do to my mother? What did you do to the pretzel guy? Tell. *Me.*"

"Bea," Sam said, putting a hand on my shoulder. I shook him off.

"You're going to tell me everything," I hissed at Kathy. My voice was low and growly and full of so much rage, I almost didn't recognize it. But I was practically shaking with anger now, I couldn't believe this woman, this woman who claimed to be my mother's *best friend* . . .

Anger pulsed through my veins like hot, molten lava—throbbing against my skin, like my whole body was about to explode. I couldn't think, couldn't form coherent emotions beyond being totally fucking mad. I wasn't completely aware of what I was doing, I just knew I wanted her to *feel* that, to understand the full force of my anger, so I picked out a tiny thread underneath: fear.

I gathered that up and projected it at her harder than I'd ever projected anything before. I *blasted* fear at her. I wanted her to go all remorseful and tell me everything. But even more than that, I wanted her to cower. To shrink from me. To fucking *fear* me.

I saw it hit, saw her eyes widen. She took a step back.

Yeah, that's freaking right, lady.

"I . . . I . . ." she said, blinking rapidly.

"My mother," I said. "The pretzel guy. What. Did. You. Do?"

She swallowed hard and took another step back, and I felt a vicious stab of triumph. This was it. I was going to get my mom back. And I was going to get revenge on whoever had trapped her in the Otherworld. Power thrummed through me, deep and dark and potent. *Yes.*

She swallowed again and something I couldn't quite grasp flickered across her face. Then she drew herself up tall and her expression turned steely.

"You're being very rude, Beatrice," she said. "I think your mother would be extremely disappointed in you."

My jaw dropped. *What the frak.* She was supposed to cower and go all meek and apologetic and tell me everything she knew.

"Bea, maybe we should go," Sam said. I ignored him.

Okay, I was just going to have to try harder. I rolled my neck, gathered up all that fear, and pushed it at her with all my might. I waited for her to step back again, for the fear to take hold.

Instead she moved closer, until we were practically nose to nose. "Stop that, Beatrice."

Before I could even register that, I felt something shove against my mind. *Hard*. It was like the feeling I was projecting was being thrown back at me.

What . . .

Did Kathy . . . could she do what I did? Did she have my power? Was she secretly an evil being from the Otherworld?

Well, whatever was happening, I needed to kick her ass . . . brain. Ass-brain? Brain-ass? "*You* stop it," I growled, mentally shoving the fear back in her direction. "And tell me what you did to the fucking pretzel guy."

"I didn't do anything," she said, giving me a sweet-as-pie smile that didn't reach her eyes. "He simply couldn't handle the competition—"

"That's so odd. Because it seemed like he was doing bang-up business, while you're barely selling any of these ass-ugly cat-hair crafts—"

"Whatever something *seems* like isn't always the reality," she said, sounding out each syllable.

"What? That doesn't even make sense!" I pushed the fear at her hard—and felt that responding shove against my mind again.

Okay, seriously. What the fuck.

I shoved back with all my mental might—and then we were simultaneously pushing each other, our minds deadlocked, trying to find purchase. I redoubled my efforts. I wasn't about to back down.

I'd never had to fight back against someone else trying to emotionally project at me. Sweat beaded my brow, and a red haze descended over my vision. Everything was going fuzzy around the edges, like the world had narrowed and now only consisted of me, Kathy Kooper, and our mental stand-off. A high-pitched whine echoed through my ears and I winced. Everything hurt.

I was vaguely aware of the sound of glass shattering somewhere to my right, and I hazily wondered if it was the sound of my brain breaking apart. Then I heard Sam's voice in my ear, though it sounded like he was so far away, trying to yell at me through a tunnel.

"Bea!" he shouted. "*Bea.*"

I turned to the right and saw a row of Kathy's glass vases exploding in quick succession: *BAM, BAM, BAM!*

I heard screaming and saw people running, and then I saw that other things were breaking apart, too: the abandoned pretzel stand was crashing to the ground, the woman with the bootleg t-shirt business was scrambling away from her collapsing stall.

"We need to get out of here," Sam said, shaking my shoulder.

"No," I said, my voice raw and hoarse. "No, we *can't—*" I whipped back around and saw Kathy Kooper running in the opposite direction. She looked over her shoulder and gave me a mean smile.

"We'll meet again, Beatrice," she yelled. "Count on it."

I gathered up whatever shreds of emotion I still had—I didn't even know what they were anymore, they were messy and fragmented—and threw them at her as hard as I could.

I felt that responding mental shove, and it hurt so bad, I gasped. Everything went fuzzy around the edges again, and the red haze descended over my vision again and it was all too much and I felt myself falling and falling and falling, Sam screaming my name. And then everything went black.

CHAPTER FIFTEEN

"IS SHE WAKING up? I think she's waking up—"

"Shhhh! Lower your voice. If she's *not* waking up, she definitely needs rest—"

"Don't crowd her, darlings, we still need to make absolutely sure she's not injured—"

My eyelashes fluttered open, and I was greeted by a swirl of faces staring down at me. I blinked a couple times, trying to make them come into focus, and took stock of my surroundings. I was back at HQ, in my bed, and I felt like I'd been smacked on the head by a very large mallet. Evie and Nate were perched on either side of me, Aveda and Scott were leaning against my dresser, and Lucy was draped over a rocking chair. They all looked worried. Sam was there, too, hovering around in the background.

"What happened?" I said, sitting up and rubbing my temples. "*Ow.*" My head hurt like hell. "And can I get, like, a vat of ibuprofen up in here?"

"On it," Scott said, heading for the bathroom.

"Sam called us," Evie said, reaching over to take my hand. "We came out to the Market and got you and . . ." She swallowed hard, her gaze sweeping over me, like she was trying to convince herself I was okay. "How do you feel?" I could tell she wanted to reach out and put a hand on my forehead but was trying to tamp down on those Momming instincts.

"My head feels like I spent last night drinking an entire liquor cabinet, but otherwise . . ." I took stock of my various body parts. Scott came back into the room and handed me a couple pills, which I dry-swallowed. "Yeah, I don't think anything's broken, bruised, or otherwise amiss. But oh my god, you guys . . ." I sat up straighter, my eyes going wide as my afternoon replayed in my head. "You will not believe the craziness that went down today. Let me recap Bea's Super Awesome Superhero Adventures for y'all."

I told them about my Ferris wheel side trip to the Otherworld, my thrilling escape from the gigantic mecha Spider, and my run-in with probably evil mastermind Kathy Kooper. I may have exaggerated and embroidered just a teeny bit here and there, like when I described how I'd bravely jumped out of the way of the Spider's tentacles slamming onto the ground, or when I mentioned that Kathy's eyes seemed to have an evil, supernatural glow about them. (I saw Sam raise his eyebrows at that one.) But, you know, it *had* been pretty exciting—I was just emphasizing that fact.

"So I guess I passed out," I said, my brow furrowing as I reached the end of my tale. "But what happened after that? Did Kathy Kooper, like, magically teleport herself back to her evil supervillain lair or what?"

"She slipped away in the chaos," Sam said, stepping forward. I noticed then that his face was pale and drawn and very un-Sam-like. "I didn't know what was going on between you two, just that all of a sudden stuff started exploding around you."

"Was it affecting the entire Market?" I said. "Like, was the whole thing crashing down while we were having a brain battle, or what?"

"It was pretty much just in your immediate vicinity," Sam said. "All those vases in her booth exploded, and the pretzel stand and that t-shirt stall next door came tumbling down." He shook his head, like he was trying to remember. "It was enough to freak out folks around those booths. They probably thought it was an earthquake or something. There was some running for the exits, but it didn't quite escalate to a stampeding mob."

"Just enough mayhem for Kathy to get away," I said, my eyes narrowing. "Argh. You should have chased her, Samuel."

"I wasn't going to leave you." He met my eyes, and his gaze was so unnervingly intense, I squirmed. "You passed out, Bea. I didn't know if you were okay or what."

"I am," I said, sitting up tall. "I mean," I turned to Nate and Scott, "I assume you guys examined me from both medical and magical standpoints. I'm fine, right?"

"We did," Nate said, frowning. "And you are *mostly* fine." He hesitated. "When we pulled you out of the, hmm—let's call it the between dimension, perhaps?—back at Pussy Queen, we did so because your heart rate spiked so high, and some of your other vitals were very alarming. The tests we did on you afterward indicated you were mostly back to normal, but that you'd experienced a moment of . . ." He turned to Scott. "Can you explain this?"

"It was like a moment where your brain and body were completely overwhelmed by Otherworld magic," Scott said. "From what we can tell, it was a very brief moment. But if you experience that overload for any longer, we don't know what will happen to you."

Nate nodded. "When we examined you at the Market, it looked like you'd just experienced the same thing—a brief moment of magical overload. After hearing your account of what happened at the carnival, it would be logical to hypothesize your trips to the Otherworld and to that between dimension are overloading your system somehow. You're fine right now, but if you go to either place again, you may not be." He met my eyes, giving me his most serious of ultra-serious looks. "We cannot risk sending you there again until we know more about what we're facing. And I would suggest you do your best to not follow the lead of mysterious voices trying to take you there. It's too dangerous."

"Please, Bea," Evie said, her voice shaking. "Listen to Nate. I don't know why you thought it was a good idea to go off by yourself to creepy carnival land in the first place, why you let the voice lure you—"

"I'm not possessed if that's what you're thinking," I grumbled. I looked at Nate. "Right? Still not possessed?"

"Still not possessed," he affirmed.

"I was the only superhero on the scene," I continued. "I had to investigate. Anyway, I protected myself with my powers, didn't I? Do I need to repeat the part where I stood tall and screamed, my cape dramatically blowing behind me in the wind—"

"Yes, I got that," Evie said. "But—"

"And why was I the only one there, anyway?" I barreled on. "We were all supposed to go to the Market, but you and Aveda and Lucy dropped out at the last minute to do something more important. What was it?"

"Rose and I went to scan your mother's grave site," Lucy said. "I know there's not an actual body or anything in there since you scattered her ashes. But we thought that perhaps the site might have some of her, I don't know, essence. That we might be able to pick up a clue. But unfortunately, there was nothing."

"And Evie and I were also doing something important," Aveda said, giving Evie an encouraging look. "Very, very important."

"Right," Evie said, her gaze shifting to the side. "We were . . . um. We went with Lucy and Rose."

"You did?" That surprised me. Evie *never* wanted to visit the grave site. It was too much for her.

"Yes," Evie said. "I didn't want to . . . um. Upset you. Until we knew something for sure. Anyway. When you're the only superhero on the scene, you also have to take certain precautions. And given what Nate and Scott's tests revealed, you can't just go jumping into the Otherworld again. No more following weird voices."

"And no more doing spells to try to connect you," Scott said, giving me an apologetic smile.

I frowned, unsure how to respond. How could I convince them the Otherworld was where the answers were? The Otherworld was where *Mom* was.

"Have you noticed any other changes in—well, anything,

now that you've returned to our world?" Nate asked. "Anything unusual or even just different?"

"No," I said. "Nothing."

Okay, so that wasn't exactly true. My ability to implant thoughts directly into people's brains had happened right after the first time I'd visited the Otherworld. And this time . . . I mean, could the reason Kathy and I had caused so much destruction during our face-off be due to yet another change? Did I get little level-ups and new features to my power every time I crossed over? Well. I sure as hell wasn't telling them about any of that. They were already trying to block me from my quest. I didn't need to give them even more fuel.

"I get the message," I muttered, crossing my arms over my chest and slumping against my pillows. "But listen: we have to figure out how to find Kathy, because she's clearly doing some messed up shit. She somehow banished that pretzel guy to the Otherworld, and she may have done the same thing to Mom. And she also appears to have some kind of superpower—"

"Hold up, darling," Lucy said, raising a hand. "We've got a bunch of stuff to cover here, and we need you to back up to the beginning of your—what did you call it?"

"Bea's Super Awesome Superhero Adventures," I said. "That will also be the name of the animated TV series. Oh, they better get an Asian girl to voice me, though, or I will start the mother of all internet campaigns—"

"As Lucy was saying," Aveda said, sounding impatient. "I think we need you to go back to the beginning. So, a creepy voice told you how to enter the Otherworld this time?"

"Pretzel Guy," I confirmed. "And I was definitely there physically this time. Then when the mecha Spider attacked, I think I was back in that between dimension. Only this time, unlike at Pussy Queen, I could actually scream."

"Maybe the supernatural energy in that area is active rather than dormant," Nate said. "That might contribute to why the between dimension seemed different this time."

"Even if you were in the between dimension, the way

the ride attacked you sounds somewhat like what's been happening with the Wave Organ," Lucy said, cocking an eyebrow. "A location being weaponized."

"Down to a person disappearing into thin air," I mused. "First the tourist at the Wave Organ and now Pretzel Guy. So maybe Kathy spirited the tourist away, too? Does she need to trap someone in the Otherworld in order to weaponize a location?"

"And why was there this huge break between trapping your mom and trapping people now?" Scott said.

"Also, was there any *result* from trapping your mother all those years ago?" Aveda said, her brow furrowing. "Because these weaponized locations seem to be an entirely new thing."

"For all we know, trapping people physically could be a new element as well," Nate said. "We still do not know if she trapped your mother's body or merely her consciousness."

"Or if she actually trapped Mom at all," Evie murmured. "Remember, this could be an Otherworld trick."

"Mom did say the evil that trapped her was back," I said, choosing to ignore her naysaying. "Maybe something happened now that activated Kathy's power. Or made it better."

"But what is that power?" Lucy said, shaking her head. "Bea, when you were mind battling it out, you said it felt like the two of you were projecting at each other, right?"

"Yes," I said. "It felt like she had the ability to block or, like, push back against my emotional projection—which I don't think I've ever encountered before."

"And somehow this mind battle resulted in destruction of physical objects," Nate said. "Intriguing."

"We've already talked to Rose about evacuating and cordoning off the Market for the time being, as her team did with the Wave Organ. I'll make sure she includes the carnival, too," Lucy said. "Just in case any more rides want to come to life and attempt to stomp people to death. Even if you were in the between dimension at that point, we'd best not risk it."

"And we'll do a thorough scan of the whole area tomorrow," Aveda said, nodding.

"How do we find Kathy?" Evie said, rubbing her temples. She looked very tired. "Scott, do you have a locator spell that might work?"

"I need a personal effect," Scott said. "Which I'm assuming we don't have?"

"The box!" I exclaimed. Everyone looked at me quizzically. "The box of Mom's stuff," I clarified. "I mean, I guess technically it doesn't belong to Kathy, so it might not work. But it was in her possession long enough to maybe possibly count as a personal effect?"

"Good thinking, Bug," Scott said with a warm smile. "We'll give it a try."

"If that's all we need to discuss for now, I'd suggest we clear out and let Bea get some rest," Nate said.

"I'm fine with that—get out!" I said, making an expansive gesture toward the door. "Do not darken my door again for the rest of the evening. Unless it's to send up a number three combo from that Vietnamese place on California Street. With extra meat sauce." I gave them a hopeful smile.

"I'll have Rose stop by on her way over," Lucy said, hopping up. "You deserve a treat for defeating that terrifying carnival Spider thingy."

"Can the rest of us get in on that, too?" Evie said, elbowing Lucy. She seemed to have perked up a little. "How much food can Rose carry by herself?"

"She is remarkably strong, darling," Lucy said, swooning. "But we could dispatch one of these big, burly men to help her."

"I'll go," Aveda said. "I am actually the strongest person here physically. As I've proven multiple times."

"Yes, recall the great pull-up competition of two years ago," Scott said, slinging an arm around her shoulders.

"Why did we never do that again?" Evie said, her brow crinkling.

"Because I kicked all of your asses, that's why," Aveda sniffed. "It was frankly embarrassing. For the rest of you."

"Did you all not hear the 'get out' part?" I said.

"I'm staying," Sam said, settling into the rocking chair Lucy had just vacated.

I swear I heard a *swoosh* as every member of Team Tanaka/Jupiter swiveled to look at him.

"Bea said 'get out,' young man," Aveda said, bristling. "I don't know how things work in your household, but that alpha male bullshit does not fly around here."

"If you are unwilling to leave of your own accord, we will remove you," Nate added.

"And some of your fingers might get broken in the process," Lucy said cheerfully.

"Whoa, guys, *whoa*," I said, holding up my hands. "Sam can stay for a bit. He's my friend, and we have a healthy relationship built on clear communication. I'm perfectly capable of booting him out myself."

"All right," Aveda said, still giving Sam massive side-eye. "But remember what Lucy said about broken fingers."

"Ask Rose to get an extra number three combo," I called after them as they finally exited the room. "Because I've been told that I'm 'the worst food sharer in the history of ever.'" I made little air-quotes with my fingers.

"I'm pretty sure they already know that from living with you," Sam said, leaning back in the rocking chair.

The door clicked behind Team Tanaka/Jupiter, and we were finally alone. I was struck by the quiet that descended on the room.

"Oof," I said, flopping back against my pillows. "What a freaking day."

He didn't respond, just studied me. His face still had that haunted look.

"Dude, I know it's part of the accepted social code that we no longer say this to other humans, but—you look tired," I said. "Why don't you go home, get some sleep?"

"Bea." He leaned forward and rested his elbows on the bed, staring at me with that unnervingly steady gaze. "Seeing you collapse like that today, then hearing about what you went through at the carnival while I was sitting on my ass talking to Kathy, it was . . ." He scrubbed a hand over his face. "Really fucking scary."

"I've been in plenty of scary situations before, Samuel," I said, trying to make my tone light. "It didn't freak you out then."

"I know," he said, giving me that intense stare again. "But there's something about actually . . . *seeing* you in danger up close and in person, versus watching you in danger on a clip on social media or something. And then hearing what Nate and Scott found when they examined you . . . I know you said you're okay, but . . ." His eyes searched my face, like he was trying to find a hidden injury. "I can't . . . I don't want to leave you. Until I'm sure."

"Didn't you hear Aveda?" I said. "That alpha male bullshit does not fly here. I told you I'm fine, therefore I'm fine. The end."

"Why didn't you tell them?" he said abruptly.

"Tell them what?"

"Tell them about what's been happening with your power," he pressed. "You figured out you could do that new thing when we were at the hospital and then today . . ." He frowned, leaning forward. "What if the Otherworld is changing you in some way? What if it's dangerous? I mean, they already said you shouldn't go back—"

"That falls into the area of things that are my business," I said, crossing my arms over my chest. "Sam, look: ninety percent of this superheroing gig is dangerous. And scary. That's what I signed up for, what I wanted. If you can't handle that, don't come with me when I have a mission. Or, you know, stay in the car."

"Because somehow I'm still going to be driving you everywhere for the duration of your tenure as a superhero?" he said, cocking an eyebrow. I was relieved to see a little of his usual challenging vibe creeping back in.

"Well, yeah," I said, matching his challenging look with one of my own. "Why else would I keep you around?"

We stared at each other and now we were back to our usual state, the competitive spark flaring between us.

"You know," I said, leaning in closer, "if you are going to insist on hanging out for a bit, why don't we circle back to a conversation we were having earlier today, before all the craziness started."

"Which one is that?" he said. I noticed his eyes were lingering on my mouth.

I leaned closer still and lightly brushed my fingertips against his throat. He took a sharp breath. "You were making some very interesting claims while we were walking to Kathy Kooper's booth," I said. I arched an eyebrow. "You know, when I shared the little fantasy I had last night? I'm curious to find out if they're true."

"I thought you said I was being cheesy," he said, his eyes never leaving my mouth. His voice had taken on that husky quality that thrilled me deep in my bones. "You couldn't stop laughing."

"Do I look like I'm laughing right now?" I slid off the bed, stood, and put my hands on my hips. "I'm going to take a shower before our food gets here. Join me if you feel like proving just how good you are at certain things in real life—it's gonna be tough, though. 'Cause you were *very good* in my fantasy."

I turned and swept into the bathroom before he could react. I felt giddy as I turned on the shower. Was this really happening? Had I really just dared one of my best friends to come get naked with me? I stripped out of my superhero outfit, wrapped myself in a fluffy bathrobe, and pulled my hair on top of my head. Steam filled the bathroom as the water heated up, and I stared in the mirror, watching a veil of mist descend on my reflection. As the seconds ticked by, a tiny niggle of worry pierced my giddy bubble. What if he didn't take me up on it? What if he just went home? What if I was standing here trying to be all sexy and psyching myself up for more illicit fun times, but the reality was that I was just wasting water while Sam booked it outta here? What if—

The door creaked open, interrupting my runaway train of thought, and I couldn't stop the grin of relief spreading over my face.

I stayed facing the mirror, watching his reflection approach me. He'd already taken his shirt off. I made a big show of allowing my eyes to roam every sharp ridge of muscle, the hard expanse of abs I'd stared at for longer than I cared to admit in the photo he'd texted me.

"You are such an ogler," he said, coming up behind me and putting his hands on my waist. His voice still had that husky tone, and I shivered.

"You're giving me a lot to ogle," I retorted.

He slid my robe down one of my shoulders and pressed his lips against my neck. His mouth was warm—warmer than the steam clouding the room, even, and he took his time tasting my skin. My head lolled back against him, and tingles danced up my spine as he lazily nibbled at my neck, my earlobe. God, that felt good.

"Why did you put your hair up?" he murmured against my skin.

"I—*mmm*. Oh, god, please keep doing that. I put it up when I'm not showering for, like, purely getting clean purposes," I said. "The dye comes out and makes a mess all over the tub and then I have to clean it up—it's a whole thing."

"Too bad," he said, toying with a rebellious strand that had come loose from my topknot.

"Mmm," I said again. I was really having trouble forming anything resembling a coherent thought. "So is my hair down in your fantasies? Because I'm assuming that photo I sent you inspired some fantasies about me, too."

He turned me around in his arms and pulled me against him, his mouth brushing against mine. "I'm more interested in *your* fantasies right now, Beatrice." He kissed me deeply. I sighed against his mouth. I was about to melt into a puddle on the floor. Then he made that little growl in the back of his throat again, and every single one of my nerve endings felt like it was set on fire.

"Can I take this off?" he whispered, his hands going to the belt of my robe.

"Yes," I managed.

He kissed me again as he undid the belt and slid the robe off. I gasped as his hands brushed against my bare skin. He pulled away from me slightly, his gaze taking me in. He looked so intense, so *hungry*.

"Now who's ogling?" I said, arching my back so he could get a better look.

He ran his knuckles lightly between my breasts and down my torso, inspiring a wave of goosebumps.

"God, you're gorgeous," he murmured.

I flushed—I'd expected him to respond with a quip, a joke, or something smug about who was the better ogler. You know, something *familiar*. But the way he breathed out those words, soft and reverent, like maybe he wasn't even aware he'd said them out loud . . . I didn't know what to do with that. Except get him in the shower immediately.

"This is hardly fair," I said, grabbing his belt and pulling him close. "I'm totally naked, and you're still wearing pants." I slid my fingers lower, thrilled at all that delicious hardness covered only by thin layers of fabric, and felt a surge of triumph when he groaned. "Although it kind of seems like you're in danger of coming out of these pants."

"So take them off," he growled.

I needed no further invitation. I tried to keep my hands from shaking as I undid his belt buckle and slid off his jeans and boxers all in one go, kneeling in front of him.

"Oh, my," I breathed. I couldn't help but linger on my knees, taking him in. He . . . well. Let's just say that now I totally understood where some of that smugness was coming from. I skimmed my fingertips over the tip of his cock, and my mouth watered.

He slid a hand down the back of my neck. "Get up, Beatrice," he said. "This is about your fantasy, remember? And in your fantasy, I'm pretty sure I was the one on my knees."

Holy. Shit.

"Maybe I'm revising my fantasy," I said, eyeing him. I should have been embarrassed at how breathy my voice sounded, how I was practically drooling all over him. But I was too wrapped up in how good I felt, the steam misting against my skin. And this fucking beautiful man in front of me, telling me he wanted to make all my dirty thoughts come true.

"No revisions," he said firmly. He slid his hand from my neck, held it out in front of me, and helped me to my feet. Then he pulled me close again, his lips brushing against my earlobe. "And I want to make *you* come first."

"I'm not sure who wins that point, then," I said, trying to keep my tone even, trying not to betray the fact that my knees were practically buckling. "Maybe we both do? Bca . . . uh, Sam . . . oh, fuck, I can't remember the scores right now."

"I am definitely about to win this point," he said, his lips moving to my neck. "Get in the shower."

I should have challenged him on the whole points thing, but I really, really wanted to see what was going to happen once we were in the shower. I actually couldn't think of one single thing I wanted more right now. I broke away from him and walked to the shower, making a big show of it, throwing him a little smile over my shoulder. I climbed in and sighed as the spray misted my back—every sensation felt heightened, dialed way up. He stepped in after me, and I took the opportunity to ogle him again, because *damn*. My earlier assertion that us getting naked together in real life would inspire a giggle-fest had been sincere, but now I couldn't imagine that happening. He was studying me again with that intense hunger, like he wanted to taste me all over, lick me everywhere. That look did things to me. It was like an exciting new version of us constantly challenging each other. And it meant giggling was about the farthest thing from my mind.

He framed my hips with his hands and pressed me against

the steamy tiles, leaning in close and claiming my mouth with his. "Tell me about your fantasy," he said against my lips.

"I told you already," I murmured. His beautiful chest muscles brushed against my breasts, and I gasped as my nipples, already so aching and sensitive, hardened.

He pulled back and gave me something resembling the typically smug Sam Fujikawa grin. "I want you to tell me again."

"Bossy," I said between kisses, trying—and probably failing miserably—to sound put out. "You were on your knees in front of me. And your hands were on my hips, holding me in place."

He moved lower, trailing kisses down my neck, over my collarbone. Every brush of his lips was hot as a brand, so searing it felt like he was leaving marks on my skin. Heat pooled between my legs, and I squirmed, the need almost too much to bear—if he didn't touch me there soon, I was going to explode.

He moved lower still, slipping one of my aching nipples into his mouth and sucking slowly, like it was his favorite thing in the world. Like he was really savoring the taste, the sensation. I made a sound I didn't know a human being could make.

"That . . . was not in the fantasy," I managed to gasp out. "I thought you said no revisions."

"Are you complaining?" he murmured, his hand drifting up my side to cup my other breast. His thumb brushed over my nipple, and I gasped again, my hands going flat against the tiled wall—like that was going to keep me upright somehow.

"I-I just think that counts as cheating," I said, closing my eyes and losing myself in pure feeling, in his mouth and hands teasing indecent sounds from me. "You know, if you're trying to get that point and all."

"I'm trying to get *extra* points," he growled. "And this strategy already seems to be pretty fucking successful." Then he captured my nipple between his teeth, and I nearly blacked out.

He kissed his way down my belly, finally lowering himself

to his knees and grasping my hips with his hands. He gazed up at me as he caressed my thigh, lifting one of my legs to drape over his shoulder. He was looking at me like he had when he'd first seen me naked—like I was the most beautiful thing he'd ever seen. He looked so earnest, stripped of all his usual smug, his *beaucoup fromage*. Maybe I could understand, just a little bit, why he'd been worried about me falling in love with him.

"Beatrice," he said softly. "Tell me what you want."

"Show me," I whispered. "Show me how good you are with that tongue."

He trailed his fingertips over my hipbone. "Can I use fingers, too?"

"Yes," I gasped out. I guess he wasn't *that* opposed to revisions.

He dipped his head low and pressed his mouth against me and . . . oh, *fuck*. My head lolled to the side, and my hand grasped his shoulder to steady myself. Forget those inhuman sounds I'd made before, now I was just outright moaning. He knew how to stroke me with his tongue *just right*, long sweeps contrasted with smaller, more intricate moves, all designed to bring me right up to the edge without sending me over.

I dug my nails into his shoulder, holding on for dear life as he licked, sucked, stroked. I was glad he had me pressed so firmly against the wall, that he'd thrown my leg over his shoulder to spread me wider, because otherwise I surely would have collapsed right then and there.

The water continued to stream down on us, making everything hotter and wetter. He brought me to the edge again and again, overwhelming me with his tongue and the hot slide of his skin against mine. Then, just when I thought I couldn't take any more pleasure, he slid two fingers inside of me. Shudder after shudder cascaded through my body, and I was practically sobbing with need.

"Sam," I cried out. "*Please*. I need . . . I need to . . ."

He pressed his tongue firmly against the exact right spot and curved his fingers the exact right way, and I screamed, my orgasm shattering through me as I dug my nails into his shoulder so hard I drew blood.

He stroked me down from my peak, slowly bringing me back to reality. But even then, I was so blissed out, I could barely stand. Things blurred together as he turned off the water, patted me dry with a towel, and carried me to my bed.

"Mmm," I sighed, stretching out on the sheets like a cat. "Forgot about . . . our food . . ."

I heard him pad over to the bedroom door, open and close it.

"They left it for us outside," he said. "I guess they knew you were busy."

"I'm not even hungry right now," I said, burrowing under the covers. I felt all glowy, like I was floating on a fluffy post-coital cloud. "Come get in bed with me."

He slid between the sheets, wrapping his body around mine, and undid my topknot, running his fingers through my hair as it cascaded around me.

"Oh, no," I said, my fingertips brushing his scratched up shoulder. "I think I did that."

"It was worth it," he said, pressing a kiss against my temple, and I felt the smile in his voice.

"My fantasy was pretty awesome," I said, my words slow and lazy as I reached down to stroke him. "But don't we need to take care of you now?" After all the pleasure he'd given me, it was a thrill to feel him harden against my palm. "There are condoms in my bedside table."

"Slow down," he said, his tone laced with amusement. "We'll get there." Then he kissed me: long, slow, and deep.

I don't know what I'd expected. I guess for things between us to be fast and crazy and passionate, some kind of high-speed Olympics of fucking. But he took everything slow, took so much delicious care with every single kiss and touch. And when he finally slid inside of me, murmuring my name in that sweet, reverent way he had, I couldn't help but think that this entire night wasn't anything like my fantasy.

It was totally, extremely, mind-blowingly *better*.

CHAPTER SIXTEEN

I AWOKE TO my phone buzzing on my bedside table and Sam trying to find his pants.

"Are you attempting to slip out of here unnoticed?" I asked him, letting out a huge yawn and reaching for my phone. "Because Lucy isn't actually going to break your fingers. I gave the okay for you to be here, remember? And your pants are in the bathroom."

"I . . . thanks. I'll get them in a sec," he said, giving up the pants hunt and sitting on the edge of the bed. He looked distracted, his eyes not quite meeting mine.

I'll admit, I was a little disappointed he was already up and almost outta here. I'd been hoping we could have a repeat session of last night's fun before being forced to get into our respective daily tasks that didn't involve mind-blowing sex.

"And no, I'm not trying to sneak out," he continued. "I have to go have brunch with my siblings. They're both in town, and I can't weasel out of it. And believe me, I tried. That means I have to go home, change, and prepare for them to make me feel worthless about anything I might foolishly consider to be an accomplishment."

"Oh, ugh." I sat up in bed, silencing my phone and pulling the sheet around me. "I'm sorry, dude. Do you want me to come with you?"

"That's all right," he said, scraping a hand over his face. "I can face Ms. Bore and Mr. Brag by myself." I'd only met

Ms. Bore and Mr. Brag a couple times and it had been mercifully brief. Emily and Alex Fujikawa both boasted multiple advanced degrees, impressive careers, and jet-setting lifestyles. Emily, an accomplished lit professor, was engaged to some boring finance guy and lived in a restored Brooklyn brownstone straight out of an interior design Pinterest page. Alex was a plastic surgeon catering to the Hollywood elite, married to a hot socialite who had more money than she knew what to do with. He owned a full rainbow of thousand dollar polo shirts. They both had eventual plans for two-point-five kids with their respective picture perfect partners. And they both looked down on Sam and his supposed lack of accomplishments with a full-body snootiness that made me want to strangle them.

"I know you *can* face them, Samuel," I said, arching an eyebrow. "I'm saying you don't have to."

"Really, it's okay," he said, giving me a slight smile and patting my blanket-covered foot. But his expression was strained around the eyes. He stood and headed for the bathroom.

I frowned after him and picked up my phone. Okay, so maybe he was preoccupied with the prospect of gritting his teeth through a highly annoying brunch. I couldn't blame him for that. But I was disappointed that there'd been zero acknowledgment of the incredible time we'd had the night before. I'd expected, I don't know, a sly grin, maybe a smug comment about how many times he'd made me come. An update to the points total, certainly. I mean, he *definitely* had a lot to brag about, and Sam Fujikawa wasn't one to let any bragging opportunity slip by.

Unless . . . My frown deepened. Maybe it hadn't been as incredible for him? He'd certainly given me plenty of reactions that indicated otherwise. But wasn't that what he excelled at—making every woman he slept with feel like she was the momentary queen of his universe? Wasn't that why he was so popular? Wasn't that *his* superpower?

I chewed on my lower lip, tossing my phone back and forth

from hand to hand. I knew there was no way he could have faked certain . . . responses to me. But could he have faked all the stuff that made me so weak in the knees—the growls, the intensity, the way he had looked at me like I was so fucking beautiful . . .

Ugh, why did that matter? We'd said this whole thing was us doing what we excelled at: having fun. And once it stopped being fun, we'd stop doing it. But . . .

I cast a look at the bathroom, where he was rustling around, trying to locate the missing pants.

It is a truth universally acknowledged, that when you're having this kind of fun with someone, it always stops being fun for one person before it stops being fun for the other. The thing was . . . usually I was the one who got to "eh, this isn't fun anymore" *first*.

This was definitely one point I did *not* want to lose to him.

I looked at my phone, trying to distract myself. There were a ton of messages from Leah, which had apparently been piling up all morning. I scrolled through them, my grip on my phone tightening as I took in the information.

"Sam!" I called out, momentarily forgetting about the weirdness between us. "Come back out here, I think we've got a lead on finding the poet-artist girl from the Wave Organ!" I stood up on the bed, draping the sheet over myself like a toga and bounced up and down a couple times, re-reading Leah's messages.

"For real?" he said, coming back into the bedroom. He still wasn't wearing pants. I tried not to get too excited.

"Leah took Pancake to his favorite café out by the Marina—it's not too far from the water?"

"Pancake has a favorite café?" Sam said, his brow crinkling. "Like, a human food café?"

"Yes, Samuel, Pancake has very expensive taste, and he can't get enough of the croissants from this place," I said. "Anyway. Leah saw a teenage girl drawing on a big sketchpad and being the curious artistic soul that she is, she glanced at what the girl was doing. The drawings were like the ones

I described—outlandish mythical creatures punctuated by emo poetry."

"There could be more than one teenage girl with that art style," Sam said.

"True, it's a possible false alarm," I said. "But I trust Leah's artistic assessment—and that girl's poetry-mythical-creature mashup is actually pretty unique. Since we have precious few leads on tracking her down, I think it's worth going down there."

"Did Leah try to talk to her?" Sam asked.

"She was going to, but then Pancake barfed up his croissant, and she had to clean it up. By the time she was finished, the girl was gone," I said. "But she asked the café staff about her and they said she's a regular. In any case, I have the perfect plan for us."

"Us?" he said, trepidation creeping into his voice.

Still holding my sheet-toga around me, I gestured to him expansively with my phone.

"Tell Ms. Bore and Mr. Brag to meet us at this café for brunch. We'll scope the scene, see if Poet returns, see if we can pin her down. And this way, your meal will be inherently less awful because we'll be on an important mission. Your suffering will be for a *cause*." I put my hands on my hips and stared off into the middle distance, affecting a dramatic pose. The sheet slipped a little, and I shifted my dramatic pose to ensure it stayed up. If he'd seemed more receptive to a repeat of last night's shenanigans, I would have let it fall off entirely.

I tried to glance at him out of the corner of my eye and was relieved that he seemed to be regarding me with amusement, his strained, distant look from before melting into something more familiar.

"Ms. Bore and Mr. Brag are not going to be happy about this," he said. "They made a reservation at a very expensive, schmancy brunch place."

"Then this will have the added bonus of irritating the shit out of them," I said, grinning at him.

"Sounds like a mission I can get behind," he said, heading back into the bathroom. "Hold on, I'll text them."

I was about to respond, when my bedroom door flew open and Aveda Jupiter marched in—clad in black leather pants, hair pulled into her sleek power ponytail, commanding expression in place. I half expected dramatic music to accompany her entrance.

"Didn't you have a whole thing with Evie where she taught you about knocking being part of the social code?" I said, sitting back down on the bed.

"Ugh, that's right," she said, her face twisting with regret. "Sorry. I forget sometimes when I'm especially amped about a mission." She smiled at me. "You and I get to go on another exciting mentor/intern adventure this morning! Scott tried the locator spell and couldn't find Kathy—we're going to head over to the Market to search her booth, see if we can find any clues. Shruti is going to join us as we may require her talents. Meanwhile, Rose and her team are going to scan the area, including the carnival." She sat down on the foot of my bed with a decisive *thump* and leaned in, regarding me keenly. "This will be more great practice getting into the nitty gritty of an investigation, Bea. And a chance to truly explore one of my favorite superheroine lessons: sometimes the key to a particularly twisty mystery is found in the most mundane of places."

I nodded, trying to look like I totally got that. The truth was, I didn't really get a lot of Aveda's superheroing "lessons": they sounded like inspirational sayings she was making up on the spot. And the bonding I'd hoped for hadn't exactly materialized yet.

I was momentarily tempted to mind-mojo her to leave so I could get some more sleep (or maybe talk pantsless Sam into some more . . . something else), but then I realized that even if her aphorisms didn't totally make sense, the proposed mission did. If I could track down Kathy, maybe that would help me find Mom. And hey, the Market had taken me to the Otherworld once—maybe it could happen again? Yes, so the rest of Team Tanaka/Jupiter had forbidden me from trying to jump through to our favorite demon land, but maybe it would just *happen*, I'd be transported without doing anything, and they couldn't really protest *that—*

"Bea?" Sam chose that moment to emerge from the bathroom (wearing pants—bummer).

Aveda's eyes went wide. "Oh," she said. "Well. I didn't realize . . . *well.*" She rose from the bed, her posture stiff. "Hello again, young man."

"Sam, I'll meet you for brunch with Ms. Bore and Mr. Brag later—and I'll text you the address of the restaurant," I said, stifling the giggles that were threatening to spill out of me. "I need to go on another mission first. And Aveda, I'll meet you downstairs in ten. Sam was just leaving. He needed to find his pants."

"Yup," Sam said, looking like he would rather be anywhere else. He patted his thighs. "Found 'em."

"Excellent," Aveda said. "Good for you."

Then, at a loss for anything else to say, she shuffled out of the room, ponytail twitching.

I waited until she was out of earshot to release the mighty cackle I'd been holding in. And I tried not to dwell on the fact that instead of trying to challenge me or laugh with me or fall back into bed, Sam just gave me a half-smile and went looking for his shirt.

🔥

Aveda and I borrowed Lucy's car, picked up Shruti, and booked it over to the East Bay. On the drive over, I chattered to them about Leah's possible Poet-sighting and my plan to follow up later. Aveda said she approved of my initiative-taking—and, thankfully, didn't press me about the half-naked Sam she'd found in my bedroom. It wasn't until we reached the Market, which was now empty and cordoned off by police tape, that I realized something was off.

"Evie didn't want to come?" I said, as we approached Kathy's booth. "I know she's not a morning person, but this mission is directly related to our mom."

"She had other things to do," Aveda said, waving a dismissive hand. "There's a lot to investigate, and we needed to divide and conquer."

I frowned. There was *a lot* to look into, but it was weird to me that Evie hadn't wanted to come. I didn't really get what was going on with her—she seemed withdrawn and reluctant whenever the Mom angle of the investigation came up, yet she'd been willing to do stuff like visit the grave site and go through the letters with me. Maybe it was because she was embroiled in her own complicated web of feelings and didn't really believe we were going to find Mom at the end of it—not like I did. She hadn't connected with Mom the way I had during my first trip to the Otherworld, hadn't heard that familiar musical voice echoing through her head. But still. If there was even the slightest possible chance we could be reunited with our mother, why wasn't she jumping in with both feet at every opportunity?

A memory bubbled to the surface: Evie and me at Mom's funeral, wearing hastily thrown together all-black outfits. Mine had involved a way-too-big cardigan over a t-shirt—to try to conceal the fact that I was wearing a t-shirt, I guess? We hadn't had the time, energy, or money to shop for anything fancier.

I'd cried through the whole thing, wiping my runny nose and puffy eyes on my cardigan sleeves until they were encrusted with snot. Evie sat next to me, back posture perfect for the first (and maybe only) time ever, staring straight ahead. And her eyes stayed totally dry the whole time.

I'd always wondered why she hadn't shed a single tear. I knew she hated crying, but wasn't that the time to do it? Or was she already thinking ahead and resenting Mom for leaving her with an unruly, snotty-sleeved kid?

"All right," Shruti said, bringing me back to the present. "Where should we start?" She cocked her head, studying Kathy's booth. "This is quite the mess."

It really was. Shards of the broken vases from yesterday were scattered on the ground, and Kathy's cat-hair crafts were strewn all over the tables, mixed in with her button and key jewelry. The colorful scarf tablecloths were rumpled and askew beneath the unorganized jumble of goods, and one of them had a huge rip down the middle, exposing the weathered wood of the table.

"Bea, you're the only one of us who's been here before. What do you think?" Aveda said.

I scanned the mess again. "See that back area?" I gestured to the far left, where the janky cardboard partition sectioned off a corner of the booth. "I think that's where her register's set up. Maybe there's something there?"

"Hopefully something with less cat hair," Aveda said, wrinkling her nose at Kathy's craft table.

The three of us made our way over to the corner, and Aveda shoved the cardboard aside to reveal Kathy's bookkeeping set-up. In comparison to the rest of the booth, it was actually quite organized: an old school paper calendar, a neat stack of receipts, and a trio of pens were lined up perfectly straight on top of a battered secretary desk. A bulletin board, propped up to one side, was pinned with a collage of photos. And a small cabinet with a single drawer was tucked underneath the desk. It looked like it had been painted a brilliant robin's egg blue at one point but now was all chipped and faded.

"That drawer looks promising," Aveda said, cocking an eyebrow.

"Wouldn't it be amazing if it contained a handy piece of paper that said, 'here's the answer to everything, you're welcome'?" Shruti said with a laugh.

"Ha! Why do I feel like that's not going to happen?" Aveda said, shaking her head. She reached down and tried the drawer. "Locked, of course. Go for it, Shruti."

Shruti took a deep breath, zeroing in on the rusted lock of the drawer. Her hair grew longer, its dark expanding tendrils reaching outward, floating through the air and snaking into the lock.

"I do adore this particular element of your power," Aveda said, giving Shruti an admiring smile. "It's like you're one of those super cool ladies who organizes multimillion dollar bank heists, only you use your skills for good."

"That's me—a heister who's never realized her full heisting potential," Shruti said, winking.

While Shruti worked her way through the lock, I studied the photo-filled bulletin board. Most of the pictures were from the era when Mom and Kathy had shared booth space— laughing, greeting customers, displaying their various crafts. There was only one current photo of Kathy. She was by herself, holding up a cat-hair craft and giving the camera a wan half-smile. The pretzel stand loomed in the background, mobbed with customers.

"Wow, look at your mom," Aveda said, leaning over my shoulder and tapping one of the older photos. "I forgot how beautiful she was. How vibrant and *happy*. Looks like she and Kathy had some good times together."

"It was pretty much impossible not to have a good time when Mom was around," I murmured. "She had a way of coaxing the good mood out no matter what."

"Why didn't Kathy stay in touch with you and Evie after your Mom passed?" Aveda mused. "It looks like she remembers her very fondly. And . . ." Aveda scanned the bulletin board, filled with so many images of Mom. ". . . a lot."

"I don't think Evie had the time or energy to maintain ties with any of Mom's friends after Dad left," I said. "And Kathy always kept a certain amount of distance, never had much to say to us. I don't think she knew how to talk to kids, really." I frowned, cocking my head at the newer photo of Kathy. "It doesn't look like Kathy's made many friends in the interim. Maybe it's lonely, working the booth by herself every day, trying to hawk those terrible cat-hair crafts. Maybe that's what made her go all evil."

"Maybe," Aveda said.

We studied the bulletin board for a moment, the silence punctuated by the soft clicks of Shruti's hair picking the lock.

"Bea," Aveda said slowly. "We're going to solve this thing, I promise. If your mother's out there, we *will* find her."

"I know Evie thinks it's not her; that it's some demon force, fucking with my head." My gaze locked on a photo of Mom with her head thrown back, laughing uproariously at something, her hair shining in the sunlight. *Where are you?* "Evie just wants you to be safe," Aveda said. "We all do. Being part of a true superhero team means looking out for each other."

"Then when do I get to be *recognized* as part of the team?" I said, trying to suppress the whine creeping into my voice. "I know I'm still at the intern trial basis stage, but I've already had so many newsworthy adventures. Like, a Maisy write-up of yesterday's mecha Spider mayhem would have been off the freakin' chain—"

"Except nobody was there to see it," Aveda said. "And even if they were . . ." She hesitated, sizing me up. "Bea, I didn't forbid Maisy from writing about you because I was trying to hide your light or suppress your ever-growing awesomeness or something."

"Then why?" I said, my brow crinkling.

She hesitated for a long moment, studying me. "I did it because you deserve room to mess up."

"You think I'm going to mess up?" I bristled.

"*Everybody* messes up." She shook her head in exasperation. "I want you to be able to wear bad outfits, and not say the perfect thing every time, and have a meltdown about getting a freaking zit without zillions of people commenting on it or trashing you or giving their hot take. And none of those things are even 'messing up,' exactly, but once you're a superheroine in the spotlight . . ." She shook her head again. "No matter how confident you might be, you're going to have moments where you feel like you can never be anything less than perfect."

"Especially as a superheroine of color!" Shruti called out. "We always feel like we have to represent well or risk letting down our entire community." She grinned at us. "Sorry, this lock is super tricky, and I've *almost* got it." Her face twisted into a look of renewed concentration.

"Shruti is right," Aveda said. "I never felt like I had space to be anything less than perfect. And as a burgeoning superheroine who is also my intern—not to mention someone I consider an honorary little sister—I want you to have that space."

I didn't know what to say, so I just stared at her. She was looking at me with something that wasn't quite her usual imperious look. It was still commanding and full of attitude, but shot through with streaks of deep vulnerability—the Annie Chang side of herself she didn't let many people see.

I realized then that even though her not-entirely-inspiring "superhero lessons" didn't always make sense, Aveda was making a valiant effort to guide me. She really wanted me to be the best superheroine I could be. She was hoping to shield me from some of the hurt she'd dealt with when she first got the gig—all those not-so-fun sides of being a hero that I hadn't considered before diving in headfirst. And as for that bonding I was after . . .

"You think of me as a sister?" I said, my voice small. I'd always imagined she saw me as sort of an Evie add-on.

"Of course I do," she said, looking offended at the idea that she'd see me any other way.

"Guys!" Shruti cried out.

We both turned to look at her.

"Sorry to interrupt a truly lovely discussion," she said, grinning. "But I think I've finally cracked this dang lock."

We heard a final click as she pulled the drawer out from the blue cabinet, and the three of us crowded around to see what was inside.

"A document?" Aveda said, cocking an eyebrow and pulling out a yellowed, crumbly bit of paper. It looked thick, like some kind of old school parchment.

"What are these markings?" Shruti said, tapping the parchment. "They look almost like, I don't know, runes of some kind."

"I think that's actually an Otherworld demon language," I said, studying the markings. They were a series of faint lines and dots marching across the page, impenetrable. "Nate and his demonologist colleagues have seen stuff like this before, but they've never been able to decipher it."

"Is there anything else in here?" Aveda felt around the bottom of the drawer, then stopped, her eyes going wide. "Wait. This thing has a false bottom." She moved the extra piece of wood out of place to reveal . . .

"More papers?" Shruti said.

I peered inside. It was, indeed, a whole mess of papers. But these weren't the yellowed parchment of the weird demon thing we'd found. No, these were neat, official, eight by ten documents, carefully stacked. And emblazoned with my mother's name.

My heart nearly stopped.

"They're Mom's hospital records!" I shrieked. I pulled the records free and brandished them in the air. "Look, there's her death certificate. This is the missing part of the file! The *end* of the file." I frowned, running my fingertips over my mother's name. "What the hell is Kathy doing with *this*?"

CHAPTER SEVENTEEN

MY SECOND MISSION of the day had barely started and I already regretted it.

After determining there was nothing else of interest in Kathy's booth, Aveda, Shruti, and I had hauled the hospital records, parchment paper, and the blue cabinet back to HQ. Nate and Scott were going to see if they could use a combination of scientific and magical tests to produce further clues. My mind was stuck on what it all meant, my head swirling with possibilities. But I had to shove those thoughts to the side to focus on my current mission. Which wasn't going so well.

As planned, I'd met Sam at the Lazy Daisy, the café where Leah had spotted Poet. The place was packed with a wide range of the Bay Area's more colorful characters, from cantankerous seniors to young artists angsting into their coffee to a loud gaggle of teenagers crowded around a tiny corner table. There was a constant buzz of chaotic energy running through the place, an endless soundtrack of silverware clinking and servers yelling "BEHIND YOU" as they contorted their bodies to move around each other.

The café's design enhanced the chaos—cramped seating, low ceilings, and a collection of whimsical teapots haphazardly placed everywhere. Normally I would've loved a spot like this, but Poet was nowhere to be seen, and Ms. Bore and Mr. Brag were already doing their damndest to make this brunch as unbearable as possible.

"Really, Sam, we gave up a five-star eatery for this?"

Emily said, making a face at her clearly sub-par cappuccino. "I know you're all about that Bay Area quaintness, but I hoped we could catch up in a more . . . sanitary environment."

"Sammy likes to keep it real," Alex said, making finger guns at Sam. "I can dig on that. But, you know, I'd love more protein shake options." He frowned at his food. "Aren't you San Francisco types all about that crunchy granola stuff?"

"Not all of us," I said. "Some of us are all about potatoes."

"So funny," Alex said, transferring his finger guns to me. "I've always thought she was so funny, Sammy. Why haven't you two ever gotten together?"

"We're friends," Sam said, his voice tight. "As I've told you every time you ask me that. Also, she has a name, and you can address her directly instead of talking about her like she's not here." He used his fork to stab at his food with more force than necessary, his eyes on his plate. Being around Emily and Alex always made him tense up in a very un-Sam-like manner. I gave his knee a gentle squeeze under the table, trying to let him know I was there for him. If he *wanted* me to be there for him, that was. I still wasn't sure *what* he wanted after his weird, distant demeanor this morning, and I was trying not to dwell on it or let it bother me.

After all, I needed to focus on the mission. I kept craning my neck to see if I could catch any glimpse of Poet. I was also scoping out the various servers, to figure out if one might be willing to talk to me about the teenage clientele. Though I could always soften 'em up if they were surly.

"So Bea," Emily said, in that fake bright voice that indicated she was pretending to care about a random detail of my life. "Your hair. It's so . . . quirky. Like a comic book character's. I just read the most *interesting* academic article about how the colorful hair streak—or brightly colored hair, period— is a marker of the rebellious Asian girl stereotype in media. Apparently, creators started adding it to signify that *their* Asian girl character isn't the docile, submissive stereotype— but in doing so, they created a whole *new* stereotype! Isn't that hilarious?" She let out a peal of brittle laughter.

"Oh, um, yeah, that does happen sometimes," I said, trying to keep my tone mild. "I've read some books by white people that totally do that. But I think that mostly applies if said Asian girl character only has the one personality trait, as expressed via that hair streak. If the hair streak is supposed to stand in for her *entire* personality, you know? Whereas I am a real person. With tons of personality traits."

"Wow, that was so articulate," Emily said, shaking her head, like she couldn't believe I was capable of such a thing. "But don't you think you have a responsibility—you know, being out there working retail, being so visible to so many— to represent well?"

"I dye my hair because I like the way it looks," I said, with the brightest, sweetest smile I could muster. "If someone thinks I'm a stereotype because of that, they can fuck off."

"Emily, give it a rest," Sam said, glaring at her.

"Just trying to engage in stimulating brunch conversation," she said, rolling her eyes at him.

"It's not stimulating," he grumbled. "It's you being a jerk."

"So Mom and Dad still haven't talked you into going back to school, eh?" Alex said, clapping Sam on the back in what he probably thought was a jovial manner. "You know Em and I both have connections all over the Ivy League. We could put in a word—"

"That's okay," Sam said. "I'm still not interested. Hey, do you guys want more coffee?"

"Oh, Sammy, you're still so young," Emily said, shaking her head. "And you're so smart. You were always the smartest of us."

"You were," Alex said, nodding emphatically. "You had so much potential. You could've taken it all in the little contest Em and I have going on, accumulating advanced degrees."

"Oh, shut up, Alex, it's so embarrassing when you boast about that stuff," Emily said, laughing way too cheerily. It was clear that she didn't find it embarrassing at all.

I shot a disbelieving look at Sam, but his eyes were firmly

trained on his food. He seemed determined to weather this conversation by not responding to either of them.

"There's still time for you to get out there and really *do* something with your life," Emily continued. "I know you say you're happy hanging out, fixing people's cars—"

"Oh, buddy," Alex interjected, "if you could take a look at my new Maserati while we're in town? It's making this clinking noise. I'd be much obliged."

"Is it the, um, photos you're worried about?" Emily pressed. "The ones in that silly calendar? I know you're probably thinking they're the sort of thing you want to actively hide from a grad school application, but a lot of admissions offices actually like that kind of . . . color."

"We just think it would be great for you to broaden your horizons in general," Alex chimed in. "Get out, see the world, meet new people . . ."

"Yes," Emily urged. "Maybe meet someone special." Her gaze dartcd to mc as if to say: *Not like this weird-hair, weird-clothes, unmotivated bad influence and bad representing stereotype you're always keeping company with.*

"We just want you to be happy, Sammy," Alex said, suddenly looking solemn for no reason.

"We do," Emily said, pressing her lips together and looking down at her food like she was about to get super emotional over the dire state of Sam's future.

I shoveled hash browns into my mouth and looked at Alex, then Emily, then back at Alex again. Were they for real? They had always talked down to Sam and treated him with a certain level of disdain, but this display of faux concern was a new tactic—and it had my blood boiling. Who were they to tell him how to live his life when they clearly didn't know him at all? He didn't just "fix cars"—dissecting the inner workings of engines was his passion. He wasn't embarrassed by his calendar photos—he was proud of them. And he was *still* the smartest of all of them—that wasn't even up for debate.

I turned to Sam, hoping to see him straighten in his seat,

about to fight back. He *usually* fought back. But today, he seemed listless, like he was just going to take whatever they slung at him, let them diminish him until he was ground down to nothing. The only time he'd spoken up was to defend me. He was slumped in his chair, poking at his food with his fork.

For some reason, that made me even madder. As much as I rolled my eyes at his cockiness, his smugness, his heartthrob swagger, seeing it all taken away was unbearable. And if he wasn't going to fight back, I would.

I gathered up all my rage and indignation and projected it directly at Ms. Bore and Mr. Brag: *I can't believe I'm such a pompous asshole*, I thought. *I'm sorry, Sam.*

"I can't believe I'm such a pompous asshole," Alex said out loud.

"Yes," Emily said. "I'm sorry, Sam."

Their faces had that glazed, docile look, and I felt a vicious twist of triumph.

Sam's head snapped up. "What . . ."

You heard me, I thought at them. *Pompous. Asshole. And I'm not just sorry for this time, I'm sorry for every time I've made you feel small or diminished or less-than.*

"You heard me," Alex said, his voice taking on a monotonous quality. "Pompous. Asshole."

"And I'm not just sorry for this time," Emily said, mirroring his tone. "I'm sorry for *every* time I've made you feel small or diminished or less-than."

Sam turned to me, a million different emotions playing over his face. "Bea," he said. "Stop it."

I leaned back in my chair and examined my nails. "Stop what?"

"You know what," he hissed. "Stop. Now."

But we're her puppets, I thought at them. *And we kind of deserve it for being such complete and utter tools.*

"But we're her puppets," Alex said.

"And we kind of deserve it for being such complete and utter tools," Emily added.

My triumph surged, power coursing through me. *That's right, assholes.*

"*Bea.*" Sam grabbed my hand, and pulled me to my feet. "Outside."

He placed a hand at the small of my back and steered me through the chaos of the café, toward the exit. I didn't protest. At least I'd gotten him to finally take action and get away from his awful siblings.

We exited onto the sidewalk. I noticed the big gaggle of teenagers who had been crammed into the corner table lingering outside. A few of them gave us curious looks, but most seemed engrossed in their conversation.

"Why did you do that?" Sam said, crossing his arms over his chest. I realized I had never seen him truly angry—he was usually much too busy being all heartthrob-esque and smug for that. But right now, he looked . . . well, angry. Really angry.

"They were being awful to you," I said, putting my hands on my hips. "They don't respect you at all. And you just sat there and took it, and *I* couldn't take that, I had to fight back—"

"How I handle my siblings is my business," he retorted. "And anyway, this isn't a demon-infested battlefield. This is *brunch*. You can't just go around mind-controlling people because they aren't doing what you want them to. What happened to your *code*, Beatrice?"

My face flushed. "My code is evolving," I said. "That's what has to happen when your powers evolve, Sam, your superheroing code evolves with it—"

"And that's another thing," he said, shaking his head in frustration. "What's happening with your power? You need to talk to Evie—"

"Now who's telling whom how to deal with their siblings?" I snapped. "How I deal with Evie and this superheroing gig is *my* business—"

"Not when it puts you in danger," he said. He scrubbed a hand over his face, overwhelmed with frustration. Then he stepped forward and put his hands on my shoulders. His face was intense and earnest, and he was staring at me like he could see my every thought. "Bea, when you passed out yesterday, it was really fucking scary."

"You already told me that," I grumbled.

"And I'm telling you again because you refused to talk about it last night," he said. "Your power totally overwhelmed you in that moment. Or maybe it was the Otherworld magic overwhelming you, like Nate and Scott were talking about. You need to figure out what's going on. And you can't keep doing stuff like *that*—" He gestured back to the restaurant, where Emily and Alex were probably wondering what had happened to their loser brother and his loser friend. "—until you figure it out."

"Samuel, I'm currently on a mission to liberate my mother from the Otherworld," I said, shaking him off. "I don't have time to stop and figure things out."

"I'm worried about you—"

"Why?!" I glared at him. "You don't need to be. We're not . . . like that. With each other."

"Like what?"

"You know what." I crossed my arms over my chest. "We have fun together. We sometimes compete with each other— also all in good fun. But we don't fight like this. We don't *worry* about each other like this."

He shook his head. "No matter what happens with . . . whatever we've been doing, we'll always be friends. And friends worry about each other. You messed with Emily and Alex because you were worried about me."

"No." I shook my head emphatically. "I messed with them because it was *fun*."

"I don't believe that," he said.

I shrugged. "Believe what you want."

I turned on my heel and walked away, tears burning my eyes. Why had I said that? It was a total lie. Was I really so afraid of giving up ground, of ceding any points to him? Was I pushing him away because he'd seemed so distant this morning? Or did I not want to admit that yes, I had done it because I was worried about him, because I had felt a burning need to defend him?

Whatever the case, I needed to get away from him right now. I needed to clear my head. Our "just for fun" entanglement was messing with me, distracting me from my quest to free Mom. Talk about being distracted by the *ultimate* shiny thing.

I hustled down the street, wrapping my arms around myself to shield from the chill of the marine layer. In the distance, I spotted the gaggle of teenagers who'd been loitering outside the café. They were walking now and seemed to be moving forward as one, like a little amoeba of hormones and feels. They were still chattering eagerly and were clustered around something. I picked up on snippets of their conversation as I got closer.

"Wow . . ."

"So cool . . ."

"Your best one yet . . ."

"You are, like, the greatest artist of all time . . ."

"And writer! Don't forget writer . . ."

I stopped cold in my tracks. The teenage amoeba had stopped too and was now just straight up blocking the sidewalk. I craned my neck to see what they were clustered around, what they were all raving about. But I had a sneaking suspicion I already knew.

There, in the middle of the circle, was Poet. Her squad had been so crammed into the corner table at Lazy Daisy, I must have missed her. She looked very different than she had a couple days ago. Her stringy hair was swept off of her face, her eyes were lit up with excitement, and she was beaming broadly. She was holding up her sketchbook, flipping through the pages, and her friends were responding to every single page with loud exclamations of adoration.

But . . . wait. Hadn't she told me she was super unpopular? That she had no friends and everyone thought her art was weird and nerdy? Had she sensed my former outcast status and lied about that to bond with me or something? But if she was channeling the spirit of my mother, why would she do that? None of this made sense.

"Hey!" I called out, standing at the edge of her little friend/fan circle. I waved, trying to get her attention. "Hey, um, cool artist girl! Remember me? From the Wave Organ? I kind of saved your life and stuff, and then we had a totes weird encounter—"

She spotted me then. Her big grin faded immediately, and all the color drained from her face. Then she clutched her sketchbook tightly to her chest and ran.

"Hey!" I yelped. "What are you . . . I just want to talk to you!"

I darted around the teenage amoeba and sprinted after her.

"Oh em gee," I heard one of them exclaim. "She's so mysterious—it totally enhances her artistic persona!"

"What the hell, Poet," I growled, increasing my speed as she rounded the corner. I followed, keeping her in my sight. She was fast, but I was gaining on her. I concentrated on a feeling of exhaustion, of pure *I want to stop* and sent it spinning at her full force. And then I sent that specific thought for good measure: *I want to stop. I want to stop. I want to—*

NO.

The thought smacked into my brain. It was like a big brick wall smashing into my *I want to stop* directive. And it hurt about as bad as if I'd run into an actual brick wall.

"Guuuuuuhhhh . . ." I stopped, doubled over, and clutched my head. I tried to straighten up and saw Poet running off into the distance, getting farther and farther away from me. I sent the thought in her direction again, but my mental throw felt weaker, like I was haplessly tossing a crumpled tissue at a wastebasket.

I want to—

NO.

The brick wall thought smacked into my mind again, and I screamed out loud.

Fuck. Okay. So either Kathy Kooper was hiding out somewhere around here, or Poet also had the ability to push back against my mind with hers. Even more reason to catch her, but I'd have to do it the old-fashioned way. I gathered all my strength, focused my mind, and started running after her again.

She was much farther ahead of me now, and she seemed to be heading for the water. I followed her to the same waterfront path I'd sprinted down only a few days ago, when I took note of the Golden Gate, the majestic views. Hmm. Actually, she was duplicating that route pretty much *exactly*. Was she heading for the Wave Organ?

"It's closed down right now!" I bellowed after her, even though I knew she probably couldn't hear me. "There's no place to hide over there if that's what you're thinking!"

With the Organ closed, there would be relatively few random tourists lingering around, and I could keep eyes on Poet pretty easily. As we got closer to the Organ, I saw a couple of Rose's team patrolling and scanning the area.

"Hey!" I yelled at them. I waved my arms around and pointed at Poet. "Stop that girl!" They looked at me quizzically. They probably couldn't even hear me. I was just a flailing girl in a slip dress screaming into the void. They turned away and went back to their patrolling and scanning business.

Poet had nearly reached the cordoned off area around the Organ. I frowned. Where was she going? Surely Rose's people would stop her if she got too close.

BRRRRRRRRRRR

Out of nowhere, there was a roaring sound in my ears, the same as I'd heard yesterday in the Otherworld—the sound of a plane descending overhead. I looked up at the sky. No planes. So . . .

BRRRRRRRRRRRRRRR

The sound was so loud, I had to clap my hands over my ears. I tried to keep running even as the roaring got louder and louder, even as it threatened to overwhelm all of my senses. Poet was still running ahead of me in the distance. I looked around wildly for Rose's people, but they had moved out of sight.

"Please!" I screamed at Poet. "I just want to talk. I just want . . ."

But it was no use. The roaring was so loud, I couldn't even hear myself scream.

I clamped my hands more firmly over my ears and kept Poet in sight. I was determined to catch up with her, to get *answers*, to ask what connection she had to Mom—

BRRRRRRRRRRRRRRRRRRRRR

The roaring was unbearably loud now; it felt like it was slamming directly into my eardrums. My vision started to blur, Poet turning into a fuzzy dot in the distance. The landscape around her started to blur too.

Wait a minute. How was this . . . this noise making my vision blur? And where was the noise coming from?

I stopped for a moment, hands clamped firmly over my ears, and watched Poet get even farther ahead of me. And standing still, studying the beautiful seascape in front of me, I realized it *was* blurring. There was a very distinct spot where everything was fuzzy, wavy, almost like it was in motion. And it looked like there was a veil over it. A fog.

BRRRRRRRRRRRRRRRRRRRRRRRRR

The roaring was making it impossible to think. I started to run again, but Poet was really too far ahead of me now and nothing made any sense.

All of a sudden, Poet jumped into the air, aiming herself directly at the blurry, veiled spot. And she disappeared.

My jaw dropped and I stopped in my tracks again.

Then, before I had time to allow any rational thoughts into my brain, I sprinted forward, hands still clamped over my ears, the roaring still overwhelming everything, and jumped into the air, just as she had—

WHOOM

I half expected that wind whooshing in my ears sound this time. I was pretty much ready to fall through that starless night. I had a hunch I would land on the soft, velvety surface that I could feel but not see. But I had no idea what would come next. I stood up carefully, ready this time for the heavy press of the weighted atmosphere. I could already see a blurry, person-shaped form standing just a few feet from me. Maybe my eyes were getting used to adjusting to the Otherworld?

Hello? I thought, reaching out with my mind. *Is anyone there? Poet? Pretzel Guy? Someone with a real name, even?*

"Did you bring my wallet?" the blobby figure said out loud. It was starting to take more of a shape now, just as Pretzel Guy had. Maybe I'd be able to actually stick around long enough to see who it was for more than two seconds before being dumped back to Earth or the between dimension.

"What?" I responded out loud. "Your wallet? Can we maybe start with something more basic, like: who are you?"

"I need my wallet," the figure said, its voice developing a stubborn cast. "I lost it the other day. Besides having all my stuff in it, it has a ton of sentimental value. I've had it since college."

"That is truly tragic, but there are more pressing issues to get to here—" I cut myself off, frowning. Why did that sound so familiar? Where had I just heard someone complaining about . . .

It came to me in a flash. Tori, the tourist we'd interviewed two days ago. The one who'd said her friend had disappeared while looking for a missing wallet. With sentimental value.

"Carmen?" I said out loud. "Are you Carmen?"

"Yes," she said, sounding supremely irritated. "Look, do you have my wallet?"

"Forget about the wallet for now," I said, my impatience rising. I took a few labored steps toward her, the atmosphere pressing down on me with every move. "I mean, uh . . . trust me, we're looking for it. Can you tell me how you got here? And do you know where 'here' is?"

"It was that girl," Carmen said. She was starting to come

into focus, to look more person-like. She seemed to be wearing a uniform of tourist clothes, a Golden Gate Bridge t-shirt and baggy jeans. At least she hadn't gotten stuck here wearing a giant pretzel costume. "That girl brought me here," Carmen continued. "Or at least, I think she did."

"Let me guess," I said. "Messy hair, glasses, kind of a sulky look? Toting a giant sketchpad?"

"Yes," Carmen said, nodding vigorously. "She was sketching by the ocean and asked me what I was doing. I told her I was looking for my wallet, and she offered to help. And then . . ." Carmen scrunched her face up, like she was trying to recall the exact details.

I wanted to reach out and give her shoulder an encouraging pat, but I knew the act of making any sort of movement at all would take forever, thanks to that Otherworld atmosphere pressing down on me again. And I didn't know how much time I had before I was dumped back into our world.

"What happened next?" I said, trying to sound encouraging.

"I'm not sure," Carmen said. "I remember she turned to me at one point and took my hand, and she had the oddest expression in her eyes. And then she said something like, 'you want to come with me.' And in that moment, I did. I absolutely did. I could think of nothing I wanted more, even though just before that, all I'd wanted was to find my wallet."

Holy frakballs. Poet had mind-mojo-ed her. Somehow, she and Kathy Kooper had what sounded an awful lot like a version of my power. And they were using it to spirit people over to the Otherworld and weaponize locations. Were they trying to take over the whole city?

"Where did the girl go after she left you here?" I said. "And when did you realize you actually didn't want to go with her?"

Carmen's brow furrowed. "I remember walking with her, holding her hand. I remember hearing this sound all of a sudden, like . . . like . . ."

"A plane overhead?" I said.

"Yes," she said, nodding. "Just loud and roaring in my ears. And I remember everything getting blurry around me and then all of a sudden, I was here."

"What does 'here' look like to you?" I said, realizing that she might not be seeing what I was. After all, even the way I saw this bit of the Otherworld seemed to change every time I was transported here. And . . . hmm. Both my voice and Carmen's didn't have that odd distorted quality that had plagued my conversation with Pretzel Guy. We sounded like we were conversing normally. Interesting.

"Darkness," Carmen said. "And it's hard to move. Though I try to take a short walk every now and again. Even though I can't actually see much. I tried to find a way out when I first got here, but no matter how far you walk, it's all the same."

"Endless darkness," I murmured, a shiver running through me. How awful, to be trapped in this freaky nightscape for days on end—and to not even have a way to mark when a day ended. Had Mom been trapped here for the past ten years? The thought was almost too horrible to comprehend.

"When I get tired, I just lie down and sleep," Carmen continued. "I keep hoping that girl will come back and take me to meet up with my friend, Tori. And that she'll have my wallet."

"Have you ever encountered anyone else?" I said. "Any other people?"

"I did have a lovely chat with a man dressed in some sort of weird food costume," Carmen said. "He didn't have my wallet, either. Oh, and there was . . . Oh, heavens. There's that sound again."

BRRRRRR

She was right. The roaring was back, a low hum in my ear. That meant our time was probably about to get cut short.

"What were you just about to say?" I said, trying to make my voice louder. "Right before you noticed the sound?"

BRRRRRRRRRRR

Argh. It was already getting louder.

"I ran into another person one day," Carmen said. "A woman."

My heart skipped a beat.

"Was she tall?" I said, talking as fast as I possibly could. "With long, dark hair and a kind of musical voice—"

"No," Carmen said, raising her voice to be heard over the roaring, which was getting louder and louder by the minute. "She was short, she had little glasses, and she spoke in a monotone. She kept talking about how much she misses her dog and . . ."

BRRRRRRRRRRRRRRRRRR

Now the sound was amping itself all the way up, and I could barely hear her. I kept my arms at my sides, resisting the urge to cover my ears.

"Talking about what?" I shouted, desperation rising in my chest. "What besides her dog?"

". . . os . . . al . . ."

"What?!?" I screamed as the roaring reached a fever pitch.

"HOSPITAL!" she screamed and then the by-now familiar whooshing sound was in my head again and I was lying on my back on the grass by the waterfront, hands clamped over my ears. Rose and one of her team members knelt next to me and peered at me with great concern.

"Bea," Rose said, laying a hand on my arm. "What's going on? I just got here. My deputy said she saw you disappear into thin air and then all of a sudden you were lying on the ground."

I sat up and, for what felt like the millionth time in just a few days, took stock of my body. Everything seemed to be in order, except that my head really, really hurt.

"Rose," I said, trying to piece together the weird, fragmented conversation I'd just had. "I think I just got a clue. And I have no idea what it means, but I'm sure as hell going to follow it."

CHAPTER EIGHTEEN

"BEA!" EVIE THREW her arms around me, then pulled back and put her hands on my shoulders, her eyes lit with concern. "Rose told us what happened! Why didn't you come back to HQ? You need to be examined—"

"And why did you want us to meet you here?" Aveda said, gesturing to the intimidating exterior of San Francisco General. She crossed her arms over her chest and gave me her best steely look. "Beatrice, being on a team—especially as a very junior member—means communicating clearly with your teammates about everything. Your text was very vague. Rose was the one who filled us in on how you *disappeared into the freaking Otherworld*! Didn't we just have a very involved discussion about you not doing that anymore?"

"I . . . uh, didn't have any control over it," I lied. "I got sucked in, it was very sudden. And I feel fine now."

"But—" Evie began.

"I'm sorry my text was vague," I said. "Issue me some superhero demerits or something later. But I think I may have just gotten a serious lead on something and time is of the essence."

The truth was, I'd been so excited about this potential lead, I hadn't been able to contain myself. The possibility that I was closer to finding Mom outweighed everything else. If it had been up to me, I would have booked it to the hospital and pursued this mission myself without stopping to tell Evie and Aveda, but Rose had insisted. And also filled them in on some extra context, since all I'd said was to meet me at

San Francisco General ASAP. And then I'd added a few choice emojis to convey the urgency.

I didn't have Sam on hand as my usual chauffeur (and I really didn't feel like calling him after our dust-up that morning), so it had taken me longer than anticipated to get all the way from the waterfront to the hospital. I'd had to take three buses, and Evie and Aveda ended up arriving before me.

"We don't have a demerits system in place," Aveda said, getting a strange gleam in her eyes. Uh-oh. Evie always referred to that look as Aveda's Idea Face. "But we could start one."

"Also something for later," I said. "For now, just listen."

I gave them the bullet points: how I'd chased Poet, how I believed she'd led Carmen into the Otherworld, how Carmen had told me about this familiar-sounding other woman she'd encountered on one of her aimless walks.

"I believe that woman was Edna—the officious desk jockey who works here," I said, gesturing to the building. "Especially since she kept talking to Carmen about the hospital. I don't know how she got trapped in the Otherworld too, but I'm working on a theory."

I put my hands on my hips and gazed up at the building. It was so tall, so solid, and it seemed to develop an ominous presence the longer I stared at it. Almost like it was staring back, daring me to try something. I faced Evie and Aveda. "I think this is where Mom was taken," I said. "I think Kathy Kooper did it, while she was visiting Mom one day. I don't know why she took Mom's records, and I don't know if she was trying to weaponize this location or what. But I need to go in there and see if I can hear that weird voice again—see if it's Edna or Mom or someone connected to her. And if I do that, maybe I can . . ." I cut myself off abruptly. I'd been so into my theory, I'd forgotten that at least part of my proposed mission was bound to be met with protests.

"Bea," Evie said, shaking her head. "You are *not* doing anything that might lead to you being transported to the

Otherworld again! And anyway, I thought you just said you didn't jump in on purpose."

"But now you want to *try* to jump in on purpose using the knowledge you've gathered from your previous encounters," Aveda said.

Was it my imagination or did she actually sound . . . admiring?

"Do you *approve* of this?" Evie said to her. "Annie, don't encourage her. Didn't you hear what Nate and Scott said last night? It's too dangerous."

"I know," Aveda said. "But it's also bold. Risky. Demonstrates a tunnel-visioned determination to get to the heart of our current supernatural dilemma." Her mouth quirked into a half-smile. "It sounds like something I'd do."

"Oh, no," Evie said, scrubbing a hand over her face. "I think you and I need to have some long discussions about what constitutes good, responsible mentoring."

"If 'responsible' means 'never taking any risks ever,' we're going to end up with the most basic, boring mentees ever," Aveda said, rolling her eyes.

"You don't have to be a daredevil to be a superheroine," Evie argued.

"No." Aveda sniffed. "But it doesn't hurt."

"Hey," I said, snapping my fingers at them. "Mentee, standing right here. Listening to everything you say. And you two sound like bickering parents."

"As if we needed to be more co-dependent," Evie sighed.

"Aw!" Aveda said, slinging her arm around Evie's shoulders. "Come on, we can raise this adorable Superbaby, you and I. I'm Fun Dad and you're Stick-in-the-Mud Mom."

I expected Evie to laugh, but she stiffened and a weird shadow passed over her face. Aveda seemed to pick up on it too.

"Sorry," she murmured, dropping her arm from Evie's shoulders.

Evie's gaze went contemplative as she studied the building. "I guess we're here. We might as well go inside, see if we can find anything out. But Bea." She touched my arm. "No jumping into the Otherworld, please."

"Okay, okay," I muttered. But deep down, I knew something with absolute certainty: if the opportunity presented itself, I was taking it. We were so close to finding Mom now—I could feel it. And I was more than ready to take a risk or two to find her. They could give me all the demerits they wanted later.

We passed through the sliding doors and entered the aggressively beige hallway. Something was immediately off. It was as beige and blah as ever, but the atmosphere was different than it had been my previous visit. I scanned the blah-ness, trying to figure out what it was, but I couldn't quite put my finger on it. Maybe it was just my amped up state of mind—maybe *I* was what was different. Then we rounded the corner, and my jaw dropped. Edna wasn't behind the reception desk—I'd expected that. I'm not sure who, if anyone, I'd expected to see in her place. Maybe Kathy, looking all evil and shit, surrounded by cat-hair crafts? Or Poet, sketching away?

Instead, a familiar figure rose to greet me.

"Bernard?" I said, my brow furrowing. I quickened my stride to the reception desk and felt Evie and Aveda pick up the pace behind me.

"Hello," he said. "Ms. . . . Tanaka, is it?"

On the surface, he looked the same as when I'd first encountered him in the basement archives: squat frame, combover in place, tie with a soup stain on it. But his entire demeanor was completely different. Instead of looking at me with an utterly downtrodden expression, he greeted me with a big, dopey smile that was super confident—smug, even.

"Hi Bernard," I said, as we reached the desk. "Did you get a promotion?"

"Indeed I did," he said, beaming at me. "Edna was fired for improperly filed paperwork, and yours truly has been such a dedicated soldier for the past twenty years. There really was no other choice. The front desk is now my domain." He let out a raspy chuckle.

"Congratulations," I said, my eyes scanning the desk. Edna's puppy picture had been removed. Bernard had wasted no time making himself at home—his vast pen collection was now spread out all over the desk and it looked like it had multiplied since I'd last seen it. Pens of every conceivable size and color were stuffed into an army of mugs, which were in turn packed into every available microcosm of space. It looked like a rainbow honeycomb. A super disorganized, hoarders' paradise of a rainbow honeycomb.

"How can I help you today?" Bernard asked, dopey smile still on full display.

"Oh, uh . . ."

I need to talk to some dead and/or trapped people who seem to be communicating with me through a kind of fucked up interdimensional telepathy. Can you help me out with that?

"We are conducting an important supernatural investigation, Mr. Bernard," Aveda said.

"It's just Bernard," he murmured.

"And this hospital is a location of interest," she continued. "We need to do a thorough search of the premises and yes, I can get a warrant in cooperation with the San Francisco police department, but as the result will be the same, it would be much more expedient for you to allow us to search now."

Hello? I said in my head, trying to reach out with my mind. *Is anyone there? Mom? Edna?* I felt ridiculous. But how else was I supposed to reach out to people who had very limited ways of communicating? Maybe I should try writing on the hospital bathroom wall.

"Oh, dear, I'm afraid that just won't be possible," Bernard said, reaching down to rearrange some of his pens. "You see, we're going through renovations. Currently on a skeleton crew. The majority of our patients had to be moved elsewhere for now. Most areas are restricted at the moment, even to me."

I frowned, looking around, taking in the beigeness and the blah-ness once again. *That* was what was off. There was no rush of nurses bustling around, no patients complaining, no usual chaos of the hospital. It was deadly silent. And except for us and Bernard, it seemed to be empty. Like it had been abandoned or something. I shivered.

"That should make things even easier to search, then," Aveda said, giving Bernard a smile that contained way too many teeth. "No people getting in the way."

"I'm sorry," said Bernard, shaking his head. "You will simply have to return when renovations are complete." He plucked a green pen with a gold-rimmed cap from one of his mugs and twirled it through his fingers.

"And when will that be?" Evie said, laying a hand on Aveda's arm.

"A year and a half," Bernard said cheerfully.

"I don't think so," Aveda said.

You may proceed with your search. No questions asked, I thought at Bernard. He looked confused for a moment, then shook his head, like he was trying to get rid of a fly that had landed on his nose.

You may proceed with your search. No questions asked. I projected the thought harder and mixed in a feeling of overwhelming friendliness, openness. *You may proceed with—*

"No."

I started. That had come from Bernard, who was now staring at me, all traces of his dopey grin wiped away.

"Um, what?" Evie said, cocking her head at him.

"That is very rude, young lady," he said to me. "And I will thank you to knock it off."

And then I felt that push against my mind, that mental brick wall.

"Oh, frak, no," I hissed, slamming my palms down on the desk. I hadn't been at all prepared when Kathy and Poet had tried to counter my mental whammy, but I wasn't about to let nebbishy, milquetoast-y, pen-obsessed *Bernard* get the better of me.

And what the hell was going on with Bernard, anyway? Was he working with Kathy?

I pushed back with all my might, envisioning my mind as a massive wrecking ball crashing through the brick wall Bernard was trying to put up. He responded with force, slamming his brick wall into place, gripping his pen so tightly, his knuckles turned white.

"You . . . are going to do . . . whatever I say . . ." I hissed at him.

My palms were pressed into the desk so hard, I was sure they were going to leave a mark. Sweat beaded my brow, and I concentrated so hard, I could practically feel a vein popping on my forehead.

"Bea," Evie said uncertainly. "What's happening?"

"Is he trying to mind-control you?" Aveda barked. "Do you need us to subdue him?"

"Nothing . . . you can do . . ." I managed, still sending my mental wrecking ball at Bernard with as much strength as I could muster.

As with Kathy, it felt like our minds were locked in battle, pushing against each other. My vision tunneled and went hazy around the edges, and my head felt like I was slamming it into an actual brick wall over and over and over . . .

CRASSSSSSHHHHHHH

Behind me, I heard a window shatter. And another one. And another—

"Bea." Evie grabbed my arm, her voice spiked with fear. "Please . . ."

I heard a loud *SNAP* and jumped, my concentration disrupted. My eyes went to the source: Bernard's hand, which was clutching his now broken pen, blue ink staining his fingers.

"Look what you made me do, Ms. Tanaka," Bernard hissed. "I've had this trusty refillable rollerball since 1972. Nobody makes this exact model anymore. That was . . . " He carefully set the pen down on his desk, then met my eyes again. ". . . very, very rude."

I'd never have guessed this meek little man was capable of such rage. But the way he was looking at me dripped with such full-body anger, such hate, it seemed to pulse through the air, pressing against my mind yet again. I threw up my own mental brick wall, trying to protect myself. Out of the corner of my eye, I noticed one of his bushels of pens floating free from the mug it had been sitting in, levitating through the air. I did a double take.

"Aveda," I said, "are you—"

"We'll just have to take care of that rudeness, now, won't we?" Bernard snarled.

"Evie, Bea: get behind me!" Aveda bellowed.

But before I could even begin to comprehend what was happening, Bernard's mighty pen collection floated up from the desk—a mass of metal and plastic clacking together and forming into an angry cloud of office supplies. It looked like a nerdy swarm of bees.

"What the hell!" Evie yelped. "Annie, can you grab on to them . . ."

"On it!" Aveda barked.

The pen swarm tightened in formation. I could see it resisting Aveda's efforts, trying to get free. Then, one by one, the pens started to expand in the air.

"Oh, shit," Evie cried out. "It's like the Wave Organ! They're getting bigger . . ."

"I don't think I can hold them all," Aveda growled.

Evie held up her hands and sent her fireballs spinning outward. Aveda grabbed on to them with her telekinesis, and they formed a dancing flame trail in the air, attempting to surround the pen swarm. But there were too many pens, they were too unwieldy, and they were growing by the second.

"Now, ladies," Bernard said, hiding behind his pen swarm. "Really, there's no need for this drama. If you all would just conduct yourselves with a bit more *decorum* . . ."

The pen swarm danced around Evie's fire, and clacked its way toward us. I never would have imagined *a bunch of frakking pens* to be so menacing, but . . .

WHOOSH

One of the pens had grown to be as tall as the ceiling. It broke from the pack and swung toward us.

"Shit!" Aveda threw up her hands to fend it off. The force of her telekinesis managed to move it just far enough, and it swung through the empty air.

I gathered up every emotion I felt—fear, anger, frustration—channeled them through my bloodstream, threw my head back, and screamed. The pen that had just swung at us shattered at our feet.

"Nicely done, Bea," Aveda said.

"Thanks. One down, a billion to go."

CLACKCLACKCLACK

The rest of the pen swarm advanced on us, and some of them were still growing. We were seriously about to be smashed into the ground by writing implements.

"All right, keep it up," Aveda said, her voice like steel. "Maybe together, we can—"

"We can *what*?" Evie interrupted. "Annie, these things are going to kill us before we can contain them all—we've gotta get out of here."

"Retreat?" Aveda spat out. "Never. Besides, there could still be civilians in here—"

WHOOOOOOOOSH

One of the pens that had grown particularly giant swung at us again, nearly clipping Evie's shoulder. She yelped and jumped out of the way.

"Evie!" Aveda screamed. "Get *back*!"

"There's no one else here," Bernard called out. His dopey grin had turned into something oily and dark. "Just us chickens. And you should thank your lucky stars I'm here for you. I'm going to teach you how to be proper young ladies with proper respect for—"

"Oh, *fuck* that," Aveda snapped.

And then she stepped to the right and whirled into her repertoire of powerful fight moves, laying into the pen swarm with a dazzling array of spinning backhands and roundhouse kicks. Most of the pens stayed upright, and she had to dodge away from their massive, swinging forms, but a few snapped and went down.

"Evie," she barked, slamming her fist into yet another pen monster. "Most of these things are made of plastic—try melting them!"

Evie sent her fireballs spinning through the air, targeting a purple pen that'd grown almost as tall as the ceiling. It tried to advance on her, but started melting on the spot.

"That's it!" yelled Aveda. "Pummel, pummel, pummel!"

Evie kept the fireballs going, and the purple pen oozed into a sad pile of melted plastic. Brow furrowed in concentration, she turned to another pen and sent even more fireballs its way.

I focused on another giant pen, a pen that swung at Aveda as she dodged out of the way to punch one of its inky friends. I sent my scream in its direction, putting all I could into it. It shattered into a zillion pieces. So I turned to another pen and screamed again. And again.

One by one, the pen army was going *down*. I felt a surge of triumph as I watched Aveda snap another one in half. My throat was raw from all the screaming, but I kept it up, fueled by adrenaline and the sense that we were finally turning the fucking tide in this extremely weird battle.

"Well," Bernard said, making a tsk-ing sound, "I do not like this at *all*. You are most certainly the rudest young ladies to ever come in here. I think I'll be taking my leave now."

BRRRRRRRRRR

Oh, shit, I knew that sound all too well by now. That overwhelming buzzing in my ears . . . I winced and snuck a glance at Evie and Aveda, but they didn't seem to be affected. How were they not hearing this?!

I tried to ignore the buzzing, tried to just keep screaming, but it was *so loud,* and that could only mean . . .

I looked around frantically for Bernard. He was running down the hall, away from his desk. In the distance, I saw the world going all wavy and distorted, that veil descending over one particular spot. I glanced at Evie and Aveda again. The pen army was nearly decimated, and it looked like they could handle the few that were left.

I took off after Bernard.

"Bea!" Evie shrieked. "What are you doing?!"

I ignored her and chased after him: down the corridor, past the windows we'd shattered with our brain battle. The roaring in my ears was almost unbearable now, but I pushed past it and kept him in sight. As he reached the end of the corridor, everything around us turned wavy and distorted, and just as he was about to run right into a wall, he leaped into the air and disappeared.

I clenched my jaw in determination, poured the speed on, and reached the end of the hall.

I'm coming, Mom, I thought as I leaped into the air.

I was preparing myself to once again enter darkness, to be smacked to the ground, to get used to the heavy atmosphere, when all of a sudden, I felt my body being yanked backward and pulled through the air.

"What!?" I shrieked.

And then I landed on my ass on the cold linoleum hospital floor, and Evie and Aveda were looming over me, looking none too pleased.

"Ow!" I said, giving Aveda an accusing look. "Why did you do that?! Why did you . . . telekinesis me?! I was *so close,* I was going to find her, I—"

"Beatrice." Aveda shut me up with her frostiest, most imperious Aveda Jupiter look. "What did we just say about teamwork?"

CHAPTER NINETEEN

I WAS BURROWING into another good sulk. I could practically feel the dark tendrils of anger swirling around me, wrapping me up in a nice little package of seething resentment.

"You shouldn't have stopped me," I growled for the thousandth time, glaring at Aveda. "That was my chance to find Mom. And now it's gone."

We were back at HQ, huddled around the kitchen table. Nate and Scott had brought cheeseburgers and fries for everyone, but no one was really eating. Even Evie, who placed French fries above everything except spam musubi in her messed up version of the food pyramid, couldn't seem to get past picking at the food in front of her.

"We told you it was too dangerous to jump into the Otherworld," Aveda said, also for the thousandth time. She glowered at me.

"No, *you* said it was bold," I countered. "Risky. Like something you would do!"

"I was commending your creative thinking, but I wouldn't have actually done it," she retorted. "Not after we discussed it as a team and agreed amongst ourselves that—"

"So why, when *I* try to do it—" I pressed on stubbornly, ignoring her.

"Because I asked you not to," Evie cut in. She looked up from the French fry she was playing with. Her voice was low and measured, her face pale and drawn. But I knew from the flash in her eyes that she was furious. "I specifically asked you not to do that *one* thing. And then the minute you had the chance, you went and did it." She shook her head and went back to playing with her sad, limp fry.

"Darlings," Lucy said gently. "Perhaps we should save the arguments and accusations for after dinner. A lot happened today, and it sounds like we need to debrief. Perhaps a 'just the facts' approach on the science of the situation might help us decompress a bit?"

"I agree with Lucy," Nate said quickly.

"Thirded," Scott chimed in.

"I didn't realize we were voting on this," Aveda said.

Evie shrugged and wrapped her sad fry corpse in a napkin. "Fine."

"Baby," Nate murmured, putting his arm around her. "Please eat something."

"Don't manage me," she grumbled.

"Rose and her team cordoned off and scanned the Market," Lucy pressed on, determined. "Nothing untoward happened there today, but they did pick up active supernatural energy on their scans. So we thought it best to keep the whole thing shut down and monitor the area, as with the Organ. If Kathy shows her face—"

"We won't find her," I muttered, crossing my arms over my chest. "She's escaped into the Otherworld. That's why we haven't been able to find Poet, either. It's a super convenient hiding place, especially when your superheroing superiors won't let you even *try* to—"

"In any case," Lucy interrupted. "If she returns for any of her illustrious cat-hair crafts, Rose will be waiting."

"I've been doing analysis of the Market scans all afternoon," Nate said. "Once again, the origin of the energy was not the Pussy Queen portal. So I—"

"You compared the scans from the Market with the ones we took at the Wave Organ," I said. "And while their origins don't match the Pussy Queen portal, they do match . . . each other."

Nate gave me a half-smile. "Yes."

"And if you took scans of the hospital," I said, "those would match, too."

Nate nodded. "That is a very good hypothesis. It would appear that all three locations are similar types of entry points to the Otherworld—"

"Places where there's active supernatural energy present," I said, "and where the walls between our worlds are especially thin. But they all seem to need one additional element to realize their full potential—a human prisoner. Delivered by the three people who seem to be able to leap into the Otherworld: Kathy, Poet, and now Bernard at the hospital. Pretzel Guy said Kathy banished him there, Carmen described being led by Poet, and I'm pretty sure Bernard somehow trapped Edna."

"Though to be clear, you never actually saw Kathy make the leap, right, Bug?" Scott said. "She just ran off?"

"Yeah, that part is an assumption," I said, my brow furrowing. "But I'd say it's a reasonable one since no one's seen her since, and your spells aren't picking her up."

"And our leapers all seem to have some version of your emotional projection power, Bea," Aveda said. Her voice was still frosty, but it seemed she'd decided to take Lucy's cue and discuss topics that didn't involve yelling at me. "With all of them, you felt like they were pushing back, right? Like you were doing some kind of mental battle."

"Yeah," I said, frowning.

"None of the superpowers we know of have duplicates, right?" Scott said. "The powers that made their way into human bodies?"

"That's correct," Nate said. "At least from what's been documented over the years, and what I remember from my time with Shasta. Humanoid demons have multiple powers, but when Shasta's raiding party was killed coming through that first portal and their powers migrated to humans—"

"The humans who received these powers only got one power each—one per customer," I said, remembering. "And every power we know of is unique."

"So are the leapers demons in disguise?" Lucy asked.

"Or some new kind of demon-human hybrid?" Aveda said.

I shook my head. "We don't have enough data—"

"—to make that determination," Nate finished, nodding at me.

"But there is something . . ." I hesitated. There was a thought pricking around the outer edges of my consciousness, and I was trying to figure out a way to voice it without giving away the fact that I'd very possibly been granted power level-ups upon visiting the Otherworld. "All three of these people seem to have very recently gotten something they wanted out of life. In the case of Kathy and Bernard, it had to do with the person they likely imprisoned: Pretzel Guy's stand went down and thanks to the disappearance of Edna, Bernard got promoted out of his basement purgatory. And as for Poet, she suddenly got really popular."

"So . . . what? The Otherworld granted them a wish, like some kind of messed up fairy godmother?" Lucy said.

"No," I said slowly. "I'm saying: maybe it was visiting the Otherworld that *gave* them a version of my power. Then they might be able to mind-mojo enough people to *make* their wish come true."

"But how did they get to the Otherworld in the first place?" Scott said.

"Perhaps it has to do with the walls being especially thin in certain spots," Lucy said. "Perhaps they tripped and fell right in. In any case, it sounds like we'll need to cordon off and patrol the hospital too. Ugh, poor Rose. Her team is getting stretched thinner and thinner by the day."

"Did you guys find anything interesting in the stuff we brought back from Kathy's booth at the Market?" Aveda asked, turning to Nate and Scott.

Oh, right. So much had happened since this morning, I'd nearly forgotten all about the contents of the little blue cabinet: the hospital paperwork and the parchment with the strange symbols.

"No," Scott said, frowning. "All we can take from that is . . . I guess Kathy stole some of your mom's hospital file, for some reason? There was nothing off or incriminating about the records she stole. It's just the final paperwork."

"Maybe Bernard gave it to her," Aveda said. "Since he appears to be all evil. Though that doesn't really answer the question of why."

"I tried using my enhanced observational powers on the parchment with the runes, but it's not telling me anything," Nate said. "It does look like bits of the Otherworld language we've encountered before, but we've only encountered it occasionally, and no one has ever been able to decipher it. I've sent it to a few of my demonology colleagues to see if they can make heads or tails of it."

"Ugh," Aveda said. "This is so frustrating. How do we defeat Kathy and Co.? And free these poor trapped people?"

"And find Mom," I murmured.

"Every time we get close to one of our probable bad guys, they jump into the freakin' Otherworld," Aveda continued, thumping a fist on the table.

Silence descended. The smell of grease from our uneaten burgers permeated the air. It felt like there was some kind of cloud over the whole table.

"It appears no one is in imminent danger, correct?" Nate said. "All three of these locations are being heavily monitored. Perhaps the best course of action is to sleep on it?"

I shook my head and started to get up from the table. "I need to go back to the hospital. I'll go with Rose's team. I was *so close* to Mom, I could feel it, and if I could just—"

"*No.*"

Evie, who had been silent throughout our whole discussion, playing with her fry corpse, stood up and faced me. She was still pale, and her eyes sparked with fury.

"You're not going anywhere," she said.

"I am not a child anymore, Evelyn," I bristled. "I believe we've covered that in great detail. Therefore you can't *ground* me."

"Bea . . ." She looked overwhelmed with frustration. "When we promoted you to superhero, you promised to listen to me and Aveda. To not just charge in whenever it might suit you. To follow our lead."

"Well, sometimes I don't agree with your lead," I shot back. "Why does it matter if whatever I'm doing accomplishes our end goal: to figure out what's going on with this freaky Otherworld shit, and to free whoever's trapped there and keep the bad guys from trapping more people?"

"Because you could hurt yourself," Evie spat out. "Or worse."

"Okay, so I messed up today," I said. "I freely acknowledge that. I should've talked to you and Aveda more about leaping into the Otherworld—"

"It's not just today," she interrupted. "You followed that weird voice at the Market and almost got trampled by a rogue carnival ride. You chased Poet down to the Wave Organ and leapt into the Otherworld there, too. You just can't seem to help yourself, you always have to choose whatever the most dangerous option is—"

"No, I'm choosing the option that will get us *answers*," I retorted. "And ya know, the reason I was by myself at the Market is you and Aveda were way too busy doing more important things—so you left all the grunt work to me. You guys treat me like a total afterthought—"

"No," Evie said. "We treat you like a trainee. Which is what you are. And all of this stuff is just showing me why we were wrong to even do that—"

"Don't you want to find Mom?!" I blurted out.

She shook her head. "What?"

"Mom," I said, my voice urgent. "This isn't just another superhero mission. We have the chance here not just to save a bunch of Bay Areans from getting trapped in some super boring demon dimension—we could actually *get our mother back*."

"That's not the point," she said, shaking her head again. "That's not even what we're talking about—"

"Yes, it is!" I exclaimed. My throat clogged, and I felt the tears pricking my eyeballs. "It *is*. I would do anything to get her back, Evie—anything. And now it's possible she's alive and we can get her out and you won't even give me the chance to do that because you're so set on . . . on . . ."

"Bea." Evie pressed her lips into a thin line. Her face now had an almost grayish cast to it, making the dark circles under her eyes stand out even more. She looked more exhausted than I'd ever seen her. "I'm tired. We'll talk about this in the morning."

"No." Frustration was rising in my chest, demanding to be heard. "We'll talk about it *now*. Stop trying to dismiss me. Stop trying to . . . to dictate everything. I know you're used to everything being on your terms—"

"Excuse me, what?"

"Even when Mom died," I pressed on. "When she was *dying*. You wouldn't let me be around her. You kept taking me out of the room. You made sure I wasn't there when she died—and maybe that's when it happened, that's when Kathy sent her to the Otherworld. I could have saved her. If you'd just let me *be* there—"

"I was protecting you," Evie said.

"You were *depriving* me," I shot back. "Of those moments I could have had with her. It's so fucking unfair. And I don't even know why. *I* was the one who was wrecked when she died. You were so . . . calm. So *cold*. You didn't even cry at the funeral—"

"I didn't cry at the funeral because I was used to suppressing every single emotion I had at that point," Evie said, her hands balling into fists at her sides. "So I didn't set everything on fucking fire. That doesn't mean I didn't feel anything. And after that . . . I couldn't be sad, Bea. I didn't have the time to be sad. I didn't have the *luxury* of being sad. Because everything I had, every drop of energy and strength, went into taking care of you." She stepped forward so we were nearly toe-to-toe. Her voice shook, and I could see the sheen of tears in her eyes. "You want to talk about unfair?"

she spat out, her voice low and furious. "You *got* to be sad. I didn't."

Tears were freely streaming down my cheeks now, but I was too angry to even begin to respond to her. I crossed my arms over my chest and glared.

"I took care of you," she said, her voice still shaky. "I somehow managed to keep both of us alive. And now, all you can do is shit all over that by willfully putting yourself in danger over and over again."

In an instant, all of the fight seemed to go out of her. Her shoulders slumped, and she took a step backward. Her eyes went to the floor and her face seemed to go even grayer.

"I . . . I don't feel well," she said quietly. "I'm going to bed."

Nate wordlessly appeared at her side, wrapped her in his arms and led her away. As she shuffled out of the kitchen, I thought she'd glance back at me. A last look of disappointment or sisterly rage or sadness.

But she didn't look at me at all.

CHAPTER TWENTY

I THOUGHT ABOUT going back to the hospital. I couldn't deny that I still wanted to, down to my very core. But something stopped me from making the actual move. So I went back to my room, flopped on my bed, and stared at the twinkle lights. Tonight, their spell somehow didn't seem as potent.

The look on Evie's face—that mix of anger and hurt and disappointment—kept flashing through my brain. Much as I chafed at so many of her attempts to parent me, I just couldn't bring myself to let her down even more than I already had. At least not tonight.

You got *to be sad. I didn't.*

I'd thought that as I'd gotten older I'd developed a better understanding of the sacrifices she'd made to raise me. But apparently there was a lot I still hadn't grasped. A memory bubbled up: me at thirteen, her at twenty-three. About a year after Dad left. She'd sold our childhood home and much of its contents, moved us into a tiny apartment, and was attempting to work her way through grad school. I was deep into my teenage loner phase and had worked my way from feeling searing pain 24/7 to that dull, dead inside feeling. A comfortable numbness.

My numb state had felt at least sort of like an improvement. There was one night I got it in my head that I absolutely needed to make a peanut butter, jelly, banana, and chocolate chip sandwich. Both Evie and Dad thought this concoction was super gross, but it was another special thing Mom and I did together. When I was still in my "everything hurts all the time" phase, I wasn't able to even think about that sandwich. Even imagining the flavor made me a little queasy. But that night, it had finally sounded delicious again, and I wanted to seize the moment. So I toddled into our miniscule apartment kitchen, opened the fridge, pulled out the peanut butter and stared at the jar for a full minute, an avalanche of emotions crashing through me.

"Evie?" I called out, my voice quavering.

"Yeah, Bea?" she said, appearing at the kitchen door.

I waved the jar around. "This is creamy peanut butter. Where's the chunky?"

"Uh. The creamy's what we usually get?" she said, her brows drawing together.

"No," I said, shaking my head emphatically. "Mom and I *always* got the chunky. That's what we like—um, liked for our sandwich."

She gave me a weary, confused look. "Bea, you haven't made that sandwich in . . . I mean, it's been a long time. You don't really eat peanut butter—"

"Yes, I do," I said, my voice twisting. Even then, I'd realized how irrational I sounded. But I really needed her to get it. "I totally do. I love peanut butter."

"—so I just got the kind I like," she continued, as if explaining things to a small child. "We can get both kinds next time we go to the store."

I just kept shaking my head. "I need to make my sandwich *now*."

"Well, I can't go to the store now," Evie said, her patience wearing thin. "I have a paper to finish and I'm going to be up all night as it is."

"But . . . but . . ." My eyes filled with tears, and I could feel my face getting all red.

"Bea." Evie stepped forward and took the jar from me. "Really, what's the problem? It's just peanut butter."

That's when I'd burst into tears.

They weren't quiet, tasteful tears. No, we're talking full-body sobs, the kind of cry that reverberates through every part of you. I'd slumped to the floor, curling myself into a little ball, and sobbed. My state of comfortable numbness shattered on the spot, and I was back to drowning in hopeless pain.

It wasn't just peanut butter. It was the *wrong* peanut butter. It was peanut butter that took me farther away from Mom, from the sandwich that had been a special bond between us. And I'd needed to make that sandwich *now*. The idea that there was this small obstacle denying me from this one tenuous connection I still had with my mother broke me completely.

I heard Evie let out a long sigh. She hadn't said a word, just sat down on the floor next to me and stayed there until I stopped crying. At the time, she'd seemed dispassionate— like she was the weary parent, waiting out a child's tantrum. But now I could see more clearly: I was breaking down so fully, so messily, there was no room for her to do the same.

A soft knock on the door startled me out of my reverie. I couldn't imagine who in this household wanted to talk to me at the moment.

"Come in," I called out.

Nate entered the room, shutting the door behind him.

"Bea," he rumbled. "May I speak to you for a minute?"

"Of course."

He crossed the room and sat down in the rocking chair next to my bed. It was a little small for his hulking frame, and I bit back a giggle as he shifted around, trying to find a comfortable sitting position. He finally settled for perching himself on the edge. I noticed he was holding a sparkly purple folder like the one he'd left for me a few days earlier.

"Kai, my colleague in Maui, located another person who nearly drowned after walking into the ocean," he said.

"She saved a *third person*?" I said, incredulous.

"Someone else saved this person," he clarified. "But it was in the same general area of beach. She conducted an interview with this latest survivor and I was wondering if you could take a look at it, as you did with the previous interviews."

"Well, sure," I said, sitting up straight and reaching out for the folder. He handed it to me. "But do you really want my expertise on . . . anything? Considering the astonishing lack of judgment I've apparently shown since getting my super-heroing stripes."

"I do not think there's much danger you can get into reading through a report," Nate said. His mouth quirked into an amused half-smile. "Though if there's a way, I'm sure you will find it."

"Was that a *joke*, bro-in-law?" I said, raising an eyebrow.

"My attempt at one." His brow furrowed. "Was it not good?"

"It was pretty good, actually," I said, laughing a little. "Though it might be kind of soon for that punchline since Evie and I just had that fight an hour ago."

"I see," he said, smiling. He paused, studying me intently. "Bea," he continued, his voice thoughtful. "Can I ask you something about your and Evie's fight—ah, not the one to-night. The one from a few days ago, right before she agreed to you doing the superhero internship."

"Gotcha," I said. "That level of specificity is necessary considering that Evie and I have enough fights for a very long highlights reel. Yeah, you can ask me whatever you want."

"Evie mentioned the work you and I had done together—all the scientific research and related work," he said. "And how you eventually drifted away from it."

"Ah, yes, when she was listing the various things I've picked up and dropped, proving that I have the attention span of a gnat," I said.

"That is . . . not exactly how I would put it," Nate said. "But when you stopped having as much time for our work, I did wonder why. I didn't ask at the time because you drew a boundary and requested that all of us respect it. But you were so good at the work, and you seemed genuinely ab-sorbed by it. Did something about it stop interesting you?" He leaned forward, his face creasing with concern. "Did I make it boring?"

"What? No!" I exclaimed. "That wasn't it at all. I just . . ." I hesitated, my eyes rolling upward to study the twinkle lights. "I think I realized you didn't really need me. I mean, I was a great assistant to you, I could definitely enhance the work you were doing and type up reports and stuff. But that's all I'd ever be if I kept on that path. Like, a Nate add-on."

He frowned. "I never thought of you that way."

"No, I know," I said quickly. "But I thought of *myself* that way. And I was kind of tired of being everyone's little sister. I wanted to find something that was just mine. I wanted to become who I was supposed to be. I wanted to—"

To fill the hole inside myself I can never seem to fill. To find that missing piece.

I swallowed hard and skipped over that part. "Anyway," I continued. "I thought that was being a superhero. I mean, it helped Evie and Aveda with their various identity crises. But maybe I was wrong about that, too, since I seem to be fucking up at every turn."

"Beatrice." Nate leaned forward again, resting his elbows on his knees. "I am not a great expert on the human psyche. It took me years to express my feelings to Evie, and even then, we had some growing pains." He smiled at the memories. "But if I may make an observation: I believe that you are already who you are supposed to be. And that person is quite incredible."

Unexpected tears sprang to my eyes. "I mean, nah," I said softly, trying to brush it off.

"If you pursue what calls to you at a deep, visceral level, what inspires passion in you—well, you will make that incredible, too. And the rest, whatever you feel is missing, will come."

"That's a nice thought, Nate," I managed, blinking back tears. "But I don't know how I can be all incredible when I can't seem to go more than an hour without disappointing my own sister."

"When we love someone that much, our other feelings about them tend to be equally strong." He reached over and squeezed my hand. "That's how it is with you and Evie. And I know that, too, will work out."

"Thanks for all these votes of confidence," I murmured.

"To be clear," he said, "I would also rather you didn't jump into the Otherworld. We expressed to you that it is potentially dangerous—I could not live with myself if anything happened to you. But . . ." He paused, studying me. "I understand why you were so compelled to do it."

He gave my hand one more squeeze, then stood and crossed the room. He stopped when he reached the door, hesitating.

"Bea," he said. "I spent much of my life with no family. Except for—"

"—an evil, heartless demon mom who did weird experiments on you?"

"Yes. I don't know if I have ever expressed what a great honor it is to be part of *your* family. Thank you."

"It's your family now, too, Nate," I said. "I don't think we'd have it any other way."

He gave me a final, gentle smile and left.

I flipped open the folder he'd left me, but I couldn't concentrate and the words blurred together. I tossed it to tne side. I'd look at it later. Emotions whirlwinded through me, and I twitched around, restless. If I liked running, I'd have gone for a run to burn off some of this unwanted tension and tire myself out so I could at least get some sleep.

But I *really* just wanted to go back to the hospital. I wanted to find Mom. I wanted to fix *something*. I turned the day over in my mind, rewinding to the beginning, to my mission with Aveda and Shruti, the disastrous brunch with Sam and his annoying siblings . . . Hmm. Wait a minute.

Maybe there was one thing I could fix.

♦

"I'm sorry," I said as soon as Sam opened the door to his apartment. I stepped inside and threw my arms around his torso, hugging him hard. He stayed in position, one hand holding the door open, the other hanging at his side. "I was a jerk," I said into his chest. "I shouldn't have tried to mind-control your siblings. Although they are, in my opinion, even bigger jerks. And you're right, I did it because I care about you. I couldn't stand to see them treat you that way. Please don't be mad at me." I turned my face to look up at him and gave him my most contrite expression.

He let out a long sigh, and I was relieved to see his mouth quirk into a half-smile. "Come in, Bea."

"What are you making?" I said, releasing him and stepping farther inside. "Something smells amazing."

He shut the door behind us and headed for the kitchen. I followed.

"Uncle's been schooling me on the finer points of okonomiyaki," he said. "I've almost got the batter down, but it needs work."

His kitchen table was set for one, a plate bearing the delicious concoction of batter and egg and squid and noodles and sauce flanked by chopsticks and a glass of wine. A warm, hearty smell wafted through the kitchen, and my mouth watered.

He crossed to one of the kitchen cupboards and pulled out an extra plate as I sat down at the table.

"Oh, you don't have to—" I began.

"Yes, I do," he said, giving me an amused look as he sat down next to me. He carefully cut his okonomiyaki in half and slid it onto the extra plate. "Because if I don't, you'll stare at me with those big, sad puppy dog eyes for the duration of this meal, and I can't take that. Plus, unlike you, I am the *best* at sharing food." He passed me the plate. "Bea: 1276, Sam: 1166. I don't have any more of that grapefruit shit, though."

"I can share your wine."

"Can you now?" he said, pushing the glass so it sat right between us.

"How was the rest of brunch?" I said, popping a big bite of okonomiyaki into my mouth. "Mmm, oh god," I groaned.

"I disagree with your assessment, this needs no work at all. It is perfection."

"Thank you. And the rest of brunch was the usual horror show of Alex showing me pictures of his latest luxury car purchases and Em getting wasted on mimosas and navel gazing about how she really needs to finish that novel she's been working on so she can finally show up Maia Weatherspoon at the next faculty mixer."

"Who's Maia Weatherspoon?"

"I actually don't know," he said. "I never ask because I assume it will make the story go on even longer."

I laughed and took a sip of wine. Mmm. That was actually pretty delicious. Not as good as pink drink, but it would do.

"Bea," Sam said, setting down his chopsticks and meeting my eyes. "We need to talk more about today. I know you said your code is evolving, but what you did to Alex and Emily . . . that was messed up. You know you can't just go around using your power to get stuff you want or make people do what you want. You *do* know that, right?"

"I know," I murmured, my eyes going to my plate. "I'm sorry."

"You've said before that the time you used your powers on Evie . . . well, it made you never want to use them in that way again," he pressed. "And this is so many levels beyond that."

"I shouldn't have done it," I said, toying with my food. "I just . . . I'm overwhelmed right now. With the investigation and being promoted and Mom and everything that's been going on. I . . . I didn't think. They made me so mad. They dismissed you so hard. And you don't deserve that, Sam. You *don't*."

He covered his hand with mine. "Regardless," he said, his voice gentle. "That wasn't the way to fix it." He squeezed my hand. "I will say: Even though I don't believe in mind-controlling my siblings to give in to my every whim, I am touched by the, uh, sentiment behind it. No one's ever stood up for me like that before."

"Probably 'cause you seem like you don't need it, what with that constant overconfident swag," I said, meeting his eyes. "Anyway, don't you usually do a good job of standing up for yourself? That was my impression from the stories you've told me of y'all's epic fights."

"Usually, yes," he said. "But today . . ." He scrubbed a hand over his face. "I don't know. I was looking across the table at them, and it was like something clicked into place. Alex's wife cheats on him regularly, but he won't leave her because her father's connections are part of the fabric of his rich, important person life. He just keeps buying more cars to soothe himself. And Emily really wants to be a novelist, but she can never actually finish her book, so she spends most of her free time seething with jealousy and talking about how so-and-so writer person doesn't deserve their success. They're both fucking miserable."

"And that's why they have to overcompensate so much," I said, pointing my chopsticks at him. "I see. Very astute, Samuel. So when they shit all over you for your supposed lack of accomplishments, they're just trying to lift themselves up by pushing you down. And meanwhile, you're over here living a reasonably happy life."

"Something like that," he said, giving me a tired smile. "But watching them also made me realize that *I* do that sometimes. The overcompensating thing."

"You never do it to hurt anyone or push someone else down, though," I said. I touched his arm. "And I will fully deny this if you ever try to bring it up in front of anyone else, but I kind of enjoy your ridiculous displays of overconfidence. You know, the swag."

"I am absolutely going to bring that up in front of everyone we know." He flashed me a smug Sam grin.

I smiled back. "Look, I'm not trying to poke at you the way your siblings do, but why *did* you stay here after graduation? I mean, you had a high school transcript that's the stuff of Asian parent dreams. You could have gotten a scholarship anywhere you wanted to go. You too could have been a d-bag doctor with a hot wife who cheats on you and a garage full of penis cars."

He shrugged. "I never wanted that. I love the city. I love being able to work on engines all day. And since I'm the one who's around for my parents, they still like me the best—even though Alex and Emily have way more fancy accomplishments."

"Ah!" I said, jabbing my chopsticks in the air. "That is so classic Asian petty. I love it."

His grin widened. "But . . . I dunno. Brunch did get me in a contemplative head space. On the surface, those two have so much to brag about, but their lives are actually weirdly small. And I *am* mostly happy, but I don't want mine to be small, too. I don't want to exist in the . . . what did you call it? Swag?"

"*Swaaag*," I said, waving my chopsticks around and injecting my voice with a little extra panache. "Make your life bigger, then. I believe in you."

He looked at me for a long moment, his expression turning serious in a way I couldn't quite read. "I'm working on it." He turned back to his food. "How was the rest of your day, after the longest brunch ever?"

"Oh, man, where do I even start?" I filled him in on my pursuit of Poet, my Otherworldly adventures, the pen battle at the hospital, and my fight with Evie.

"Wow," he said. "You and Evie can never have a fight over, like, who gets to pick the pizza toppings, huh? You guys always go for the deep cuts."

"First of all, I always pick the pizza toppings," I said. "Because I have the best taste. Second of all . . ." I pushed my now-empty plate away and rested my head on the table with a heavy *thunk*. "I don't know why she doesn't seem to want to find Mom as badly as I do. Maybe she doesn't believe it's Mom—even though I know in my bones that it is. Or maybe she thinks it's an impossible task—even though she's accomplished so many impossible tasks. I don't know. I'm the one who always holds out hope, I guess. To the extent of foolishness."

"You're not foolish." He reached out to stroke my hair and gave me a slight grin. "Impulsive, loud, bad at sharing food—"

"Okay, I get it," I said, giving him a look. "I just wish I could convince her of how important this is, how we can't go around being so *cautious* if we want to figure this out. But no matter what . . ." My chest tightened and I swallowed hard. "Whenever she looks at me, it's always *that* look. The one that says I'm disappointing her. I should have gone to college. I should be doing her proud. I should be able to focus on something for more than a millisecond." I shut my eyes, the wine swirling around in my brain. "I should be a way better, more responsible superhero. And I should be more aware of the fact that I'm the reason she never got to have the big, grieving catharsis I had after Mom."

There was a long pause. I kept my eyes shut, enjoying the drifting blotches of light floating around my vision.

"Did you?" Sam finally said.

My eyes opened. "What do you mean?"

"Did you get to have the big, grieving catharsis?"

"Of course I did," I said, my brows drawing together. "I broke down, I cried, I tantrumed. I started wearing really goth-y makeup—you were there for that part. But Evie never got to tantrum about anything because she had to be the adult."

"Bea." He smoothed my hair away from my face. "I don't think either of you got to process something that's, like . . . a really intense, life-changing loss. There was too much going on, with your dad leaving and Evie trying to keep you guys afloat and you being twelve fucking years old. You both did the best you could. You both *survived*. And whatever happened or didn't happen during that time is not your fault."

"No. You're wrong." I sat up and crossed my arms over my chest. "It *is* my fault. I drained her in every possible way. She was there for me the whole time, and I never really saw it. I *have* to fix that."

My voice kept getting thicker as I talked, tears rising in my throat. But somewhere in the back of my mind, a realization crystallized: There was *a way* for me to fix it. It was the same thing that was going to fix that big hole inside of me. The same thing that was going to fix *everything*. Evie couldn't see it because she'd never had time to see it— because she'd been giving everything to taking care of me. So I'd just have to show her.

"Bea . . ." Sam began, but my runaway train of thought had left the fucking station, and I was determined that it reach its destination.

"If I can get Mom back, I can fix it." My voice was way too loud and my face felt hot and my chest felt tight—but I kept watching him. I needed him to get this for some reason, I needed him to *see*—

He reached over, grabbed the edge of my chair, and dragged it closer to him. I remained in my defiant, arms-crossed position, refusing to help even a little.

"Just because you acted out doesn't mean losing your mom automatically stopped hurting you," he said. "It's *still* hurting you."

"*No.*" I blinked hard and tried to keep my tone steely. I felt like I couldn't breathe. "I mean, even if it is, it doesn't matter. Now I need to make it better for Evie."

He cupped my face, his eyes searching mine. "You don't have to act like something's okay when it's pretty clearly not okay. You don't have to do that with me."

Dammit. He *really* wasn't getting this. How could I make him understand?

"Let me tell you a story about peanut butter," I said.

Then I burst into tears.

My instinct was to curl into a ball in the chair, let it swallow me up, let my sobs consume me the way they had on the kitchen floor so many years ago. But Sam gathered me in his arms and pulled me into his lap, stroking my hair and making little soothing sounds. I buried my face in his shoulder and cried.

"I-I can *feel* you looking at me all sad, like you p-pity me," I managed between sobs. "Please don't. *Please*. I've always been able to count on you *not* to look at me that way."

"I'm not looking at you that way," he said, his voice soft against my ear. "I'm looking at you like a friend who cares about your general well-being and wants you to be happy."

I sat up straight, meeting his gaze and scraping the back of my hand over my eyes. He was looking at me with such sweet earnestness. No trace of Calendar Sam. It reminded me of the way he'd looked at me the night before, when . . .

"Is that why you like giving me all those orgasms?" I said abruptly, my voice tremulous. "Because you want me to be happy?"

He laughed, surprised. "I like doing that for many reasons."

"Then why were you so weird this morning?" I blurted out. "I was all afterglowy and ready for round two and you were like . . ." I made an exaggerated crabby face.

"Bea." He shook his head. "Trying to follow your train of thought is like trying to follow a locomotive that's careened wildly off the tracks and is now crashing its way through a previously scenic meadow. Or something."

"I'm trying to talk about anything but my mom," I said, my voice wavering again. "Indulge me?"

"I . . . I was a little preoccupied with my impending terrible brunch. But also . . ." He trailed off, considering, then reached up to brush my hair off my face again. "Last night was amazing," he finally said. "But I wasn't sure if you wanted a round two. Or if you ever would."

"What?" I said, shaking my head. "How could you think that? Did you hear the sounds you got out of me last night?"

"Yes," he said, giving me a half-smile. "But you're always talking about how quickly you get bored."

I searched his face. He still had that sweet, disarming earnestness, but now there was something else. A trace of real vulnerability underneath it all. Had he really not known how badly I'd wanted to get naked with him again? Had cocky Sam Fujikawa actually experienced a moment of *doubt* when it came to his sexual prowess? Something about that stabbed straight to my heart, made me want to wrap him in my arms and keep him safe forever.

"I'm still finding plenty that's of interest," I said, winding my arms around his neck. "I'd love to have you, ah, make me happy all over again."

"Oh, really?" he said, smiling.

"Yes. But first . . ." I scanned the table, zeroing in on his plate with its half-finished okonomiyaki. My plate was, of course, empty. "You know how else you could make me happy right now?"

He picked his plate up off the table and handed it to me. "Let the record show that I am once again the best food sharer. I should get, like, infinity points for that."

"No infinity points," I said, leaning against him. "But I'll grant that you win pretty much every point awarded tonight."

I spent the next hour cuddled up in his arms, eating okonomiyaki. And after that, he made me happy again right there on the kitchen table.

CHAPTER TWENTY-ONE

TWO DAYS LATER, Evie and I still weren't speaking to each other.

It was super weird, but after we'd lasted a whole twenty-four hours with only the most basic "pass the salt" type pleasantries exchanged, it felt like an invisible wall grew between us, which only became more insurmountable as time went on. Aveda sat me down and told me I was "on probation" as far as superheroing went until further notice. I saw a flicker of conflict in her eyes, like she didn't totally agree with the decision, but was still willing to go along with what Evie wanted when it came to her unruly little sister.

I hadn't protested. If they were so dead-set against taking the action we needed to find Mom, then there was no use in me being part of their team anyway. I tried to pursue leads on my own. I went out to the Wave Organ again, attempting to find that entrance to the Otherworld. I snuck over to the hospital—but unfortunately couldn't figure out a way inside since Rose's team was now patrolling every inch of the place. I left more notes in the It's Lit bathroom, hoping Mom would attempt communication again. None of my efforts bore fruit.

I knew Team Tanaka/Jupiter was following their own avenues of investigation, but they weren't getting very far, either. They couldn't track down Kathy, Poet, or Bernard (because they were all hiding out in the Otherworld, duh). Rose and her team kept up their patrols—nothing much was happening at the previously weaponized locations. Further investigation of the hospital revealed that all patients and personnel except for Bernard had been mysteriously relocated to other local hospitals the day before Evie, Aveda, and I had battled the pen army. When interviewed, none of them could remember exactly why—my guess was that Bernard had mind-mojo-ed all of them so he could finally be alone at the big front desk with all his beloved pens and his very own handy Otherworld portal.

On the plus side, no *new* locations had been weaponized. So yay for that.

But I was starting to feel a little desperate, so I brought two potentially exciting projects with me to my shift at It's Lit. First, I'd convinced Nate to let me borrow the parchment we'd discovered in Kathy's blue cabinet, the one with the mysterious runes. None of his demonologist pals had been able to make heads or tails of it, but I thought maybe the combined brain power of me, Leah, and Sam would be able to crack it. And then, because that just wasn't enough, I'd also brought Rose's demon trap to tinker with—the one Sam and I had, um, been distracted from.

"I dunno, Bebe," Leah said, shaking her head. We were crowded around the register area with Sam. Pancake was sacked out on his special pillow, snoring loudly enough to be a distraction. His back left foot was raised in the air, like he was hoping someone would be kind enough to give him belly rubs while he slept. "We've been staring at this for an hour, and we still don't even know where to start."

"Dangit, I thought you'd be our secret weapon," I said, elbowing her. "I mean, the extremely intricate made-up dragon language is one of your most treasured parts of our favorite dragon-shifter lady book."

"I know," she said, shaking her head in frustration. "And I'm fluent in Klingon and Dothraki, too. Made-up languages are one of my jams. But this . . ." She pointed to the parchment. "I can't find, like, a root. A place to start. Most languages have a key that will at least begin to unravel them, but this one . . ." She trailed off again, then looked up from the parchment. And her eyes immediately narrowed.

"Gak," she said, making a face at Sam and me. "You guys are . . ." She waved her hand at us.

"What?" Sam said. I realized that he'd wrapped an arm loosely around my waist, pulling me against him.

"I could take the ridiculousness," Leah said. "But now you're being casually affectionate. Like . . . love-y."

"Excuse me!" I yelped, just as Sam said, "We are *not*."

Leah rolled her eyes and looked like she wanted to say more, but Nemesis Nicole chose that moment to wander in.

"Hey," she said, approaching the counter.

"What, no empty coffee cup?" I said.

"No." She cocked her head at me. Hmm. She looked strangely listless today. I mean, she was never the most exciting person to be around, but there was usually a spark of fire behind that beige suit. And her hair part, always so perfect, was crooked.

"What's up with you?" I blurted out.

"Why do you care?" she said, instantly suspicious.

"I don't," I retorted. "But you approached the counter. So I assume you want something."

"I . . ." She frowned, her expression going a bit unsure. Her eyes wandered to the parchment, now lying next to Pancake's snoring form. "What's this?"

"Nothing," I said. "Top secret superhero business you're not supposed to look at. It's classified."

"Oh, really?" she said, rolling her eyes. "Because I still haven't seen a single mention of you on Maisy's blog, Bea. So I don't know why you expect me to believe—"

"There's a *reason* for that," I said, my face getting hot. "One of my very important superheroing mentors is trying to protect me—"

"Anyway," she interrupted. "I was just going to ask: why are you reading it sideways?"

"Wait, what?" Leah said, her eyes going wide.

Nicole reached over and rotated the parchment ninety degrees. And Leah's eyes went even wider.

"Oh my gosh," she said, clapping a hand over her mouth.

"Of course. We assumed we were supposed to read this page vertically. But it's actually *horizontal*."

"Yeah," Nicole said, tapping the parchment. "I'm surprised you didn't see it, Leah. It looks like it has a similar root to the dragon language in that dragon-shifter lady book you recommended to me. Which I read in one night, by the way."

"Um, what?!" I exclaimed, my eyes going from Leah to Nicole and back again. "You recommended *our* book? To *her*?"

"Bebe," Leah said, her eyes glued to the parchment. "I think I've got this. Can you just give me some silence for a minute?"

"And since when do you recommend books to her?" I pressed. "Since when do you guys talk in a friendly manner at all?"

"Come on, Bea," Sam said, patting my shoulder. "Let's go work on the trap."

"Fiiiiiiiine," I spat out, stomping toward the back room.

"You're welcome!" Nicole called after me, her tone smug.

I pushed Sam into the back room and slammed the door behind us.

"Can you believe that?" I raged. "Can. You. Believe. *That*. How could she—"

"Leah or Nicole?" he said.

"Nicole, of course," I sputtered. "Leah and I *hate* her, she's always so rude. And she totally used to make fun of me for reading that book and now suddenly she loves it?! I . . . she . . ." I huffed over to the work table containing the disassembled pieces of the trap. My face was on fire, and the anger that had overtaken me so quickly pulsed through my bloodstream, hot and irrational.

"Bea." He came up behind me and wrapped his arms around my shoulders, brushing his lips against the top of my head. "Leah isn't going to abandon you," he murmured against my hair.

"What?!" I pulled out of his embrace and turned to face him. "Were you even listening? That's not what I—"

"Yes, it is." He tapped my forehead. "You've got your forehead crinkle." I batted his hand away. "What you were actually saying, underneath all that rage, is that you're scared Leah's going to decide she likes Nicole way more than you and replace you as her best friend."

I sucked in a long breath, then slumped against the work table, sulking. "Why would I think that? I mean, that's ridiculous."

"It's ridiculous because Leah would never do that," he said, his voice gentle. "But it's not ridiculous for you to go there. Because . . ." He trailed off and met my eyes. His gaze was so tender, I had to look away.

"Because so many people *have* left me," I finally said, toying with the ends of my hair. "My mom, my dad. Nemesis Nicole, way back when. Even Evie seems to have given up on me."

"I'll never give up on you." He leaned against the work table and reached over to take my hand, lacing his fingers through mine. "Promise."

"But what if you stop having fun first?" I blurted out.

He shook his head. "What?"

"You know, in this little fun-having . . . thing we're doing," I said, my face flushing. "One person always stops having fun first. What if it's you?"

I didn't know why I was lashing out at him. Maybe because some residual traces of that anger were still pulsing through me. Maybe because he'd hit so precisely on one of my central issues.

Or maybe because ever since I'd cried on him and blabbed all my Mom feelings a few nights before, I'd felt more sensitive around him, more exposed—he'd seen me naked in more ways than one.

"Bea—"

"You have all your rules," I barreled on. "About no second

dates and not leaving clothes behind. And now that we're apparently being all *casually affectionate—*"

"*Beatrice.*" He gave me an exasperated look. But didn't stop holding my hand, I noticed. "I have those rules because . . ." He hesitated, then shook his head, like he was giving up. "Well, because having rules is easier than finding out that once the novelty of getting to touch the abs from the calendar wears off, there's not much else of interest."

I goggled at him. "What?"

"Look. Women like sleeping with me. Most of them would be more than happy to sleep with me more than once." He gave me a light version of his *beaucoup fromage* grin. "But the truth is, once they get to know me even a little bit, they realize I'm not the muscles from the calendar, or the hot mechanic who likes to take his shirt off for no reason—I'm not the guy they've projected all their fantasies onto. And that means they're not really interested in spending time with me, unless we're spending that time in bed."

I raised an eyebrow. "So you're just like . . . a disposable piece of meat to them?"

"Thank you for making me sound like the blue plate special at Mel's Diner," he said, chuckling a little.

I studied him. He was trying to laugh it off, but there was that streak of vulnerability underneath. I could tell it really bothered him. He couched his himbo tendencies in a careless player lifestyle, but could it be because people refused to see him any other way? "Well," I finally said. "I already know you. And I already like you. So there."

He grinned. "I already know you and like you, too."

I rested my head against his shoulder. Our fingers were still interlaced, our palms pressed together. The warmth of his body next to mine soothed me, draining the last of my anger over the whole Leah/Nemesis Nicole situation.

"I trust us to stop having fun at the exact same time," he said. "If anyone can do it, we can."

I laughed, but something about that stirred uncertainty in my gut, made my skin prickle.

"We keep getting distracted from actually working on the trap," he said, making his tone light. "Is Rose going to kill us?"

"That would be way against her entire personality," I murmured.

"Guys!" Leah burst in, then stopped abruptly, frowning when she saw Sam and me all cuddled up. Something passed over her face, like she was having some sort of realization. But it was gone so fast, I thought maybe I'd imagined it.

"Sorry," I said, raising my head from his shoulder and releasing Sam's hand. "I should have put a Casual Affection Alert sign on the door."

"I think I've decoded this." She brandished the parchment, then held up another piece of paper with her swoopy handwriting all over it. "Or sort of decoded it."

"Holy shit, you're a genius," I said. "Demonologists have got *nothing* on hardcore dragon-shifter lady book enthusiasts."

"It's, like, a plea," Leah said, waving the paper around. "From a daughter to a mother. The daughter is about to embark on a big adventure that will take her far from home. Her mother is against it, and the daughter is trying to explain all the reasons she absolutely *needs* to go."

"We're sure this is demon language from the Otherworld?" Sam said. "Because that sounds like a very human story."

"Some stories are universal," I said, thinking of all the times I'd begged Evie to just let me be a grown-up.

"This demon girl talks at length about how all her powers will protect her in the 'alien realm of the humans,'" Leah said.

"So she was coming *here*?" I frowned, considering that piece of info, an idea sparking in my brain. "Oh, shit. Was she one of Shasta's raiding party—the humanoid demons who came through the original portal?"

"Exactly what I was thinking!" Leah said, stabbing an index finger in the air. "And there's something else. Bebe . . .

one of the powers she describes having: 'great influence on the minds of others,' being able to reach out with her brain and 'gift' people with the feelings she wants them to have—"

"Oh, double shit," I said, my eyes widening. "*I* got her power when she died!"

"Yes!" Leah said, nodding vigorously. "So why the hell did Kathy Kooper have this in her possession?"

"And *how*?" Sam said. "Is it a souvenir of one of her trips to the Otherworld, or what?"

Trying to make sense of it all, I stared at the parchment Leah was still holding. I'd hoped to end the day feeling like I'd made progress on multiple projects that would also somehow contribute to my overall quest to save Mom.

Instead, all I had were more questions, I wasn't sure where to go next, and I was still banned from superheroing for the foreseeable future.

If I were one for giving up, now probably would have been the time to do it.

CHAPTER TWENTY-TWO

I AM, OF course, *not* one for giving up, so I kept on my quest as best I could. I shared with Nate what Leah had discovered about the demon daughter's note. He was super excited that Leah had actually decoded some of the mysterious demon language, even though the note didn't lead us in any new directions as far as finding Mom. And the weaponized locations seemed determined to remain frustratingly mundane. No more mecha carnival rides chasing people.

Evie and I were still icing each other out, so for the next week, I found myself spending more and more time away from HQ. I threw myself into helping Leah plan the Art Jam, which now appeared to be reverting back to its original purpose of simply being a fun event at the store. I wasn't holding out much hope that Poet was actually going to show up—why go to an Art Jam when you can chill in the Other-world? And I spent almost every night at Sam's place. We ate delicious food, we played with the inner workings of the trap, and we continued to have the best sex I'd ever had in my life. It was like a tiny pocket universe of fun, and escaping into it kept me from dwelling on things with Evie or obsessing over why Mom wasn't communicating with me.

Leah joined us for dinner a couple times, but usually had something else to do, often involving her mom and the lizards. I always asked if she wanted me to come help her, but she always said no. I wondered if Leah was making up some of these other commitments, if she felt excluded from our little pocket universe. Ever since Sam and I had added benefits to our friendship, it seemed to have created an odd imbalance in the group, and I was eager to correct it. I redoubled my efforts to find her a love match, but she always brushed me off.

"Come on," I said, as yet another prospect headed out the door of It's Lit. "He was totally cute. And I only mind-mojo-ed him a little, I'm pretty sure he was already checking you out. You could have at least invited him to stay for Art Jam." The Jam was that evening, and Leah and I were in the midst of decorating. Pancake was supposed to be "helping," but was mostly just running around getting underfoot and fucking up the giant swaths of butcher paper we'd laid out on the floor.

"Bebe," Leah said, shaking her head. "Stop. How many times do I have to say, I do not want to be set up by you."

"Why *not*?" I said, a whiny thread creeping into my voice. I arranged canisters of markers, paintbrushes, and other arting implements on a table. Then I added a few unicorns from Charlotte's collection to my display, so it looked like the unicorn posse was watching over the art supplies. "Is my taste that bad? Or off? Describe to me your perfect person in detail. Give me something to work with."

Leah shook her head, setting out a bunch of crafting supplies on another table. "I . . ." She blew out a long breath, turned, and studied me, as if sizing me up. "I'm going to tell you something," she said. "And I need you to not act a fool about it."

Pancake chose that moment to throw himself on top of my foot, whining for attention like he was being murdered. I scooped him up in my arms.

"Of course," I said, stroking Pancake's ears. "You can tell me anything, Lee."

She took a deep breath. "I—"

"Hey." Of course Nemesis Nicole chose that moment to waltz up, book clutched to her chest. "I was wondering—"

"We're having an important, work-related conversation,"

I snitted at her. "Your coffee refills and other annoying demands will have to wait."

She blinked at me, her gaze sliding from me to Leah and back again. "Oh, uh . . ."

"It's all right," Leah said, stepping forward to take the books from her. "You're looking for the next one in this series, right?"

"Yeah." Nicole gave her a tentative smile. "You were right, the chemistry between the two fairy queens was off the charts. And the banter—"

"The *banter*," Leah said, clapping a hand to her chest and pretending to swoon. "What did I tell you? I die."

Um. What the fresh hell was going on here? Leah was *still* recommending books to her? My head swiveled back and forth between them, like I was watching a really intense tennis match. And I could swear Pancake's head was doing the same.

"Why don't you go hang out in the café while I find it for you?" Leah said.

"Great." Nicole's smile widened, and she reached up and absently tucked her hair behind her ear. "Thank you. And thank you for loaning those to me, I promise to keep them in totally pristine condition." She turned back to me, gave Pancake a little pat on the head, and then headed for the café.

"Uhhhh," was all I could say. Pancake looked slightly offended at my inability to articulate more than that.

Leah ignored me and started walking toward Paranormal Romance.

"Excuse me," I said, following her. Pancake squirmed in my arms, but I didn't put him down. "Nicole just tucked her hair behind her ear. Tucking her hair behind her ear is her tell for when she likes someone. It's been her tell since we were *twelve*. Was that . . . Are you . . . Is the thing you wanted to tell me about *you and Nicole*?"

Leah slid the book back on the shelf, pulled out the one next to it, and turned back to me. "And what if it is?"

"I . . . *we* . . . we hate her," I hissed, pulling Pancake tight against my chest. He gave a little snort of indignation. "I've told you how awful she was to me. She's awful to us *now*. She sits in that café, she never buys any books, she acts like we're her freaking *servants—*"

"Bea! Leah!" Charlotte called from up front. Her usual monotone was slightly elevated. "People are starting to arrive for the Art Jam."

Leah and I hustled up front to see several dozen people streaming in the front door, exclaiming in wonder at the decorations and the crafting stations and the reams of butcher paper spread out on the floor.

"I'll just run this over to the café," Leah muttered, waving the book she was holding.

"We are *not* done talking," I muttered back.

"Oh, I know," she called over her shoulder.

I finally set the squirming Pancake down on the floor, and he gleefully set off in the direction of the butcher paper. As I stood up, I did a double take. Evie and Aveda were filing in behind the stream of Art Jam enthusiasts, looking wary and alert. I crossed the room and planted myself in front of them.

"Why are you here?" I demanded. "I told you: nothing is likely to go down tonight, now that Poet appears to have fucked off to the Otherworld. We're all set for an evening of pretty freakin' mundane shenanigans, and there are pretty much zero ways that I, Thrill-Seeking Terror that I am, can get into trouble. Especially since you put me on probation and all."

"Relax, tiny terror," Aveda said, giving me a look.

"I'm taller than you are," I mumbled, crossing my arms over my chest.

"We came here to observe, just in case," Aveda said. "You never know what might go down—sometimes a break in a case happens when you least expect it."

"Another superheroine lesson?" I said.

"Yes." She smiled at me, surprised, then glanced at Evie, quickly schooling her features into something more stern.

"We'll stay out of your way," Evie murmured, her eyes not quite meeting mine.

"Fine," I huffed.

I turned and stomped off, trying to quash the irrational feeling that I was being babysat for no reason. People were crowding around the craft tables, chattering amongst themselves and perusing the supplies. A hum of excited energy permeated the air, stoking my irritation. I tried to shake it off.

"Bebe." Leah appeared by my side and poked me in the arm. "I saw Evie and Aveda come in; does that mean we're expecting a Poet appearance?"

"No," I grumbled. "As far as I can tell, they just showed up to bc annoying. Like your new best friend Nicole over there." I nodded at Nicole, who had returned to the bookstore area and was perched on the pink couch, looking totally out of place as she watched everyone else sift through craft supplies.

Leah blew out a frustrated breath. "So are you willing to actually listen to me about that now? Nicole and I got to talking while you were off with Sammy one night. She lost her job at the, um, paralegal place. That's why she's always here and that's why she doesn't buy the books—she can't afford them right now. And as for all the 'tude . . . I mean, she's embarrassed. She's overcompensating for feeling like nothing. She still hasn't told her parents. She has no idea what to do next, and she feels like a failure. This place, these books—they've provided a sort of safe space for her. And isn't that kind of what this bookstore is all about?"

"But she's *always* been awful," I protested. "She's awful with or without a job. She—"

"Is it so impossible for you to accept that maybe she's changed?" Leah said. "Aren't you always going on about how much *you've* changed over the years, how it isn't fair for

Evie to judge you for all the stupid shit you did when you were younger?"

"Not that that ever stops her," I muttered, shooting Evie and Aveda a look. They'd positioned themselves on the other side of the bookstore and were "casually" leaning against a vintage armoire Leah had restored and filled with tiny knick-knacks for sale. They were really bad at looking inconspicuous. I noticed some of the Art Jammers whispering and casting starstruck looks their way. Great. So not only were they annoying, they were also pulling focus from the event.

I turned back to Leah. "I just don't understand why of all the people in all the world, you have to pick *her*—"

"Bebe." Leah threw me a look of extreme frustration. "We're not ready to pledge our eternal souls to each other or something. We haven't even kissed. Or progressed beyond flirty talking about books and deep, soul-searching conversation about what the hell we want to do with our lives. But I *like* her, Bebe. I really, really do."

"I've tried to set you up so many times," I protested. "Presented you with so many better options."

"I don't *want* any of those options," Leah said, shaking her head. "I don't want someone to be presented to me, I want to choose my own person, of my own free will. Who also has *their* own free will."

"They have free will," I said. "I just offer a little encouragement—"

"Until they do something you disagree with or that annoys you," Leah said. She stepped closer to me and touched my arm. "I appreciate how protective you are of me. And of all the people you care about. But you've got to be careful with that mind mojo stuff. You're inching toward a place you don't want to go. Like, kind of a *villain* place. Where you just make people do whatever you want because it means you'll get the result you want. I don't think that's you, Bebe—that's not the hero you want to be."

"You seemed fine with my mind mojo before," I said, feeling stung. "You actively encouraged it, in fact, when I was using it on people like that annoying Ichabod guy. What changed? Are you saying all this because I used it on the suddenly wonderful Nicole?"

"Actually, yes," she said. "But not because it was her. That's the first time I've seen you, like, *control* someone. Dictate to them what you wanted them to do. And you didn't even think twice about doing it. It was freaky."

I blew out a long breath, frustration overwhelming me. "Look," I said, trying to get back to something resembling the point, "I *am* protective of you. And that's why I'm trying to discourage you from this Nicole thing. Because I *know* she'll be awful to you, she'll hurt you—"

"Actually, you don't know that," Leah said, her gaze going cool. "You don't know her at all *now*. And honestly, if you're worried about people getting hurt, you need to take a good, hard look at your own love life."

"What are you talking about?" I said. "Me and Sam? You called it from the beginning—we're enjoying the excitement of sleeping together. The fun for fun's sake. I'm leaning hard into the ridiculousness of it all. And when it's done, it's done, and things will go back to normal, and . . . I mean, are we being weird to you, Lee? Because once we decide to end this thing—"

"Bebe." Leah squeezed her eyes shut and pressed her fingertips to her temples, like she'd just been walloped with a monster migraine. "You guys are ridiculous in all the ways. I can't even begin to describe it. But whatever this thing was when you started it . . . well, it's clearly not where you're at now."

I shook my head. "What are you talking about?"

She met my eyes. "For someone who spends so much time playing with other people's minds, you sure don't know your own."

"Leeee-*aaah*." I gave her a look. "Can you please quit with the inspirational poster catchphrases and—"

"Bea."

Leah and I both whipped around to see Evie approaching,

her face tense. Aveda was right behind her, mouth set in a grim line.

"What?" I exploded, my irritation at them and Leah and stupid Nicole boiling over. "What am I doing wrong now? And how can you tell I'm doing something wrong from all the way across the room—"

"It's not that," Evie interrupted. At an apparent loss for words, she pointed toward the front entrance. Where Poet, Kathy Kooper, and freaking Bernard from the hospital were strolling in, looking like, *Oh, hey, we just happened to be walking by, and can anyone take part in this delightful Art Jam? Or are possibly evil assholes with possibly evil connections to the for-sure evil Otherworld specifically banned?*

My jaw dropped.

"That's Bernard, right?" Evie hissed. "And I haven't actually seen Kathy Kooper in years, but I'm assuming that's her? So that third person must be—"

"Yup," I said. "That's Poet."

Our evil trio stopped in the entryway and surveyed the scene, their faces dispassionate.

"Leah," Aveda said, "we need to get all the civilians out of here. But let's try to do it quietly, without any chaos or stampeding. Can you go around to all these little clusters and tell them, I don't know, that Art Jam has to be postponed to another night?"

"Check," Leah said, her eyes darting around. Her face was pinched, and she looked like she was panicking but trying to shove it down. "Um, have any of you seen—"

"Pancake," I said, realizing the little dog was flitting around the store and could easily get trampled if people started freaking out and bulldozing toward the exits. "Don't worry, Lee, I'll find him. Evie and Aveda, if you guys want to go talk to our pals up there, I can reach out with my mind and see if I can find them in the . . . what would you call it? The mental space where we've been having our little skirmishes. The brain plane. While securing the puppy."

"Good multitasking," Aveda said, nodding approvingly.

"And Bea, if this does end up escalating into a battle-type situation, consider your probation temporarily lifted. Right, Evie?"

"Well . . ." Evie's gaze slid to the side. "She could also evacuate with everyone else."

"Bea's special talents could prove to be essential to whatever's about to happen," Aveda said, her voice firm. "And anyway, we may need all hands on deck. I'm going to text Shruti."

"All right," Evie said reluctantly. "Probation lifted—for now. Let's go talk to these jerks, Annie."

Evie and Aveda made their way up to the front, where the jerks in question were still surveying the scene, not doing anything particularly evil.

"Bebe." Leah's fingers dug into my arm. Her eyes were darting all over the place. "Please . . ."

"I'll find Pancake," I repeated, gently prying her fingers from my arm. "Lee, I know we were just, uh . . ."

"Having a strongly worded discussion?" she said.

"Yes, okay, let's go with that. But I'm always here for you. And for that side-eyeing, bacon-snarfing, pain-in-the-ass little puppy. Okay?"

"Okay," she said, her face relaxing a little. "Wait. Are you mind-mojo-ing me right now? Trying to get me to calm down?"

"No," I said firmly. "Now go start telling people to get the hell out of here, and we'll talk about your terrible taste in crushes and incorrect assessment of my love life later."

She looked like she wanted to respond to that, but settled for nodding and turning to head for one of the crafting clusters. I took it as a win.

I scanned the crowd for Pancake. Where had I last seen him? Oh, right. Heading off to gleefully fuck with the butcher paper. I wended my way around all the people who were now sprawled on the floor, painting and gluing and papier-mâché-ing to their heart's content. Keeping an eye out for the pup, I reached out with my mind, feeling around for people trying to put up mental brick walls or attack.

"Oops, sorry!" I exclaimed to a woman after nearly tripping over her. My multitasking needed work.

I was getting nothing, though. The brain plane appeared to be barren. I shot a look at the entrance, where Evie and Aveda were engaged in conversation with Kathy, Poet, and Bernard. They didn't seem to be arguing, exactly, but Aveda had her hands on her hips in one of her trademark intimidating stances. The set of Evie's shoulders was tense, her fingers curling into fists at her sides, like she was just waiting to let loose with that fire.

I finally spotted Pancake, who had plopped himself down on a small expanse of butcher paper and was enthusiastically gnawing on his foot while dedicated Art Jammers painted around him.

"Oh, Pancake," I said with a sigh. "Your mom is worried sick about you. And you've got paint on your tail." He gave me a baleful look as I scooped him up, cradling him to my chest. "You're much more of a tiny terror than I am. Maybe that's why we get along so well."

I started to turn back around to check on Evie, Aveda, and the evil trio—and that's when it happened.

It was like a massive semi trailer-truck barreling at top speed slammed directly into my brain.

"Wha—" I gasped out loud, falling to my knees. Stars danced in front of my eyes and my vision blurred in and out. I clutched Pancake to my chest, even though he was barking and squirming up a storm. I tried to throw up some kind of protection, my own mental brick wall, but then the semi was slamming into my brain again, over and over and *over* . . .

I writhed on the ground, trying to curl myself into a ball, like that would somehow keep the relentless pain out. Fuck. Fucking frakballs. That *hurt*. A scream tore itself from my throat, but I couldn't even hear it. I just *felt* it, deep in my chest, in my gut, in my everywhere.

Then the pain stopped. My vision started to clear and the world started to drift back into focus in dribs and drabs. I felt Pancake, warm against my chest. I saw people running

for the exits. I heard Leah yelling at them to please calm
down, head for the café, they could barricade the café . . .
What was she talking about? Why were people running?
What was happening?

There was a slight ringing in my ears and my vision was
still blurring in and out. I tried to shake my head, but my
movements felt slow and labored, like when I was in the Otherworld. Wait . . . was I in the Otherworld? I felt something
nudge against my brain, and I pushed back hard. It flitted
away. Emboldened, I reached out again, trying to find the
evil trio on the brain plane. They weren't there, but something else was. What *was* that?

It felt like a bright, glowing light. And it wanted me to
grab on to it. I reached out with my mind and embraced it,
and then my ears started to ring even more.

Then Evie's scream pierced through the ringing: "Annie,
move her, fucking *move her* or it's going to—"

Suddenly I was lifted off the ground and swept to the side.
I slammed into a bookcase and dropped to the ground, still
holding on to Pancake for dear life.

"Ow!" I yelped.

"Sorry!" Aveda called out.

Being knocked into the bookcase seemed to shake off the
last of my disorientation, and the room came back into focus.
I was on the ground, facing the bookcase I'd just crashed into,
and Pancake was still in my arms, barking his tiny head off.

I scrambled to my feet and whipped around just in time
to see a gigantic porcelain unicorn stomping its way through
Historical Romance. For the second time that night, my jaw
dropped.

STOMP STOMP STOMMMMMMPPPPP

The unicorn was almost as tall as the ceiling and it obliterated everything it smashed into with its oversized glittery
hooves. I swallowed hard, trying to get my bearings, trying
to take in everything I could about the scene. Pancake was
still barking his head off. No way I could put him down now,
he'd be smashed to fuzzy smithereens.

Evie was by the entrance of the store, shooting fireballs at the gigantic unicorn. They smacked into its legs and the porcelain seemed to be melting slowly—but only enough to slow it down, not stop it entirely. Aveda was next to the vintage armoire, sizing up the giant beast. Probably trying to figure out if there was any way in hell she could kick its ass; it was likely too gigantic for her to trap in a sustained telekinetic hold. My eyes darted to the café, and I was relieved to see the barricade between the café area and bookstore had been pulled down. Hopefully all civilians were safe behind it. It looked like Evie, Aveda, and I (and Pancake) were the only ones left in the store area.

Where had the evil trio gone? Surely they weren't locked up in the café with all those innocent people . . .

CRASH

The gigantic unicorn smashed its hoof into the vintage armoire, breaking it to bits.

"Gah!" Aveda yelped, jumping out of the way. "Goddammit, I wish Shruti was here. Maybe she could wrap her hair around this asshole My Little Pony."

"It's more like a My Not-So-Little Pony," Evie said ruefully, sending out another series of fireballs.

"Evie, stay back!" Aveda growled. "Don't get in that thing's way!"

"I know, I know," she said, sounding a bit weary.

Huh. That was odd. Usually Evie snapped at Aveda if she felt like she was trying to "protect" her by keeping her out of the fray. It was one of the oldest parts of their dynamic. Why was she being so . . . docile?

"Guys—Evie, Aveda! I'm over here!" I called out, stepping forward. "Where'd the evil trio go? Did one of Charlotte's porcelain unicorns actually come to life and inflate itself and . . . Holy shit, this is like the Wave Organ, isn't it? Or the pens at the hospital? Sorry, that's probably too many questions—"

"That is exactly what happened, Bea," Aveda said,

darting out of the unicorn's way again. "It almost stomped on *you*, actually, but I telekinesised you out of the way just in time. As for the trio—"

"They disappeared!" Evie shrieked.

STOOOOOOMPPPPPPP

The unicorn smashed its foot into the ground so hard, I felt the entire building shake.

"Disappeared?!" I said.

"Right after Leah got everyone into the café and pulled down the barricade," Aveda called out. "They were still out here with us, then Evie and I turn around to deal with the massive fucking unicorn destroying the bookstore, and *poof*, they're gone."

"Fuck." I shook my head, trying to process. Pancake whimpered in my arms. All right, I'd process all this later. Right now was the time for action. I stepped forward, made sure my grip on Pancake was firm, and gathered up the heady brew of confusion and fear that was roiling inside of me. Then I opened my mouth and screamed.

I hadn't had *that* many opportunities to deploy my scream yet. But I was used to it having an instantaneous and devastating effect, massive monsters shattering at my feet.

That didn't happen this time.

Instead, the giant unicorn raised its head, its golden horn glimmering in the usually comforting bookstore light. Then it turned. Zeroed in on me. And, was it my imagination, or did it sort of . . . nod?

I didn't have time to contemplate that, because all of a sudden, I heard a *CRASH* and whipped around to see one of the tinier porcelain unicorns in Charlotte's collection fucking leap off the bookshelf behind me.

What the hell . . .

I whipped back around and . . . holy shit. All the porcelain unicorns were coming to life, hopping down from their perches, ready to wreak havoc on the poor bookstore. Some of them were inflating to actual horse size, some of them were staying super teeny. None seemed to be getting as massive as the gigantic one who'd started the whole thing, but this was definitely scarier than Bernard's stupid pen swarm.

"Oh, no, you bargain basement Twilight Sparkles, you are *not* going to make an even bigger mess up in here!" Aveda barked. "Aveda Jupiter will. Not. Have. *That.*"

She charged into the fray, dodging the gigantic Queen Mother unicorn, smashing her fists into the smaller ones. It was dazzling as only Aveda can be dazzling: her eyes sparkling with untamed ferocity, her ponytail swishing through the air as she twisted and turned her body into various ass-kicking shapes.

Evie followed her lead, targeting the smaller unicorns with her fire. Her fireballs crashed into a tiny duo of pink and purple unicorns that were originally salt and pepper shakers, and they melted into the floor.

Hmm. So maybe my scream hadn't worked on the first unicorn because it was just too giant? Maybe I could take down the smaller ones. I tightened my hold on Pancake and took a deep breath, gathering up every feeling I had. Then I charged forward into the porcelain unicorn melee, lobbing my screams like they were my own tiny fireballs, aiming them at the smaller unicorns. I ran toward Evie, cutting a path through the middle of the bookstore, dodging out of the way of the gigantic unicorn's stompy hoof. One of Evie's fireballs whizzed by my ear, and I dodged out of the way of that, too.

"Argh! Sorry!" she yelped.

Adrenaline hummed through my veins with every step, every scream, and I felt like I was propelled forward by some invisible force pushing against my back, giving me extra momentum. Pancake, clutched tightly to my chest, growled at the sparkly interlopers. I ran past Aveda, who smashed her fist into another unicorn. I ran past three more unicorns melting into the ground, felled by Evie's fire. I put even more force behind my screams, even though my throat was going raw and my head hurt and my ears were ringing. And weirdly,

I felt my heart lift. Because *this*, I realized, was what it felt like to be on a bona fide superhero team. All of us working together, our powers in sync, taking down an evil none of us could explain. Protecting all the people in that café who couldn't protect themselves. All of the drama I'd had with Evie faded away and there was just this amazing feeling.

This was what it felt like to be a hero.

I finally reached Evie by the door and came to a stop. My throat felt like it had been used as a scratching post by a million cats. I whipped back around, breathing hard.

"How many did I get, Sis?" I managed. "It felt like *a lot*. But I was so focused on the running and the screaming, I didn't actually see—"

"Bea," she said, her voice low and urgent as she lobbed another series of fireballs at a unicorn trying to climb onto the pink couch. "I don't think you got any of them."

My heart froze. "What?"

"None of them shattered," she said. "Annie, on your left!" she screamed. Aveda dodged out of the way of the giant unicorn yet again. "I don't know what's going on," she said to me. "But just . . . sit tight. Maybe see if you can go lock yourself in the bathroom or something until this is over."

I took a step back, leaning against the wall for support. Pancake whined, his ears flicking back and forth. My body felt like it was going numb all over. The scene in front of me went hazy, the sound receding. I was vaguely aware of bursts of flame shooting through the air and Aveda's body whirling through the unicorn mass and Evie barking at her to watch out, but it was like I was watching them on TV. I felt disconnected, removed. What the hell was going on? Why was the evil unicorn army immune to my power?

BRRRRRRRRRRRRRRRRRRR

The sound rose up in my ears, that all-too-familiar plane engine sound. I scanned the air wildly, looking for the blurry spot, or for signs of a veil of fog somewhere. Not there . . . not there . . . dammit. I mean, Aveda looked like she was rendered in perfect crystal-clear hi-def. I widened the scope of where I was looking, my eyes flicking over every single hidden nook of the store. No . . . no . . . wait. *There* it was. In the back, next to the biggest Paranormal Romance shelf. That telltale spot where everything looked fuzzy.

BRRRRRRRRRRRRRRRRRRRRRRRRRR

The sound was threatening to overwhelm me as it always did, and I gritted my teeth, determined to rise above it. I stole a glance at Evie. She and Aveda were fully absorbed in the unicorn fracas.

"All right, Pancake," I murmured to the pup. "Big Sis isn't gonna like this, but I gotta do it. Hold on tight and don't even think about trying to go rogue and throw your tiny self at these porcelain beasts."

I tightened my grip on Pancake, gathered every drop of strength and mental fortitude I could muster, and launched myself into the battlefield of unicorns. I danced around a parade of miniatures charging the bottom shelf of Cozy Mysteries, kicked aside a green-and-gold glass model jumping toward the cash register, and dodged out of the way of a life-sized horse monster galloping around the pink couch.

Aveda was in front of the massive Queen Mother unicorn, delivering kick after powerful kick to its back legs.

"Go! Down! You! Asshole!" she snarled.

I sped past her, keeping an eye on the blurry spot in the back of the store, trying not to get overwhelmed by the roaring in my ears. I made a quick detour to the bathroom, cracking the door open and plopping Pancake down on the floor. He whined inquisitively.

"Stay here, buddy," I said, scratching him behind the ears. "Stay here and don't come out until someone who is *not* a murderous porcelain unicorn comes and gets you. I love your mom, and I love you, and I really can't bear the thought of anything hurting either of you." Pancake sat back on his haunches and gazed up at me like he got it. I stood, carefully shut the bathroom door behind me, and turned to face that telltale blurry spot in the air. The roaring in my ears was still there, but it was such a constant presence at this point, I was used to it.

I glanced back at Evie, still sending out streams of fireballs at the unicorn army, her brow furrowed in concentration. I felt a stab of regret. I didn't want to hurt her, to disappoint her, any more than I already had.

We'd work it out when I returned from the Otherworld with Mom. We'd have a big family hug and she'd realize everything I'd been doing was for a reason.

I forced myself to turn away from her, screwed up all my courage, and ran toward that blurry spot in the air. Then I closed my eyes and jumped.

This time, I didn't fall into darkness and land on mysterious velvety ground. Instead I found myself plopped down in a grassy field, a vast expanse of blue sky above me. I sat up slowly, anticipating the heavy press of the atmosphere around me. But that wasn't there, either. It felt like I was just in the real world, surrounded by a bunch of mundane nature and shit. I heard rustling and turned toward the sound.

I saw long, curly dark hair. Bright green eyes. An even brighter smile. And then I heard that voice, the voice that sounded like music, the voice I'd craved so badly for the last decade of my life.

"Oh, Bug," my mother said. "You finally found me."

CHAPTER TWENTY-THREE

TEARS SPRANG TO my eyes. I couldn't believe I was staring up at her. That I was hearing that musical voice out loud instead of trying to conjure it up from cobbled-together fragments of memory. That she was actually *here*.

Yes, I'd held out hope this entire time that I'd find her. I'd been steadfast in that—stubborn, even. But to actually see her standing in front of me . . .

I opened my mouth, tried to say something, and could only manage the most pathetic of tiny whimpers. I sounded like Pancake being denied food. And as the tears broke free and started to stream down my face, I realized something: In the most secret part of my sub-conscious, I'd doubted my own hope. I'd wanted so badly to find her, but deep down, I'd wondered if Evie was right. If my hope was as foolish as it had been so many other times.

"Bug." Mom held out her arms. "Come here."

I scrambled to my feet. The tears were streaming freely down my cheeks now, blurring everything around me. But I managed to stumble forward into her arms. I slumped against her, deflating completely. It was like all the tension, all the sadness, all the pain of the last two weeks—hell, the last ten years—left my body. In her arms, I could remember everything about her, all the vibrant detail I'd lost the longer she'd been gone; the gentleness of her hands stroking my hair, her light scent of cinnamon mixed with magnolia. I could have just stayed there, being soothed, forever. It felt like coming home.

"Bug," she said, pulling back and putting her hands on my shoulders. "Let me look at you." She smiled at me warmly, her green eyes—the eyes Evie always said were so much like mine—sparkling. She was wearing an outfit I vaguely remembered, one of those hippie-dippie maxi-dresses with bell sleeves she'd loved so much. This one had a tiny daisy print. "You've gotten so beautiful. And look at this hair, like a mermaid's. It's so *you*." She laughed in wonder.

"Mom," I choked out, trying to get my bearings. I needed to get my shit together for two seconds so we could get her out of here. "I have to figure out how to get back," I continued, my words spilling out in a rush. "I mean, before it was automatic, I just hear that plane noise again, and then I get dumped back to where I came from, but I'm not sure how to take someone else with me. Do you know?"

A shadow passed over her face. "It's going to take some doing, my darling. I'll explain in a moment. First, please tell me how you are. How Evie is. I want to know everything." She clasped my hands in hers and beamed.

"We're good, Mom," I said. I was still trying and failing to get a handle on the chaotic mass of emotions crashing through me. Every nerve in my body felt like it was standing at attention, like the world around me was turned up way too loud. "I mean, mostly." It didn't really seem like the time or place to get into Evie's and my dysfunctional dynamic. "Evie's a badass superheroine, and she protects San Francisco from demons, and there are even comic books based on her adventures and stuff. And she fell in love and married the most amazing guy. He seems kind of grumpy and dour at first, but he's actually the kindest, most patient person, and he loves her *so* much. And I'm . . . um . . . ." I swallowed hard. What could I say that wouldn't make me sound like a total loser? I'm a currently-on-probation part-time superhero and directionless bookstore lackey who's in a fight with one of her best friends and sleeping with the other one? I've never, ever figured out how to not be a total disappointment to the one other remaining member of our fractured family?

"Oh, Bug," my mother said, reaching up to brush tears from my cheek. "You're in so much turmoil. I can see it written all over your face. You know, while I've been trapped here, I've been able to see snippets of your life. I know you're *trying* so hard. And you have nothing to be ashamed of."

"Th-thank you," I whispered, my voice shaky.

"I can't believe I've missed so much," she said, shaking her head. "Kathy's been catching me up. Is it true that your father—"

"Wait a minute, *what*?" I interrupted. "Oh, and, uh, yes, Mom, Dad's a total deadbeat, sorry. But more importantly: Kathy's *evil*! She tried to mind battle with me at the Market and I'm pretty sure she's the one who trapped you here—"

"Oh, no, Bug," Mom said, her brows drawing together. "Kathy's a true friend. She's been trying to help me get *out*."

I frowned. "Are you sure?"

"Of course I'm sure," my mother said, smiling.

"B-but she's trapped other people here, too," I said. "This guy who owned a pretzel stand—"

"I'm afraid you've misunderstood. Or more accurately, you've been misled." She frowned, getting that steely look Evie was always talking about—the Tanaka Glare. But it wasn't aimed at me; it seemed to be directed at whoever had been doing all this misleading. "Those people in the other dimension are dark forces, trying to imprison more people as I've been imprisoned all these years. Kathy's been trying to stop them. But they will try to trick you, Bug—you can't listen to anything they say."

I took a deep breath, trying to make sense of what she was saying. "What do you mean 'other dimension'? How many demon prison dimensions are there? And if Kathy's on the side of good, why has she been trying to block me at every turn? I mean, she basically punched me with her mind—"

"Bug." My mom took my hands in hers and gave me a gentle smile. "Slow down, love." Tears pricked my eyes again. Being able to touch her and talk to her and see her smile at me the way she had when I was little—it was all so sweet and fresh and novel. Even though I was confused, even though we were chatting in her demon dimension prison cell, I felt soothed. Like that wild, unruly piece of me, always looking for the next exciting distraction, was finally calm. Serene, even. For once, I wasn't looking for anything other than what was right in front of me. That missing piece had finally snapped into place. I felt *whole*.

"I'll explain everything when I can," Mom said, squeezing my hands. "I promise. But for now, I need you to help me get out of here. We need to stop the dark forces from imprisoning all of San Francisco here in the Otherworld. They have almost everything they need. If I don't get out soon—"

"Tell me how." I tried to rally my focus around that single question, brushing aside the million other queries I had.

"In order for me to be free, we need to trap one more dark force in the prison dimension—the place where you encountered those souls who would mislead you—"

"Hold on," I said, unable to help myself. "Back to my first question: how many freakin' demon prison dimensions are there?"

"This place is part of that dimension as well," my mother said, gesturing around her. "The Otherworld's prison dimension is sectioned off in ways I do not completely understand."

"You definitely got the nicer digs," I said, scanning the idyllic golden field. "Okay, so one more dark force: how do I find it?"

"It will be housed in the body of a seemingly regular human—but that person is rotten down to their very core," Mom said. "You'll know who it is, my darling. You'll *feel* it. And when you find them, take their hand. Compel them to go with you. The rest will come."

"I need more than that—"

"You don't," she said, smiling. "Trust your gut, Bug. I do."

Warmth washed over me again, and that lovely, soothed feeling pulsed in my chest.

"I've missed you so much," I said, tears filling my eyes again. "I've felt so lost, and I've done so many things wrong and . . ."

"And now we can make everything right," she said. She smoothed my hair away from my face.

"Mom—" My voice caught, and a sob clogged my throat. There was so much I wanted to say to her, so much I wanted to—

But before I could finish that thought, the roaring was in my ears again, and I was falling through the air screaming for my mother, and then I was falling on my ass in the middle of It's Lit, the real world coming back into harsh focus around me.

"*No!* Goddammit, no!" I screamed. I clawed wildly at the air, my eyes scanning the room, desperately trying to find that telltale blur. I *needed* to get back there. I needed to talk to Mom some more, I needed—

"Bea!" Evie was at my side, her hand on my shoulder. "Are you okay? God, what happened? Why did you jump into the Otherworld *again*? Why—"

"I found Mom," I choked out. "I found her, and now I have to get her back. And once I do that . . . everyone in San Francisco will be safe. From being trapped like she is."

I looked around again, Evie's incessant barrage of questions fading to a burble as I took stock of the scene. The unicorns were gone—or at least the ones that were still there had turned back into harmless porcelain. The shop was wrecked, busted furniture and books and other detritus tossed everywhere. The barricade had been raised, and Aveda was moving amongst the distressed Art Jam customers, making sure they were okay. Leah was huddled on the somehow still intact pink velvet couch, cuddling Pancake in her arms.

That part of me that had felt so soothed and comforted and *right* while I was talking to Mom had shattered. I was twelve years old again, in that hospital waiting room, and Evie was grasping my shoulders, and I was screaming, and my entire world was falling apart. I couldn't believe Mom had finally been right in front of me, only to be ripped away in an instant. I had to get her back. I had to save the city.

And she'd told me how.

I scrambled to my feet, still ignoring Evie's insistence that I tell her what was going on.

You'll know who it is, my darling. You'll feel it.

I whipped back and forth, scanning the room. I needed someone rotten, someone who had done bad things, a dark force . . .

My eyes landed on the pink couch again, on Leah snuggling Pancake to her chest, murmuring words of comfort in his ear. And on the figure who was now sitting next to her, putting a hand on her shoulder: a beige, blah, thoroughly annoying figure who was moving in on my best friend and was going to hurt her like she'd hurt me . . .

It was as if the rest of the room fell away. My vision narrowed as I shook Evie off and strode forward. Everything around me was nothing more than an inconsequential burble, drowned out by that shattered part inside of me, that part that felt like it would never, ever heal.

I reached the couch and held out my hand to my nemesis, Nicole Yamamoto.

When you find them, take their hand. Compel them to go with you. The rest will come.

I'll come with you, I thought at her. *Wherever you want to go.*

"Bebe?" Leah said, but she was lost in the burble, in the pain screaming through my soul.

Nicole turned to me. "I'll come with you," she said, her eyes glazing over. "Wherever you want to go."

As soon as her hand clasped mine, the familiar roaring, that plane landing sound, rose up in my ears and I saw that blurry haze appear in front of me. A stab of triumph pierced my pain. *Yes.* This was it.

Nicole stood, and I dragged her behind me, focused on the portal. Mom had said to trust my gut and that's what I'd done. Now I was going to free her from a fucking demon prison and protect everyone else in the city, and finally I'd have accomplished what I was always meant to do—

"Bebe."

Leah stepped in front of me, Pancake clutched under her arm. Her presence disrupted the about-to-be triumph I was so firmly focused on and forced my mind to hear something other than the pain and determination overwhelming me.

"Lee," I hissed, my grip tightening on Nicole's hand. "Get out of my way."

"No," she said, planting a hand on one hip and shifting Pancake so he was propped on the other.

"You don't even know what I'm doing," I growled. "Look, I'll explain later—"

"You're mind-controlling Nikki and . . . and trying to take her somewhere. I don't know the rest of it exactly, but it has something to do with the Otherworld."

"What . . ." I shook my head, not wanting to admit how close to right she was. "Since when is it *Nikki*?!" She just stared back at me, unwavering. "Look," I continued. "I can't tell you everything right now, but she has some kind of 'dark spirit' thing going on. Mom told me I'd feel it in my gut, and I absolutely one-hundred percent fucking feel it—and that means, yes, I have to take her to the Otherworld, trap her there so she can't hurt anyone. She's not a good person. She *will* hurt you, Lee, and I can't bear that. You deserve so much more than that, someone who will care for you deeply, someone who won't stomp all over your heart the first chance she gets. And anyway, this has to happen so the entire city won't be imprisoned the way Mom is. You have to trust me that this is for the greater good all around. This is part of my *code*—"

"No, it's not," Leah roared, her eyes flashing. Pancake barked in affirmation. "Honestly, Bebe, your code is *fucked* right now. You've been pushing the boundaries of what you *know* is right ever since your powers started expanding or growing or whatever it is they've been doing. You want your mother back so badly, you want to prove yourself as a hero so you won't feel so broken, and it's blinded you to what's right and what's wrong. If you trap Nikki in the fucking Otherworld, you'll have *crossed* every boundary." She stepped forward and put a hand on my arm. "You say you care about me not being hurt. I care about you not being hurt, too."

"Then get out of my way," I said. "Because I'm hurting now more than I've ever hurt before. And this—" I gestured to Nicole, who gazed at me with glassy eyes. "—will fix it. It will fix everything."

"No." Leah squeezed my arm. "You'll be sacrificing someone innocent. You say it's to save all of San Francisco, but it's actually just for you."

I shook my head vehemently. "It *is* to save people. My mother told me this is the only way."

"Your mother's wrong," Leah pressed. "And if you do this, you'll hurt forever. You'll never come back from it. I *know* you."

Tears pricked my eyes and I tried to retort, but the words clogged in my throat. *Push her aside,* a vicious little part of my brain hissed. *She'll understand later, just get this done. Get it fucking done and everything will be better.*

I squared my shoulders, tightened my grip on Nicole's hand, and shook Leah off. Then I charged forward, shoving her to the side as gently as I could manage, my eyes glued to the blurry spot in front of me. My body tensed as I geared up to make the leap, to pull Nicole with me, to finally free my mother once and for all—

I leaped through the air.

"No!" I heard Leah scream. Pancake barked, loud and urgent, and I heard him scrabbling around on the floor. My body jerked mid-air, distracted by the sound. It was enough to fuck up my grand leap. I landed unceremoniously on my ass, Nicole falling into a tangled pile with me.

"What?!" I yelped. I scanned the air wildly. The blurry spot was gone. My opening was gone. My way back to my mother was *gone.*

"Bea." Evie spun me around, her hands on my shoulders, her eyes wide with confusion. "What the hell is going on? What are you doing?"

I was vaguely aware of Leah helping Nicole up behind me, asking if she was okay.

"I need to get Mom," I said, my eyes still scanning the air. Where was that damn blurry spot? "I need to . . ."

"I think you need to explain some things to me first," Evie said, her grip tightening on my shoulders.

"No," I said, shaking her off. I glowered at her. "I'll figure this out myself. I'll save her—and this whole damn city—myself."

"You're not going anywhere," Evie said. Her face had gone from pale to flushed to uncomfortably mottled. Anger sparked in her eyes. "You need to stop throwing whatever tantrum you're throwing, and *tell me* what's going on."

"Evie!" Aveda strode up to us. Her face was concerned and her voice was smooth and placating. "Let's all just calm down for a minute. Maybe go back to HQ? Then we can have a nice, civilized discussion—"

"No," Evie snapped. "Just . . . don't, Annie. Nate's trying to manage me enough right now, I don't need it from you, too."

"We're both worried about you," Aveda said, laying a hand on her arm. "The doctor said you have to watch your blood pressure, both for your sake and for—"

"Doctor?" I interrupted. "What is she talking about, Evie? Are you sick?"

Evie shot Aveda a warning look. A *shut up* look. A look that made me realize exactly what was going on. It was one of those realizations that dawns in a slow, queasy-making way, then speeds up until it's a rollercoaster of images smashing together, things that suddenly make so much more sense when you figure out they're part of the same puzzle.

Evie complaining about "not feeling well" so many times the past few weeks, pushing away her dinner and turning green.

Evie propped up on my pillows when we were doing Mom research, her eyes fluttering closed, barely able to stay awake.

Evie grumbling at Nate while he fussed over her, trying to get her to eat something.

Evie being mysteriously absent from missions, Aveda making weird excuses for her.

Evie actually listening when Aveda barked at her to stay out of the battle fray.

"You're pregnant," I said.

She didn't have to say it out loud. Her face told me everything I needed to know.

"Bea," she began. "I was going to tell you, I just—"

"No," I said, shaking my head. "Don't explain. Don't . . . do anything."

The pain that had been screaming through me quieted to something dull and sickly and sad. My gaze wandered over the room. I saw Leah comforting a dazed-looking Nicole. Aveda stepping forward to comfort Evie—Evie, who felt like she couldn't share some of the biggest news of her life with me. And no sign of a portal, no way to get Mom back, no way out. I was just standing here in the bookstore, like I'd done so many times before. Being useless. Everyone looking at me like the big fucking disappointment I was.

All of my emotions drained away, like I was deflating on the spot. I felt so *empty*. For once, I couldn't even summon a scrap of hope. There was just *nothing*.

I pushed past Evie and ran.

CHAPTER TWENTY-FOUR

I RAN TO the one person I was pretty sure I hadn't disappointed yet.

"Bea," Sam said, opening his apartment door and rubbing sleep from his eyes.

"Sorry, were you asleep?" I blurted out, stepping inside. "I mean, of course you were, it's the middle of the night."

"What's wrong?" he said, his brows drawing together as he reached over to cup my face.

"I . . ." So many emotions were crashing through me, and I couldn't get a handle on any of them. All I knew was that there was a deep, dull throb of hopelessness underneath it all. "I saw my mom," I finally managed. "Also, Evie's pregnant and didn't tell me—because no matter what happens between us, I'm always her disappointment of a little sister who can never be trusted. And Leah is into one of the most awful people ever and stopped me from going back to the Otherworld, which would have let me fix everything. But now I can't fix *anything* and everyone hates me and I'll never be anything more than this . . . this sad person. This sad, broken, *nothing* person—"

He wrapped his arms around me and pulled me close.

I didn't cry. I felt too hopeless even for that. But I held on tight, his warmth enveloping me and making me feel some version of safe. I expected him to start bombarding me with questions about everything I'd just spilled, but he just kept surrounding me with that warmth, his hands stroking through my hair and down my back.

"Oh, sweetheart," he said softly. "That's so much."

For some reason, *that* made tears spring to my eyes. I turned my face up to his. His eyes searched mine, and I saw no trace of smug, of *beaucoup fromage*. He just looked like he was trying to figure out some way, *any* way, to heal me. Before I would have taken that as pity, would have pushed him away and challenged him to . . . I don't know, a math duel or something. Now I took it as confirmation of something I'd absorbed about him these past couple weeks: that his empathy ran deeper than anyone gave him credit for, that he was stronger than anyone knew. That I'd underestimated him the way so many people underestimated me.

I kissed him. He made that surprised growl in the back of his throat, the one that got under my skin and set all of my nerve endings on fire. Then he pulled me closer, his hands tangling in my hair, his tongue sliding over mine. He was clad only in boxers, which he must have thrown on hastily before answering the door, and I reveled in pressing against so much of his delicious bare skin. I ran my hands over his chest, thrilling in the goosebumps appearing beneath my fingertips.

"Bea," he said breathlessly, breaking the kiss. He cupped my face and stroked a thumb down my cheek, his eyes full of a million questions. "Do you need to talk or do you want me to go with you back to HQ so you can talk to Evie or . . . just tell me what you need."

I leaned into his palm, luxuriating in his touch and the warmth surrounding me. "I need to feel . . . this." I gestured between us and pressed a hand to his chest. "*Just* this. Just for a little while. Please."

He didn't ask any more questions. Just pulled me into another kiss that made my head spin. I pushed him back toward the couch and he sat down, pulling me with him. I straddled him at the waist, my hands stroking his chest, his arms, his broad, gorgeous shoulders. He slid the strap of my dress down my shoulder and nibbled at my collarbone. As usual he took his time, tasted every inch of my skin. Then he moved lower, stroking the lace of my bra out of the way with his thumb so he could slip my nipple into his mouth.

I shivered, losing myself in the sensation. The wet heat of his tongue, the pure beauty of his mouth bringing me so much pleasure. I loved the way he always looked like he *relished* tasting me, like he couldn't get enough. Like it was his favorite thing in the whole goddamn world.

I trailed my fingertips down his chest, skimmed over his abs, and then reached lower to free him of his boxers. He stroked my thighs, pushing my skirt up, every touch making my blood fizz with pleasure. We managed to find a condom in the side table next to the couch. I helped him get my panties off, and then I was rolling the condom on and guiding myself onto him, my hands on his shoulders. He gripped my hip and thrust upward, and we both gasped, our eyes meeting.

"Bea," he said, holding himself there.

"Sam," I whispered back.

I realized then that we were in the same position we'd been in that night we'd first kissed: on the couch, me straddling him, our eyes locked. That night, we'd said each other's names like we'd both just made a huge mistake. But tonight was different. And as we started to move, as he gazed at me with a wonder that brought tears to my eyes again, I figured out why.

I'd broken the one promise I'd made. The promise to never fall in love with him.

Just another thing I'd managed to totally fuck up.

🔥

Afterward, we lay in a tangle on the couch. Sam pulled a fuzzy blanket cocoon around us and fell asleep, his arm locked around me. I rested my head on his chest, listening to his heartbeat.

"Sam," I whispered after a while. "Are you awake?"

His breathing remained deep and even.

"Okay, good," I said. "I need to tell you something, and I

can only tell you if you're asleep." I closed my eyes and made my voice even softer. "I love you. I don't know how it happened. I totally broke that promise I made, and it's almost like you knew I was going to break it, like you knew . . ." My voice faltered, and I squeezed my eyes shut more tightly, trying to hold back tears. ". . . you knew there was no way I could get bored with you. That I'd only want *more* of you. There's so much to you under all that swag. You're so passionate about the things you care about. More sensitive than people think you are. You make me feel so . . . seen. Beautiful. *Treasured.* And you make me feel like I actually deserve for someone to see me that way." I opened my eyes and let the tears trickle down my cheeks. "That day at the bookstore, when you so clearly *saw* how scared I am of being abandoned . . . I think one of the reasons I always conveniently 'get bored' with the people I date is . . . deep down, I'm afraid they'll leave me. So I leave first—and the truth is, it's not always as drama-free as I like to say it is. That's just another lie I tell myself so I don't have to deal with feelings—theirs or mine. And I usually manage to leave before I get to know them *too* well. But with you, it's like we said. I already knew you. I never stood a chance." I swiped away the tears and swallowed hard. "I can't bear to tell you all of this and then have you try to make me feel better by pretending you feel the same way. That's what I think you'd do. And that's worse than pity." I pressed my face against his neck. "I love you," I whispered again. "Bea: Zero, Sam: Infinity. You win this ridiculous battle we've been having forever."

His breathing remained deep as I disentangled myself, tucked the blanket more snugly around him, and got dressed. He didn't even stir as I let myself out. It was still the middle of the night, and I caught the all-night bus home. No one was awake when I crept into HQ, and I made it to my room without incident. So there was one whole thing that had gone right in the last twenty-four hours.

I fell onto my bed and stared at Leah's painting on my wall, that wild, beautiful mermaid. Leah probably hated me.

And I couldn't really blame her. Nicole was awful, she was my nemesis, but was she really a "dark force"? Had I really felt that, or had I just convinced myself it could be true because I wanted my mother back so badly?

My gaze fell on my bedside table and a sparkly, purple folder caught my eye. Oh, right: the report Nate had asked me to look at the night Evie and I had our most recent fight. It was another meticulously documented interview by Nate's friend Kai with the most recent near-drowning victim: the third person who had no memory of how they'd ended up in the water. I'd read it the day after Nate had given it to me, but hadn't really picked up on anything new. And I'd exchanged a few emails with Kai discussing the incidents, but that had kind of been the end of it.

For some reason, I found myself opening the folder, paging through, skimming the document again. This particular survivor's account was vivid, harrowing. I'd been transfixed when I'd read it the first time, and I was just as transfixed now. I read through the whole thing again.

And then, as I reached the end, I gasped out loud.

Oh, fucking frakballs. How had I not seen it before?

I set the report aside and grabbed a notebook and pen from my bedside table. I started to scribble, my mind working overtime. Finally, the pieces were starting to come together. And the picture they were painting was more fucked up than I could have imagined.

TRANSCRIPT

Interview with Carmelo Cruz
Conducted by: Dr. Kai Alana

This interview is part of an investigative study of the recent near drownings in Makena Beach State Park. Mr. Cruz is the third individual to report an incident of this kind; he was rescued by an off-duty lifeguard out for a morning run and sustained no severe injuries.

DR. KAI ALANA: Can you tell me what you remember from right before the incident? What were you doing?

CARMELO CRUZ: I was walking on the beach, picking up seashells. I found a few of those long, twisty ones; a bunch of clamshells; and a few broken sand dollars. But I left those, because I have a shit-ton of sand dollars already.

KA: Is this something you do often?

CC: Yeah, I got a pretty sweet seashell collection, if I do say so myself. And I do. [laughs] I'm training to be a professional wrestler, and I want to have, like, a *thing*, you know? A trademark. I thought maybe it could be seashells.

KA: Like you'd make a costume out of seashells or . . . ?

CC: Nah, girl, how uncomfortable would that be? I mean I'd just be known as, like, the wrestler who collects seashells.

KA: Oh, uh, okay. Cool! So you were leaving behind the sand dollars and . . . ?

CC: Yeah, and then I stood at the edge of the shore for a minute, looking out at the water.

KA: Contemplating your day ahead, that sort of thing?

CC: I was actually imagining how that pose and scenery would look in my official publicity shots. Gotta start practicing that shit *now* so I'll be ready when the time comes, ya know?

KA: Totally! And how did you go from practicing PR photo poses to—

CC: Being in the water, screaming my dumb head off? Well, Doc, at first I didn't remember at all, it was just this big, blurry gap. But then I sat down and really tried to recreate my mental steps, ya know? And I do remember this: I was thinking about wrestling. I mean, I'm always thinking about wrestling to some degree.

KA: It's your passion, sounds like.

CC: Definitely. But that day, I was specifically thinking: What if it doesn't work out? What if I'm never good enough to go pro, what if I never get my shot? I had a bad practice the other day, like, *really* bad. There's this guy I spar with, he calls himself the Teriyaki Terror, because— You know what, it's not important. What is important is that he kicked my ass. And it made me wonder what would happen if I never made it. I mean, I don't really have a back-up plan.

KA: There's nothing else you want to do? Nothing else you love?

CC: Eh. Not really. I mean, I love eating loco moco, but I don't know if there's a career in that, really? You like loco moco, Doc?

KA: Love it.

CC: Try Okazuya and Deli, best loco moco ever. Anyway, I was thinking about this really hard, and then all of a sudden . . . This is gonna sound really ridiculous, Doc.

KA: It's okay. Don't be afraid to say it, this is a safe space. And since demonology is my area of study, ridiculous is my business.

CC: Hey, that's catchy! You should get it on a business card.

KA: I did, actually. Most people didn't find it very amusing.

CC: Aw, man, I would have given you mad props for that, Doc, I think it's hilarious. Anyway, I've tried to remember this moment over and over again, and it's still kind of hazy, but I swear the ocean was, like, whispering to me, Doc. Telling me that if I walked into the waves, I'd be guaranteed success as a wrestler. I'd achieve that dream no matter what.

KA: So you got a sense this voice was coming from the ocean. Was there any other source you could see?

CC: Nah.

KA: And was it saying these exact words to you or . . . ?

CC: It was more like this overwhelming feeling. Like all of a sudden I was convinced that if I walked into the water, I'd get the thing I wanted most in the world.

KA: That must have been very powerful.

CC: It was. It took over my brain. There wasn't room for anything else. And it was like . . . like it was also telling me I was *special*, Doc. This force, whatever it was, focused on *me*. Let me know those other wrestlers weren't important. I don't feel important very much, Doc. But in that moment, I felt like whatever was happening was all about me. I was the center of the universe. It was *awesome*. And the next thing I know, I'm floundering around in the waves, yelling for help. That part wasn't so awesome.

KA: Have you had any reoccurrences of this, felt the same message from any other sources?

CC: Nah. I've been back to that beach a few times, too—nothing.

KA: Really? You went back to that beach? Even after your experience?

CC: Well, yeah, Doc. We gotta live, don't we? And nobody ever lived a full life staying home, avoiding everything that scared 'em. I mean, I did invest in swimming lessons, though.

KA: Sounds like a wise choice.

CC: I've gotten so many more seashells for my collection. I'm thinking my pro wrestler name's gonna be The Shellinator. What do you think?

KA: I like that very much.

CHAPTER TWENTY-FIVE

I KNEW WHAT I had to do. Well, sort of.

I still didn't have all the pieces yet. But I had enough of an idea of what was *maybe* going on and what *might* work. Considering that I'd pretty much torpedoed my entire life, I had nothing left to lose by putting stock in mights and maybes. If I could save some innocent Bay Areans from being imprisoned in a shitty pocket prison dimension of the Otherworld . . . well, my life would still be torpedoed and I'd probably never be a true superhero, but at least I'd have accomplished *something*.

In a weird way, my loss of hope was freeing. From this point on, anything even remotely positive would be a nice surprise.

I didn't know if what Carmelo Cruz—aspiring pro wrestler and loco moco fan—had experienced was directly connected to what was happening here. But his words brought some things home for me, things my brain had been dancing around this whole time. For one, humans will do just about *anything* to get what they want. Even if it doesn't make sense, even it's dangerous, even if it fucks up other people. I don't know how I could have entrusted my hope to a species as broken as we are.

And as for the rest . . . well, I'd just have to try my latest experiment and see if I was right.

It was early morning when I slipped out of HQ, the sun slivering its way through the marine layer. I burrowed into the folds of my woolly cardigan and caught the bus to It's Lit.

It was way too early for the store to be open yet, so I let myself in, disabled the alarm, and surveyed the scene. It looked like things had been mostly cleaned up after I'd left. The remnants of broken furniture were piled in a corner, books had been arranged for re-shelving in haphazard stacks on the floor, and there were a few paint splotches on the walls. And of course the porcelain unicorns were lurking in all kinds of random places, although they appeared to have reconstituted themselves and gone back to being inanimate. Being surrounded by them now made me shudder. I felt like their beady little eyes were staring at me from every angle.

I stood in the middle of the store, put my hands on my hips, and addressed the empty air.

"Okay, listen," I said, making my voice firm and clear. "I don't know *exactly* how it works, but here's what I think I know. One of you Otherworld assholes figured out how to access certain locations in San Francisco through humans connected to said locations. You got the Wave Organ through Poet, you got the Market through Kathy, and you got the hospital through Bernard. You gave them a version of my power so they could mind-control people and get whatever they wanted most in life: high school popularity, or be rid of a nemesis, or more alone time with a beloved collection of writing implements. And that power also helped them lure other humans into your freaky demon prison dimension—because you need some kind of human sacrifices in order to solidify your connection to these locations and truly weaponize them."

I waited, thinking maybe I'd actually get a response. I didn't, so I kept going.

"They all took you up on your offer," I continued. "Because some humans will do *anything* to get whatever their dearest dream is. I almost did. And that brings me to the other major piece of this that I think I've figured out: For whatever reason, this grand demon plan . . ." I paused. Was I really going to say this next part out loud? I pushed doubt aside and bulldozed on. "This grand demon plan was all about *me*."

I waited again for a response. Still nothing.

"Look at the people you targeted," I said. "Kathy, my mother's old friend. Bernard, who worked at the hospital where she died. And Poet, a girl who reminded me of . . . well, me. When I was younger. You gave them a version of *my* power. You played on all my insecurities. And you put out clues that would send me on a wild fucking goose chase, because you knew I wouldn't be able to resist the chance to get what *I* want most in life: my mother."

My voice wobbled. I straightened my spine, determined to stay strong. "I don't know if that's really my mother that's been talking to me. I was *so sure* it was. But now I'm not sure of anything. I don't know if you want me because I can give you access to It's Lit—if the bookstore is some kind of key in taking over San Francisco. I don't know if you want me because of my power or . . . or if you're just making me feel special because you know I'm extra susceptible to that. I mean. I almost banished Nicole Yamamoto to a demon prison for you. And she may be my nemesis, but she most certainly does not deserve *that*. So I'm standing here, talking to the empty air like a dork, because I want you to let me into the Otherworld and tell me what the *ever-loving fuck* is going on." I drew myself up taller, trying to look fierce. Yes, I still looked like a cartoon character—mermaid hair, goth-y makeup, slip dress/cardigan combo. But I would *not* be underestimated this time. "Let me in. *Now*."

I stood there, trying to maintain my power pose. Silence permeated the room, and I should have felt silly. But after spitting all of that out, I was too pissed off to feel silly. Rage bubbled through my veins, thick and toxic, overwhelming everything else.

"Let . . . me . . . *in*," I hissed. I reached out with my mind, trying to find the brain plane. I felt that bright light again, ran toward it, embraced it. And before I knew quite what was happening, a veil descended over everything and that blurry spot appeared in front of me in the air. I didn't hesitate. I ran toward it and jumped through.

I landed in that huge meadow again, my mother standing over me.

"Oh, Bug," she said, beaming with pride. "I *knew* you'd figure it out. You were always so smart."

"Who are you?" I said, scrambling to my feet. "*What* are you? Because . . ." My voice wobbled again and I struggled like mad to keep it steady. "My mother would *not* manipulate me this way." I'd been afraid to say that out loud, to admit that whatever was standing before me was most definitely not my mother. Because then I would have to admit that yes, my mother—my *real* mother—was actually dead. There was no magical, miraculous resurrection to be had. No warm, fuzzy scenario where she came back to Evie and me and somehow mended our dysfunctional relationship and made everything better. She wasn't going to fix me. None of this had been real. My stupid hope had led me down the most wrong of paths.

"I am your mother," she said, taking a step toward me. I took an instinctive step back. "In all the ways that matter."

"Oh, for fuck's sake," I said, rolling my eyes. "So are you a shapeshifting demon robot or a hologram that has all of her memories or something? Because that's what someone says when they are totally a robot or a hologram with human memories."

"It's more complex than that," she said. She gestured to a small stone bench next to us. "Why don't we sit down and talk?"

"Uh, did you just make that *appear*?" I said. "I don't remember it being there before. Seriously, is this the demon dimension version of the holodeck?"

"Sit next to me," she said, settling herself on the bench.

I crossed my arms over my chest. "No."

"Suit yourself," she said. "I do love that stubbornness. My darling, the first thing you need to know is you were right: this has all been for you."

"Why?" I demanded.

"I wanted to bring you here. To be with me," she said, smiling angelically.

"That . . . *can't* be it," I said. "Let's go back to the beginning. How did you figure out you could access humans in our world—and through them, *locations* in our world—in the first place?"

"It was just as you theorized with your brilliant boot hole analogy," she said, angelic smile in place. "There are places where the walls between your world and mine are rubbed so very thin. One day, I realized I could see through them. And I saw *you*. That's one of my powers—to be able to connect with others' minds that way, though I can't influence them the way you can. But I could see into your brain, access all your memories, hear your every thought and feeling: your astonishing power, your hurt, your longing for me. I knew if I could bring you to me . . . well, I could make you even more amazing. Help you reach your full potential."

"And here I kept hoping for someone to finally see my full potential," I muttered, shaking my head. "Of course this is how it turns out."

"I did so many experiments, trying to reach through the walls and communicate with you," she continued. Her voice still had that musical quality. Now instead of being soothing, it was disconcerting. "But your power made your mind so strong, I could never quite get there. I couldn't get past simply *seeing* your mind. You were always thinking of your mother, your past. I saw a memory you had of Kathy, so I went in search of her." Her smile widened, and I saw a glint of maliciousness in her eyes. "And she was *perfect*—so lonely, so vulnerable. Vivian was her only friend. All she had left in life was that sad little craft stand. And when the pretzel booth went up . . . well, it was so popular, people started passing her right by. She was so afraid the stand would be taken away from her, too. It took me a long time, but her mind was susceptible, and I finally got through to her. I convinced her I could give her everything, if she would just help

me get to you. I helped her remember she had that box of
your mother's letters—"

"Wait." I shook my head. "Were those letters invented
solely for my fake quest here or—"

"They're real," she said, giving me a nod. "Kathy didn't
want to give them to you. They were her treasured mementos
and all she had left of Vivian, even though they rightfully
belong to you and Evie. I convinced her they were the perfect thing to get you started on your journey."

"How did you give her and the others a version of my
power?" I asked. My brain was whirling, trying to piece it all
together.

"Another one of my experiments," she said, beaming.
"Really, we're so alike, you and I. I had a version of your
power perfectly copied and preserved, and once I was able
to connect with Kathy and the others directly, I realized I
could pass it on to them."

"How did you have a version of my power just lying
around?" I sputtered. "And why—"

A shadow passed over her face. "We'll get to that in a bit."

"All right, so you were trying to get to me," I said, reaching for another piece of the puzzle. "Was that . . . I mean,
what are all these voices I've been hearing? Because sometimes they've helped me and sometimes they've done the
opposite, and I'm just so . . . confused."

"The voice you heard when you first went to the Market,
telling you not to buy a pretzel—the one you thought might
be me—was actually Kathy testing the waters, trying to discourage people from partaking of her rival's pretzels. And
the voice at the hospital—"

"Bernard?" I guessed. "Trying to get me to go downstairs
so I could find Mom's file?"

"Which he had already removed pieces of, to pique your
interest," she said, nodding with approval. "And then gave
to Kathy for safekeeping."

"But what about the second voice at the Market?" I said,

trying to make sense of it. "The one that took me to the Ferris wheel? I thought that was Pretzel Guy."

"It was," she said, her eyes darkening. "That was an unexpected complication. The walls between worlds were so thin, he too was able to reach through and communicate with you. He tried to lure you away, to that empty carnival area, hoping Kathy wouldn't notice. But she was so connected to her location by then, she felt it, so she used her connection to—"

"—to make a carnival ride stomp me to death in the between dimension?" I spat out. "If all this was to lure me in, that doesn't seem like the most effective tactic. And you know, Bernard also kind of tried to stop me from getting any information whatsoever."

"Everything we've done that seemed antagonistic was all to lead you down the path, my darling, to lead you *here*. Because I still couldn't reach your mind directly—it was just too strong. I was able to leave you a little note at the bookstore—the writing on the wall, which I copied so perfectly from the letters Kathy was holding on to. I spoke to you through young Poet. And your friend's spell in the bathroom helped me to talk to you briefly." She smiled. "I know you so well. I knew exactly how to hook your curiosity, how to get you to investigate things and push the boundaries of your power—"

"And my power has grown and morphed every time I've visited the Otherworld," I said. "The whole thing where I could suddenly implant direct thoughts in people, *control* them—"

"You can do so much," she said, her voice dreamy. "I suspected, but I didn't know for sure that the Otherworld would enhance your power. You haven't even begun to explore just how much yet. Just look at what you accomplished at the Art Jam—"

"Um, nothing," I said. "I accomplished nothing after Kathy and Co. showed up and made Charlotte's porcelain unicorn collection come to life—"

"No," she said, beaming at me. "They pushed *you* to make

the porcelain unicorn collection come to life. You may recall a bright light, calling for you to embrace it. Because you're the one connected to It's Lit—you're the one who can weaponize this location. You did that. Even though you didn't quite know it."

"Um, *how*?" I said, rolling my eyes. "I haven't given you your precious human sacrifice yet, so technically I shouldn't be able to—"

"Ah, I believe that's your power coming into play again—the wild card," she said, smiling slyly at me. "I had a hunch—if Kathy, Poet, and Bernard pushed you hard enough on the—what did you call it?—the brain plane?"

"Yeah," I muttered.

"So creative," she said. "I thought if they pushed you, it might spark a brief connection, might give you that ability to bring the location to life for a moment. And it did! My experiment worked."

"But back to the part where I didn't know I was doing it," I said, shaking my head. "I mean . . . what the hell was that?"

She shrugged. "Sometimes, the human connected to the location doesn't quite know what they're doing at first—remember how Poet just stood there at the Wave Organ, calling for help? She didn't realize things would get quite so out of control. In any case, in order to make your connection permanent, I needed you to finally open up your own portal at the bookstore and come here." She gestured to the meadow.

"So you set up an entire video game's worth of quests and boss levels for me," I said, trying to follow along. "And I followed along like a little puppy dog, because you knew how to take advantage of every bad habit and/or predilection that's gotten me into trouble before. But why? What happens now that we're at the *ultimate* boss level?"

"Oh, Bug." She stood up and stepped toward me. I recoiled. This Mom-Demon looked and sounded so much like Mom, I had to keep reminding myself it wasn't her. "Being here with me isn't another level to be conquered. It's your reward."

"That is a *messed up* reward, and I don't want it," I snapped. "Back to my original question: who or what are you? Underneath the Mom mask."

She stepped even closer to me and put her hand on my arm. I did my best to stay still, to stare her down, even though I wanted very badly to pull away.

"I am your mother," she said, her green eyes unnerving in their intensity. "I am the closest thing you will ever find to your mother."

"That's not an answer," I hissed.

She studied me, considering. Then dropped her hand from my arm. "I had a daughter before you," she said slowly. "She was like you. In so many ways."

"Wait . . ." A thought swirling around the edge of my brain came into focus. "That parchment we found in Kathy's cabinet—the letter Leah translated. That was—"

"From my daughter to me," she said, her expression turning wistful. "I gave it to Kathy so she could plant it as a clue to lure you. I had a feeling you or your friend would be able to translate it." Her eyes got very sad. "I begged my daughter not to go on that mission to your world. I *forbid* her to be part of Shasta's invasion party. But she wouldn't listen to me. And then—"

"She was killed instantly when she came to Earth," I said. "Along with the rest of the invasion party. And when she died, *I* got her power."

"You *are* my daughter," she said, nodding vehemently. "Don't you see? We both lost the most important person in our lives. And now we have the opportunity to get them back."

"And . . . what?" I said, shaking my head. "We just hang out here in this boring holodeck meadow for the rest of our lives together?"

"Think bigger, Bug," she said, squeezing my arm encouragingly. "You can still give me the dark soul I need so we can control the bookstore. But what you would get in exchange would be so much more. Everything you've ever wanted." She studied me again in that steady, unnerving way that made me squirm. "Explore your mind for a moment. Connect with it."

I didn't want to do anything she told me to, but my curiosity got the better of me. I took a deep breath and took stock of my brain, and I definitely felt more . . . aware. Like what I could feel with my consciousness was bigger and brighter; like I could somehow reach *more* with my mind.

"The more you go back and forth between here and the Otherworld, the more your mind—and your abilities—will expand," she said. "And that means you can finally fix everything, my darling. Everything that's made you so hurt and scared and broken all these years. You can finally be *whole*."

Unexpected tears filled my eyes. That was the desire I'd had so many times, the thing I'd wanted deep in my bones. And I shouldn't believe anything from a Fake Mom demon, but goddammit. Hearing those words out loud from a face that looked so much like my mother's . . . it was too much.

"What do you mean?" I said, my voice shaking.

"You'll be able to do anything with your mind," she said, beaming like she was super proud of me. "You can mend things with Evie. Be the sisters-in-arms you were always meant to be, caring for each other and fighting alongside each other as a formidable superhero team. Heal the wounds she's carried for so long."

"Make it so she doesn't hurt anymore. Or that she *gets* to hurt if that's what she wants," I murmured, remembering the pain in Evie's eyes when she'd told me she hadn't gotten to be sad when Mom died.

"Yes," she said, her eyes flashing. "You can help her so much. She'll finally feel like she can confide in you, like she can share everything with you. And it won't end with Evie. You can help *everyone* you love. You can get Leah her perfect soulmate, someone truly worthy of her. You can make Sam see that he should care for you as you care for him, that his life will be so much fuller that way. And *you*, my darling . . . you'll finally be as amazing you were always meant to be. A superheroine for the ages."

She waved a hand and the scenery in front of us turned into something that looked like glass, like we were gazing through a clear pane. But there was nothing on the other side.

"Whoa," I said, taking a step back.

"Do not worry, it's stable," she said. "I just want to remind you of something." She waved a hand again and the It's Lit bathroom appeared in front of us. It was like we were seeing the bathroom on some kind of gigantic, all-encompassing TV screen. We were in front of the craft wall containing people's musings and art—and the message I'd written what felt like eons ago.

I never want to be normal
I want to live an extraordinary life
I want fabulous adventures, fabulous food, and fabulous sex
I will be the greatest superhero of all time
Just you wait

"You can have all of this," Mom-Demon said. "Agree to join me, and you'll have *everything*."

"B-but what's in it for you?" I said, my eyes glued to those words I'd written, reading them over and over again. "I mean, besides getting a version of your daughter back. You get access to It's Lit and—what? You then have access to a bunch of Bay Area locations and can make them attack civilians as you please? Because that isn't really something I'm into. In case that wasn't clear."

"No, my darling," she said. "I told you: all of that was just to get you here. To get you to *me*. All I want is for us to be together. For both of us to feel whole again. Once I have access to a fourth Earthly location and imprison a fourth dark human soul, I'll be able to cross over. That part of what I told you is true. We can be in both your realm and mine. You and Evie will have your mother back. And your powers will grow greater than you ever imagined. They are already so great—greater than mine. Greater than my daughter who perished. You can do anything. Make your life whatever you want. Make the *world* whatever you want." She put a hand on my shoulder, leaning in close. That cinnamon-magnolia scent, the one that brought back so many childhood memories, swirled around me, and I felt dizzy.

Everything she was saying . . . I couldn't deny it was tempting, that it poked at a part of me longing to feel soothed and complete. The part that wanted to make things right for the people I loved. That wanted . . . so many things.

"I just need to agree to this?" I didn't even try to keep my voice from shaking. "That's really it?"

"I still need that dark soul of your choosing," she said in my ear. "Just one person, someone who's rotten to the core. All for the good of the world. For the good of everyone else."

I swallowed hard, jolting back to reality a bit. Could I really do that? Lead someone to a lifetime in a demon pocket prison? Even someone as shitty as Nicole?

But wasn't it all for the greater good? To make the world better? To be able to use my mind to heal so many? I really would be the greatest superhero of all time.

Maybe I could send over one of Sam's jerky siblings? They were both pretty rotten.

"Bug," my mother's voice said in my ear. She waved a hand again and the bathroom dissolved into another familiar setting. Now we were looking at the central area of It's Lit. Leah was sitting on the pink couch, clutching Pancake. Sam was sitting next to her, rubbing her back and looking a million miles away. Evie, Aveda, Nate, Scott, Lucy, Rose, and Shruti appeared to be searching the store, poking around every nook and cranny.

"I don't understand," Nate said. "My 'find this person's phone' function said she was here."

"She jumped into the freakin' Otherworld again, obviously," Aveda said, rolling her eyes. "Kind of the ultimate tantrum, no?"

"As if you've never been prone to stomping off and sulking when things don't go your way, darling," Lucy said, arching an eyebrow at her. "You do know we used to call that the Aveda Jupiter Tantrum, no?"

"Scott, can you do that spell where you connect with the supernatural energy in the room?" Evie said. Her voice was thin and tired, her face pinched. "Maybe we can try to find her—or wherever this Otherworld entrance is?"

"I can try," he said.

"Is this . . . are we seeing them *now*?" I managed.

"Yes," Mom-Demon said. "They're looking for you."

"Wait." Scott's brow furrowed. "I'm getting something. There is an entrance to the Otherworld here somewhere, but I don't know how to find it. And Bea . . . Bea *is* here. It's like I can sense her presence, lurking around. But she's hidden behind a layer of something, she's kind of flickering in and out, and I can't figure out how to find her exactly. I don't know." He shook his head in frustration.

"Bea!" Evie shrieked into the air. "Please, wherever you are: just come back. *Please*."

"I don't think she can hear you," Scott said.

"I don't care," she snapped, her eyes filling with tears.

"Look at her," Mom-Demon murmured. "All that pain. And you could fix it. You could finally do something for her—after all she's done for you."

I swallowed hard, blinking back my own tears. Evie kept looking around frantically while everyone else watched, helpless.

"Evie," Aveda murmured. "Don't forget your blood pressure . . ."

"Fuck my blood pressure!" she bellowed. "Bea. If you're there, just listen, please. I'm sorry I didn't tell you I'm pregnant. I was . . . I *am* so fucking scared. I don't know if I can do this. In fact, I'm pretty sure I *can't* do this. I . . . I tried so hard to take care of you and make sure you were okay, and I did such a fucking shitty job. Because you're clearly *not* okay. And it's all my fault."

"It's not," I whispered, my tears breaking free and streaming down my cheeks.

"I can't do this without you," Evie said. "I *need* you. Please come back. *Please*, Bea."

She fell to her knees sobbing. She looked like everything had been drained from her. She looked like a used-up husk of a person. She looked like I had ten years ago, when I'd collapsed on the kitchen floor over some peanut butter.

"And now she's lost her hope," Mom-Demon said. "Just as you feel you've lost yours. But think of what you could do for her—for all of them—once your power grows. You can guide their moods, their thoughts, their feelings. Constantly. You can control everything—no more nasty surprises. Look at them . . ." She gestured to the scene in front of us. Evie was still on her knees, sobbing. Nate and Aveda had moved in to comfort her. Scott was looking around, probably trying to figure out his spell. Rose, Lucy, and Shruti were conversing off to the side, their faces creased with frustration. And Leah, Sam, and Pancake were still slumped on the pink couch, staring into space, looking lost. "They're all broken in some way," she said. "You could fix them. You could fix everything. Return right now as the big savior—and with your mother!" She leaned in close, right next to my ear. "You'll finally feel whole, Bug. You'll have everything you want. And because of that, you'll get your hope back."

I studied them for a long time—all these people that I loved. Evie, who carried so much guilt it made her feel like she had no hope of being a decent parent. Sam, who put on a confident show, but secretly believed his siblings when they made him feel like the smallest person in the world. Leah, who put out so much love, but didn't always get it back.

You could fix them. You could fix everything.

I took a long, shaky breath and turned to my Mom-Demon. "Is it true what you said about my powers growing greater than anyone's? I can literally mind-mojo anyone?"

She beamed at me and took my hand. "That's right. And coming here, to my little pocket of the Otherworld—" She gestured to her meadow. "Has made them stronger than they've ever been. You should be at an all-time ultimate peak in your power."

"Okay," I said, nodding and squeezing her hand. "Good."

Then I gathered up everything I was feeling and sent it blasting her way. I'd never projected with so much pure *force* before. I visualized myself overwhelming her mind, surrounding all of her mental safeguards. Giving myself ultimate *control*.

She dropped my hand, confusion crossing her face.

"What . . ." she gasped.

"Here's the thing about hope, Not-So-Mommy Dearest," I said, my voice strained as I battered against her mind. "It's not about mind-controlling everyone so they feel good all the time, it's not about leaving nothing to chance, and it's not about me feeling fixed or whatever." I felt her start to throw up mental brick walls, pummeling against me, and I winced.

"It's about believing that no matter how shitty things get, no matter how much you fuck up, no matter how many times you end up crying on the floor over peanut butter . . ." A sob rose up in my throat and I shoved it down, throwing all of my focus into fighting back against her mental brick walls. "No matter *what*: you believe that you can work to make things better. And I *do* believe that. Because I'm lucky enough to be loved by all these amazing people. I've seen them make things better every fucking chance they get. They're out there every day, trying their hardest—no matter how shitty things get. You thought watching them in this mega-despair moment would make me despair, too. But it didn't. It did the *opposite*, motherfucker."

Mom-Demon backed away from me, glowering, her serene smile a distant memory. The blue sky above us darkened, storm clouds blotting out the sun. I sent the full force of my emotions spinning at her yet again.

"You would give up certainty?" she hissed. "The chance to have the life you've always wanted, to be secure in that knowledge—"

"It wouldn't be real," I said, stepping toward her. The storm clouds above us rumbled and lightning streaked the sky. "Taking that bargain would mean I'm *rejecting* hope—that I don't believe things will actually get better, ever, without some kind of supernatural intervention."

"Maybe they won't," she said, giving me a malicious smile.

"Not to mention," I continued, ignoring her, "that accepting your stupid bargain would mean, oh yeah, I have to *give you another human* and be totes okay with at least four people being banished forever to a super boring demon prison dimension. And you know, I'm not exactly convinced you wouldn't keep using the locations you have to attack people if they start doing something you don't like."

Her cruel smile widened. "If that's what it takes to keep people in line, to make things better—isn't that for the greater good? Isn't that part of your code?"

"Ugh." I shook my head. "You know, Leah was right: my code is *fucked.*"

The skies opened up, rain pouring down on us. Thunder and lightning crackled overhead. I redoubled my mental efforts, pushing against Mom-Demon's mind with all my might. I needed control . . .

"I don't understand you!" she bellowed. "You're always agonizing over people underestimating you—I'm the only one who never has! I believe you can be *great*! That you can be so powerful!"

"You believe I can spend my life mind-controlling everyone around me, luring innocent humans into demon-y traps, and getting the world to do my bidding!" I shrieked. "You believe I can be a *supervillain*! And that's not what I fucking want!"

And with that, I slammed my mind into hers as hard as I could. She howled in pain and the ground started to shake. I tried to plant myself, to remain in an upright position even as the rain soaked me to the bone and the earth rumbled beneath my feet. I felt her mind slam back against mine, but I persisted, pushing and pushing and pushing.

You will do as I say, I thought at her ferociously. *I am going to fix things—or at least try to—but not the way you want me to.*

Our minds locked in battle and pain bloomed at my temples, behind my eyes, fucking everywhere. I shut my eyes tight and pushed through it.

Free the people you have trapped in the prison dimension, I thought at her. *Carmen. Pretzel Guy. Edna.*

Mom-Demon fell to her knees, gasping. I felt her mind start to give against mine. I was freezing, soaked to the bone, my head was killing me, and I could barely stand up straight. The ground was still shaking beneath my feet. I gritted my teeth and pressed on.

Free them, I thought firmly. *I'm assuming that will sever your connections with Kathy and Co.—and the locations you have a hold on. But if it doesn't . . . um, do that, too.*

Mom-Demon screamed, and I heard myself screaming in return. My mind felt like it was shredding the longer I fought her with it, breaking into teeny, tiny pieces. But I had to keep going.

And when you're done with all that, send me back, I thought at her. *Send me back to the human world. And don't do this ever again. Don't reach out through the worlds again. If you find yourself even thinking about it, lock yourself up in the prison dimension. Take up a hobby or something. Whatever the demon equivalent is of crochet. And . . .* In spite of myself, I felt my heart crack a little for her—for the daughter she'd lost and the hope she'd never been able to find. *And try to find some peace.*

The sky thundered again, rain drenching me down to my bones. The ground shook so hard, it threw me into the air and I was falling . . . falling . . .

I thought I heard Mom-Demon scream one more time. I felt myself scream, too, and then it was like my brain exploded, and all I saw was blackness and all I felt was pain.

And then I didn't feel anything at all.

CHAPTER TWENTY-SIX

MY EYES CRACKED open. I don't know what I expected to see—a totally wasted demon landscape, perhaps? Mom-Demon standing over me, cackling evilly? The dark nothingness of the prison dimension?

Instead I saw twinkle lights, blinking at me overhead. *My bedroom*, I realized. *I'm in my bed.* I sat up slowly, still transfixed by the twinkle lights, and felt someone shift next to me. I looked down and saw Evie, arm thrown over her face, snoring softly. I reached over and pinched her.

"Ow!" she shrieked, batting at me. "Bea!" She gave me an injured look. "What are you doing?!"

"Just making sure I'm not in some kind of demon holodeck dimension," I murmured, leaning back against my pillows.

She sat up and threw her arms around me, pulling me into a tight hug.

"Thank god you're okay," she whispered. "Thank *god*."

"Ack, can't breathe!" I gasped. "Did being pregnant give you some kind of bone-crushing strength? Because that is one power you definitely do *not* need."

She pulled back and looked at me, brushing my hair off my face. Her eyes were full of so many emotions, like she didn't even know where to begin.

"What happened?" I finally said. "Did I just, like, reappear at It's Lit?"

"You kind of fell out of the sky," she said, studying me. "It was very dramatic. Not that you would have it any other way, of course." She gave me a slight smile. "You appeared right above the pink couch, and Sam and Leah managed to catch you—sort of. You almost smooshed poor Pancake."

"Oh, no! Is he—"

"He's fine," she said, laughing a little. "Very indignant, though. You might have to apologize a few times. With bacon."

"I can do that."

"Right after you appeared, a bunch more people kind of fell out of the sky: Carmen, Edna, and . . . well, his name is Matt, but you've been calling him Pretzel Guy?"

"Oh my god," I whispered. "It worked."

She nodded. "And then—"

"Kathy, Bernard, and Poet," I breathed.

"Yes," she said. "Rose is questioning all of them, trying to get the full story. Nate checked all of you for injuries, but everyone seemed to be okay."

"What about . . ." I hesitated. "That supposed magical overload I was getting from visiting the Otherworld, the one that kept fucking with my vitals? Did that happen again? And did it have any lasting damage?"

"Apparently not," she said, raising an eyebrow. "Scott and Nate said whatever was happening to you before doesn't appear to have happened this time—it's almost like your system *adjusted* to the Otherworld."

"Whoa!" I said. "Maybe that's why the way I moved through the Otherworld seemed to change every time, why it got easier for me to speak to people and stuff—I was totes getting used to it." I poked her. "See, you were a big worrywart for nothing."

"I wouldn't exactly call it *nothing*—"

"Maybe I can help fill in some blanks," I interrupted hastily. I recounted my adventure battling Mom-Demon—and how I'd figured out I needed to go after her in the first place.

"Wow," Evie said. "That's *awesome*, Bea. That you figured out how to turn it around and use the information she gave you to defeat her." She shook her head at me, smiling slowly. "I underestimated you so much. You *are* a hero. In so many ways." Her smile faded, and she gnawed at her lower lip. "And look, we have so much to talk about. But I also want to say I'm sorry for what I said that night. About not getting to be sad when Mom died. I put all this stuff on you, and it wasn't fair. And this pregnancy . . ." A shadow crossed her face. "It's made me doubt myself so much. I really don't know if I can do this."

"You can," I said softly. "Of course you can. But back up, please—how did this happen? I mean, uh, I understand the mechanics," I added hastily. "But . . . was it planned? How far along are you?"

"We're still early in the first trimester," Evie said, smiling slightly and patting her stomach. "And uh, no. It wasn't planned. You can thank that teeny-tiny percentage of fail that comes with any modern birth control method." She shook her head. "It's so weird. I knew immediately I wanted to keep it. But at the same time, I feel like I don't know what the fuck I'm doing. And I feel guilty for not just being deliriously happy. *Nate* is deliriously happy. What's wrong with me?"

"Tanaka girls," I said, leaning my head on her shoulder. "We have to angst about fucking everything. Did you tell Dad?"

"He never responded to the email I sent when we started investigating Mom's death," she said. "So. He doesn't get to know about this." She paused, her expression going contemplative. "I don't know if I can do this," she said again. "Especially since I'm still so bad at just, like, talking to you. About anything. I mean, I couldn't even bring myself to tell you I was pregnant. There's been so much going on, and then we kept fighting, and I didn't know how you'd react. But I still should have told you. I don't think . . ." She took a long, shuddering breath and blinked a few times. "I don't think you know that I love you. Like, deep down, underneath it all. I don't think I was *good* at letting you know that. After Mom. I'm so sorry."

"Of course I know you love me," I said fiercely, my eyes filling with tears. "But Evie . . ." I hesitated, trying to put my thoughts together. "Neither of us ever *dealt* with losing Mom. Not really. We survived. We got through it. We somehow came out the other end intact. And a lot of that was because of you." I squeezed her hand, and repeated what Sam had said to me that night I'd cried in his lap: "Any mistakes made during that time . . . well, I don't think they're entirely our fault. We did the best we could. And I think now . . ." I took a deep breath. "I think we need to try to deal with it. *Really* deal with it."

"How?" she said, her voice faint.

"Well, therapy, for one thing," I said, giving her a slight smile. "I mean, there *must* be a therapist or two in this town who specialize in superhero psyches, right?"

"Oh, for sure," she said, returning my smile.

"But also . . . We need to be honest with each other. To try to relate to each other as actual human beings who've been through a bunch of shit instead of Big Sister Who's Always Nagging and Little Sister Who's Always a Disobedient Pain."

She cocked an eyebrow. "Maybe we should go to therapy *together*? Because I have a feeling this might require a referee of some kind."

"Sounds like a plan," I said, laughing. "But I think it's all part of a process, you know? Something that doesn't have an end date, necessarily. I've been so fixated for so long on finding this big magic bullet that I think will fix me. And then I get bored and move on to something else when whatever I'm doing at the moment *doesn't* fix me. You know, what you call my short attention span."

"That's another thing," she said, wincing. "I haven't been fair to you about . . . well, what you've been doing with your life. What you've *wanted* to do with your life. My perception of how you, like, process information and how you focus and how you find new passions . . . it hasn't always been accurate. I was stuck seeing you a certain way."

"And I was stuck seeing you a certain way," I said. "That's another thing we have to work on."

"So much to work on," she murmured, giving me a slight smile.

"When Mom-Demon showed me you guys in It's Lit, I realized a lot of things. But one thing I realized *especially* is that because I get so fixated on finding that one big thing that I think is gonna fix me, I completely fail to see all this stuff I already have that makes me happy. A big, weird, extended family that loves me so damn much, and gets protective past the point of reason when I have, say, a boy in my bedroom. A best friend who shows up for me no matter what, even when I've acted like a total asshole and almost sent her crush to a demon prison dimension. Another best friend who . . ." My voice faltered. I swallowed back my tears and forced myself to continue. ". . . who I am completely in love with and is super dedicated to giving me more pleasure than I can handle. And even though I'm pretty sure he doesn't feel the same way, and we're probably going to have to stop with the mind-blowing marathon sex sessions . . . it's okay." I leaned my head against her shoulder. "Because the fact that I *can* fall in love like that? Is pretty awesome."

"Those are all good things," Evie said. "Wonderful things."

"Looking at all of you, I realized: hope comes from watching people push past seemingly insurmountable odds to do the right thing," I said. "And everyone I love does that on pretty much a daily basis. Remember when you told me how it seemed like I'd lost my ability to hope after Mom died? How it seemed like I'd somehow gotten it back in recent years?"

"Yes," she said softly.

"It was because of you." My tears rose up again, threatening to fall. "It was watching you take control of your life, after being so sad and so scared and so inside your shell. When you actually started standing up to Aveda, when you actually started admitting you have feelings, when you found a purpose and started superheroing . . ." I swallowed hard. "It was like seeing you come back to yourself. And find a *better* self—that person you were meant to be. You pushed past those insurmountable odds, Evie. *That's* what made me feel like I could hope again."

"Bea," she said, her voice tremulous.

"I love you," I said. "I love you more than anything. No matter how much we fight. No matter what else happens."

"I love you too," she said.

And then she buried her face in my shoulder and we lay there silently and cried on each other, letting out all those years of broken, pent-up feelings between us.

"I should let you rest," she finally said, sitting up and brushing a hand over her eyes. "Nate would tell me to let you rest. And then tell me *I* need to rest. But you have a couple visitors—are you up to seeing them? Please say yes, because they've been waiting for hours, and if I don't let them in now, well . . . I can only bribe one of them with bacon."

"Yes, please," I said, sitting up straighter. "Send them in."

She smiled, gave me a last hug, and got up from the bed. I tried to smooth my tousled hair as she crossed the room and opened the door. Leah, Sam, and Pancake burst in, like they'd been smushed up against the door the whole time. I couldn't help but laugh.

"Oh, Bebe!" Leah shrieked, pouncing on me. I heard Pancake racing around on the floor, yapping up a storm. Sam picked up the puppy and set him on the bed, then settled himself into the rocking chair. "Are you okay?" Leah asked, grasping my shoulders, her eyes wide with concern. "I mean, are you *really* okay? I must've asked Nate like a million times, I was probably driving him crazy—"

"You were," Sam murmured.

"And he said yes, but I want to hear it from you," Leah continued.

Pancake settled between us, curling himself into a tiny bread loaf of a dog, and started licking my hand. I scratched his ears.

"I am okay," I said, laughing. "Really. And Lee . . . I'm *so* sorry. I was such an asshole. I was so out of my head,

thinking I could bring my mom back, thinking I could somehow make everything better—"

"I know," she said, patting my hand. "I know. And I
should have . . . I don't know, found a better way to tell you
about Nicole. I think I was feeling weird and kind of left out
when you and Sammy started, uh . . ." Her eyes slid to Sam,
and he raised an eyebrow. "It's always been the three of us,
and then you guys kinda had something *extra* going on," she
continued. "But I really like Nicole, Bebe. And she totally
gets why you'd be suspicious of her. She said she's willing to
sit down with you and have, like, a whole conversation and
submit to any grilling you want before we go on a date. She
knows you care about me, and that's important to her."

"No, please, date her. If it makes you happy, date her," I
said, squeezing her hand. "But definitely let her know that if
she hurts you in any way, I will murder her. In a way that
makes being trapped in a demon prison dimension for eter-
nity look *pleasant*."

Leah laughed and cuddled Pancake to her chest. He side-
eyed her, annoyed at being disturbed from the bed. "I'm so
glad you're okay," she said, beaming at me. "Now Pancake
and I are gonna leave you two alone. 'Cause I think you guys
need to talk."

"Oh, no, we're—" I said.

"We don't need—" Sam said at the same time.

Leah hopped up from the bed, Pancake hoisted under one
arm, and held up a hand to silence us.

"You are both still the *most* ridiculous," she said. "And
that's why you probably belong together. Come on, Pancake,
I'm pretty sure we can find someone downstairs to give you
food."

"Nate's the weak link!" I called out after her as she headed
for the door. "Total not-so-secret softie."

Awkward silence descended as soon as she exited. Sam
stayed in the rocking chair, studying me intently. I looked
down at my hands.

"I heard you," he finally said, his voice low and charged. "Last night. When you thought I was asleep."

My cheeks warmed. "Why did you pretend to be asleep?"

"You were saying a lot of nice things about me, Beatrice. I didn't want to interrupt."

I fiddled with my blanket. *Don't cry,* I thought. *You've kicked ass in so many ways today. Don't let this be what breaks you.*

"So," I said, trying to make my tone nonchalant. "We should probably stop—"

"Now *I'm* going to talk," he said. "And you're not going to interrupt."

I kept my eyes cast downward. He reached over, turned my hand over, and set something in my palm. I frowned, studying it. It was an eraser. Not just any eraser, but the dopey trophy-shaped eraser he'd won during the Great Calculus Bee of Sophomore Year. The one he kept proudly displayed in his apartment.

"What . . ." I said.

"I want this on the record," he said. "So there's no confusion, ever. No fighting. No competing. Look at me, Bea."

My head jerked up, my eyes meeting his. I rubbed the eraser between my fingers, trying to figure out what the frak was going on. His gaze was intense—more serious than I'd ever seen him.

"I fell in love with you first," he said.

My heart skipped a beat. I pulled the eraser to my chest, squeezing it tightly in my fist, unsure if I was hearing right.

"I didn't realize it until that day at the Market," he continued. "When you got in the brain battle with Kathy and passed out and I thought I was going to lose you. I couldn't even process it. I . . ." He trailed off, shaking his head. "I don't know when it happened. Maybe a long time ago. Maybe the first time we competed for something or the first time you won a point over me. Maybe before that, even. But it hit me so hard in that moment, what it would be like to be without you. And later that night, when we were naked together for the first time . . ."

My blush deepened and he gave me a soft, secret smile.

". . . I knew," he said.

"*That's* why you were so weird and distant the next morning," I managed to say.

"What you said last night, about me making you feel treasured—you make me feel that way too, Bea. Like you see me in ways that nobody else does."

"I *am* apparently the only person who's not just in it for the calendar abs," I murmured.

His smile widened. "I fell in love with you first," he repeated. "I love the way you throw yourself into life with such gusto. The way you fight so fiercely for the people you love. The way you embrace everything you're doing so fully. I love that you talk too fast and that you're bad at sharing food and that I will *always* be able to find you in a crowd." He touched my bright hair—then tapped me gently on the forehead. "And I love this crinkle."

"And all this means . . . what?" I tried for an impish look, even though I was overwhelmed with emotion and my heart was beating so fast, I thought it was going to pop out of my chest. "You win another point?"

"No. You said it yourself last night: You said that I won forever. That you lost because you'd fallen for me." He tapped the eraser in my hands. "But since I was actually first on that front, it means *you* win every point. It means I'm done competing with you because you have my entire heart. And I don't need anything except yours."

I fiddled with the eraser, a slow smile playing over my lips. "Well," I said. "*That's* no fun."

I set the eraser down and took his hand, tugging insistently. He got up from the rocking chair and let me pull him into bed.

"One of the chief thrills of my life is competing with you," I said, winding my arms around his neck. I brushed my lips against his, and his arms went around my waist, pulling me tight against him. "And I see no reason why I should have to give that up."

"Hmm," he said. His hands were already sliding under my shirt, raising delicious goosebumps everywhere. "What do you suggest? I think we're a little old for Calculus Bees."

I grinned and kissed him again—long and deep and sweet. Taking it slow, like we always did.

When we finally came up for air, he brushed my hair off my face and gave me one of those looks that thrilled me so much—like I was the most beautiful thing in the world.

"I can think of a few things," I said.

DEMON ENCOUNTER REPORT

Submitted to: Sergeant Rose Rorick (Demon Unit, SFPD Emergency Service Division), Dr. Nathaniel Jones (Aveda Jupiter, Inc.), Dr. Kai Alana

Submitted by: Beatrice Constance Tanaka (Superhero-in-Training Currently On Probation, Awesome Bookseller/Science-Lover, Generally Okay Person Trying to Figure Her Shit Out)

Short Summary: Mom-Demon tried to turn me into a supervillain, but I kicked her ass.

Long Summary: This report has been compiled from information assembled by Dr. Jones, Sergeant Rorick, and their respective teams, and from interviews with Kathy Kooper, Bernard Clements, Shelly Wong (previously known as "Poet"), Carmen Ramirez, Edna Flaherty, and Matt Grillo (previously known as "Pretzel Guy"). And yours truly! (That's right, I interviewed myself. Pretty innovative, eh?!) *(Note from NJ: Yes, but next time, consider bringing in a third party.)*

Extensive scanning of the various San Francisco locations "activated" by Otherworld Demon Threat #2752 (aka "Mom-Demon") indicates they are now **dormant**—no sign of further demon activity detected. None of Mom-Demon's chosen human minions (Ms. Kooper, Mr. Clements, and Ms. Wong) appear to have retained the "emotional projection" power she gifted to them. (It has been confirmed that the version of said power Mom-Demon had preserved in her lab was a copy she made from her deceased daughter.) Report Writer still has hers because she always had it, but it remains to be seen whether or not the power "enhancements" received while in the Otherworld (such as being able to implant direct thoughts into people's minds) remain. She hasn't tested them out and has no plans to do so in the near future.

Ms. Kooper, Mr. Clements, and Ms. Wong are currently in a shitload of trouble and are being dealt with by Sergeant Rorick and the SFPD. Ms. Ramirez, Ms. Flaherty, and Mr. Grillo appear unharmed and are currently recuperating with their loved ones. (Ms. Ramirez asked Report Writer to please include a note here to say that she is *still* looking for her wallet and would like to be contacted if anyone finds it. Report Writer tried to tell her this Report is not for public consumption and including this note is therefore not especially helpful, but given that Ms. Ramirez has been trapped in a demon prison dimension, Report Writer feels it is the least she can do.)

Report Writer also confirmed with Ms. Kooper that the box of Vivian Tanaka's letters given to Report Writer and Evelyn Tanaka is the real deal—no supernatural interference involved. They're just letters. RW is very grateful to have this memento of her mother, though she kind of wishes it didn't have so much baggage attached.

As for bigger picture ramifications: Although RW mind-mojo-ed Mom-Demon into (hopefully!) never doing this again, we should not ignore the fact that the walls between our world and the Otherworld have rubbed thin enough to give demons new ways of reaching Earth. Though this incident does not appear to be connected to the near drownings in Maui, the Maui incidents contain enough suspicious markers to merit further investigation. Report Writer is in full support of Dr. Kai Alana's request to set up a mini Demon Unit in Maui to look into it. (Report Writer would also like to issue a very enthusiastic THANK YOU to Dr. Alana for sending her some of the famous peanut butter mochi from Maui Specialty Chocolates— they are truly a mouth-watering delight and RW ate them all even though she was technically supposed to share. Oops.) *(Note from NJ: We are* so *not telling Evie about that last part.) (Note from KA: Bea, I love your observational style. Thank you for sending me a copy of this. And I'm glad you liked the mochi! :)*

CHAPTER TWENTY-SEVEN

"STARBUCK. JADZIA. GALACTUS."

"Bea!" Evie shot me an amused look across the breakfast table. "We are not naming our baby *Galactus*."

"Awwwww, come on!" I protested, poking Nate with my fork. "Galactus Tanaka-Jones. It has such an excellent ring to it. Aveda will back me up on this." I turned to Aveda hopefully.

"Aveda's gunning for them to name the baby 'Aveda Jr.,'" Lucy said, letting loose with a snorty giggle. "She will *not* back you up on this."

"It was just a *suggestion*," Aveda huffed, stabbing her spoon into her Grape-Nuts.

"Save that one for us, sweetheart," Scott teased, slinging his arm around the back of Aveda's chair.

"It sounds very dignified," Rose said, giving Aveda a nod of encouragement.

"I like Jadzia," Shruti said, winking at me. I'd invited her to join us for breakfast, 'cause I had things to talk to everyone about.

It was a week after the big Mom-Demon battle, and we were all gathered around the breakfast table at HQ. Things had gone mostly back to normal. The Pussy Queen portal was still causing random demon incidents around town, Aveda and Evie were handling it, and I had gone back to working at the bookstore full-time and hanging out with Leah and Sam. Oh, and figuring out what I wanted to do with my life in general. I still didn't have all the answers, but

I was getting a better idea of the direction I wanted to head in. And I had planned on presenting it to everyone at breakfast.

I knew they weren't gonna like it, though. Which is why I tried to warm 'em up with baby name jokes. (Though to be honest, I thought Galactus Tanaka-Jones actually *did* have an excellent ring to it.)

"So, guys," I said, trying to make my tone light. "I've been doing a lot of thinking and—"

"—and you want to be taken off probation, finally!" Aveda said, clapping her hands together. "Perfect. Evie and I could definitely use some help—"

"No," I said, shaking my head. "I mean, thank you. But, no. You actually don't need that much help with the current supernatural state of San Francisco. You guys and Shruti have it handled. And Shruti somehow manages to be an awesome heroine on her own *and* leads a balanced life *and* seamlessly melds with your co-dependent dynamic when called on. Maybe because she's not related to one of you." I gave Evie a rueful smile. She smiled back tentatively. "Or maybe just because she's awesome," I said, grinning at Shruti. She grinned back and toasted me with her spoon.

"Here's the thing," I continued. "I'm still figuring myself out. I've never really taken the time I needed to do that— because I was so fixated on being a superheroine just like y'all. And then when that wasn't really working out, I went rogue and . . . well, let's be honest, I got a little drunk on my own power. I tried to control people. I flirted with supervillain territory. So I need to take a few gigantor steps back and think about what kind of hero I actually want to be. And I *do* want to be a hero. But I need to figure out what that means for *me*."

Aveda's brow furrowed. "So what are you going to do?" she said. "Back to experimenting on people at the bookstore?"

"No. That was honestly a little supervillain-y, too," I said. I took a deep breath, trying to put together everything I needed to say. "A super smart person told me recently that I should follow what calls to me on a visceral level, and the rest will come." I turned and met Nate's eyes and he gave me a half-smile. "And then another super smart person told me there's more than one way to use my gifts, and I should figure out what makes me happy." I nodded at Shruti. "You all know I love figuring out how things work and investigating science stuff and . . . well. The truth is, I've also been thinking a lot about how I've never really been anywhere outside the Bay Area. Sooooo . . ."

I jumped up from my seat and reached behind the counter, where I'd hidden my posterboard. One last posterboard. Leah had helped me with it, of course. It depicted the fine Hawaiian island of Maui in glitter (which had taken us forever because the glitter kept wanting to fall off and/or migrate somewhere else so that Maui looked more like a blobby horse's head or something). We'd drawn the ocean around it and given the waves menacing faces, like they were monsters rising up to attack the island.

"I've been emailing with Nate's friend, Kai," I said. "She and the local police department are setting up a small demonology unit to investigate those mysterious near drownings."

"Have there been any more?" Lucy said, her eyes widening with alarm.

"Just the three so far," I said. "But as we all know—"

"—three makes a trend," Evie murmured, giving me a slight smile.

"Kai really appreciated my notes on her research," I said. "And she wants to create a position in the unit for someone with my specific blend of talents. For me." I tapped the monster waves on the posterboard. "Who knows? Maybe if these bad boys try to lure anyone else, I can take 'em down with my scream. That would be a totally heroic, non-villainous use of my powers."

"If the demons of the Otherworld have figured out other ways to get through to our world—as your Mom-Demon did—it seems like this will be a necessary mission," Nate said.

"Exactly," I said, waving my posterboard around. "And I think a change of scenery, some distance from the Bay Area, will give me the space I need to figure myself out. I need to be in a place where I'm not Evie's little sister or Nate's awesome assistant or Aveda and Evie's superheroing intern. Where I can explore who I am when it's just me."

"I have a question," Evie murmured.

I met her eyes. I'd been trying not to look at her too much during my presentation, 'cause I knew she'd probably like this idea the least. She looked teary, as I'd expected. And like she was tamping down on her instincts to smother me.

"There are therapists in Maui," I said, giving her a hopeful grin. "I'm still fully dedicated to dealing with my Mom issues, Big Sis."

"It's not that," she said softly, getting up from her chair and crossing the room to me. I set down the posterboard so she could take my hand.

"H-how long?" she said, her tears threatening to overflow. "This sounds like a great opportunity, Bea, and a good plan. And I respect what you want to do—I'm so happy you've figured out that this is what you want to do. But . . ." She bit her lip, her expression turning uncertain. "I don't think I can stand to be that far away from you forever. I need you. I'm still scared out of my freaking mind that I'm going to fuck this up, remember?" She rubbed her stomach and attempted a wobbly smile.

"You won't," I said, squeezing her hand. "And anyway, you've got all of them, too." I gestured to our friends. Our family. "I don't think they'll let you fuck it up."

She shook her head, tears sliding down her cheeks, and pulled me in for a hug. "I know," she said fiercely. "But I still need *you*."

I hugged her back hard, my own tears starting to fall. Then I pulled back and rested my hands on her shoulders, giving her a game smile. "Regular visits," I said. "And my stay there will be open-ended, but it won't be forever. Maybe a year or two at most? There's only so much solitary soul-searching a girl can take. Eventually, when I'm awesomely self-actualized, I'll need to come home. And continue my journey." I put my hand on her stomach. "And anyway, I plan on being the Best Ever Auntie to little Galactus Tanaka-Jones, here. I'm going to be their favorite adult. After you and Nate, of course."

"We'll see about that," I heard Aveda mutter. I giggled.

Then they were all standing up and gathering around me, enveloping me in a big group hug.

"Oof, guys!" I exclaimed, pretending to be annoyed. "Don't squish me! I just made a pretty stirring case for my adulthood and independence. No need to revert to treating me like a baby."

"Oh, shut up, Bea," Aveda said. She was trying for imperious, but I heard the warmth in her voice. "You're *our* baby. And we wouldn't have it any other way."

"So I usually do a sweep through the café area at least three times a day for stray books to re-shelve—you've gotta get to them before someone spills on them or gets crumbs on them or dog-ears the pages. I mean, if they crack the spine, *forget it*. Do you have any questions?"

I cocked my head inquisitively at my possibly former nemesis, Nicole Yamamoto, who was taking copious notes as I led her on a tour of It's Lit—her new workplace. It was a month later, and I was leaving for Maui in two days. In just a few minutes, we were having my going away party right here at the bookstore. But first, I had to train my replacement.

"Um, yeah," she said, frowning at her notepad. "Does Charlotte's unicorn collection get dusted once a week, or do you think it's better to be more frequent? I want to make sure I'm thorough, but I'm kind of clumsy, so I'm a little worried about breaking something."

"Excellent question," I said, nodding approvingly. "Once

a week is fine, and if you break something, just blame it on Pancake." We reached the register area, where Pancake was snoozing on his special pillow. He lifted his head and gave me an irritated stare.

"Got it," she said, scribbling in her notepad. She looked up and gave me a tentative smile. "Hey, Bea, thanks for all this."

"Don't thank me," I said, waving a breezy hand. "Charlotte's the one who hired you. And I kinda owe you one after trying to drag you to a demon prison dimension and all."

"I know. But I meant . . ." She trailed off, set the notebook down, and leaned against the counter, giving me a considering look. "Thanks for giving me a chance. For not protesting me dating Leah. Or working here."

I shrugged. "Well. I actually *did* protest. At least the Leah part. But I was being kind of a narrow-minded jerk and not allowing for the possibility that you might have changed. Or that you might be going through your own identity crisis-type thing."

"Yeah, I was kind of freaked out when I got fired," she said. "I'd been on the lawyer path for so long, I guess I didn't realize it's not actually what I want."

"What do you want?" I said. "Or are you still figuring that out?"

"I think I want to be a writer," she said, scrunching her face up. "I'm going to try to write a book on my off hours. Leah drew some art for it and we might even make it a comic book. Full of fantastical female creatures who fall in love and murder people."

"Sounds amazing," I said.

"Yeah," she said. "I mean, I don't know if it's going to lead anywhere serious, but we're just having so much fun with it."

"Never underestimate fun," I said, stabbing a finger in the air. "I think part of our problem as, like, a society is we don't take fun and joy seriously enough. That we dismiss it every chance we get or consider it lesser than other stuff. But those are, like, the bedrocks of our existence. That's what makes life worth living. You wouldn't believe the number of people who come in this store who say being able to escape into a fun, joyful book saved their lives. I mean, me realizing I have so many joyful things in my life is part of what saved mine. Fun is *important*."

"Can you give my parents that speech?" she said, laughing. "Because I have a feeling I'm in for a fight when I tell them I've switched my career path from lawyer to writer."

I scratched Pancake behind the ears, regarding her thoughtfully. "When we were younger . . . I know I pulled away from you with basically no explanation. I'm sorry. I was hurting so much. I didn't have room for anything—or anyone—beyond that pain."

"No, *I'm* sorry," she said. "Because I wasn't understanding at all about your mom, Bea, and then I went and turned everyone against you and I . . . We were so young. I don't think I got what a loss like that means. How it feels. I just knew that I'd lost my best friend. And it made me lash out at you in the most immature way possible."

"Ugh, twelve-year-olds," I said, rolling my eyes. "Sooooo immature."

She laughed, surprised. "I know you're leaving soon. But maybe sometime, when you're ready, we could get together and talk?"

"I'd like that," I said, smiling at her. "In the meantime, why don't you stay for the party? I know Leah would love to have you here."

"I would love to," she said. "Thank you."

"Great," I said, nodding. "If you're cool here with Pancake, I'm gonna go freshen up before everyone arrives."

"Sounds good," she said, moving behind the register. "I'll take this time to study all the notes you gave me." She rubbed Pancake's head and cooed at him, putting on a baby voice that seemed completely at odds with her entire personality. "Who's the best doggo, the cutest doggo, is it you?" Pancake looked up at her adoringly and rolled over, presenting his belly.

"Man, really?!" I said to him, putting my hands on my hips. "She's the only one you *don't* look at with complete disdain?"

"Is that good?" Nicole said, rubbing Pancake's belly.

"It's more than good," I scoffed. "It means I should start preparing yours and Leah's wedding registry."

"What's this about a wedding?" Leah sang out, bursting through the front entrance. She bustled over to the counter, loaded down with party supplies. "Ooh, are you and Sammy—"

"No," I said, laughing. "I mean, not yet. Hey, Nicole, can you give us a moment, here? Take Pancake with you to the café?"

"Roger that," she said, scooping up the pup and heading off.

"What's up, Bebe?" Leah said, cocking an eyebrow.

"I wanted to give you something before everyone else shows up. Well, two somethings," I said, moving behind the counter and pulling out the things I'd stored below. "This is an electric paintbrush cleaner," I said, holding up the first thing. "I finally figured out how to adjust it just right. No more tedious manual brush-cleaning for you." I set it on the counter and pushed it toward her. "And this . . ." As I brandished the second item, a lump formed in my throat. "I, um, think you might recognize."

"Our favorite dragon-shifter lady book!" she exclaimed, her eyes widening as she took the rainbow-hued tome from me. "This looks like a super old copy. Maybe a first printing. Is it a collector's item?" She turned to the inside cover. "Your name is written in here," she said, her brows drawing together. "I don't . . . wait." She met my eyes, and I saw that hers were misting over. "Is this the copy your mom gave you? Oh, Bebe. I can't take this. It's too important."

"You're important," I said fiercely. "You're important to me. And, um. I don't want you to forget about me while I'm gone."

She practically leapt over the counter to pull me into a hug. "I won't," she whispered. "I never would."

We hugged for a long time, neither of us willing to let go. But I finally *had* to let go to head to the bathroom and accomplish my freshening up mission.

I shut myself in the bathroom and combed my fingers through my hair, checking my makeup in the mirror. I heard a soft knock, and then the door opened, revealing Sam.

"Hey," I said, going all mock indignant and echoing my words from so many weeks ago. "You can't just barge into the bathroom like that! What if—"

"—you had been naked or something, I know," he said, smiling at me indulgently. He shut the door behind him, crossed the room, and pulled me close. I wound my arms around his neck and kissed him. I still couldn't get enough of him—I didn't think I ever would. "Do you *want* to be naked?" he murmured against my lips. "Because I'm pretty sure we could make that happen."

"Mmm, yes," I said. "I do. But aren't people starting to arrive? I don't want to be late for my own party."

"They're trickling in," he confirmed. "Lucy brought a cake."

"Gah," I said, wrinkling my nose. "Hopefully Leah can direct Pancake over that way."

He laughed, pulled back, and brushed my hair away from my face. "I can't believe you're leaving. I mean, I tell you I love you, and you immediately decide to put an entire ocean between us. How am I supposed to take that?"

His smile was smug, *beaucoup fromage*—but now I could see what was under it, that vulnerability, that earnestness. I felt a rush of affection so deep, it almost overwhelmed me.

"You're coming to visit me in two weeks, drama queen," I said. "And many times after that, I assume. We are totally going to make our worlds bigger together."

"I can't wait," he said softly. He held my gaze for a long time, all the surface layers of his expression melting away. No Calendar Sam. No All Swag, All the Time Sam. No Competitive Calculus Bee Sam. Just . . . Sam. What was between us was still undeniably fun. And yes, now it had a deeper layer to it, the layer that came with love. But being with him, I realized, was something else I'd tried to dismiss as "just fun." The reality was, something this delicious, this wonderful, wasn't "just" anything. All of these things I'd come to treasure so much—joy, fun, love, hope—could *never* be "just" anything. These things were hard-fought, hard-won, and I had to choose to embrace them every day.

I kissed him again and let all of those things wash over me, reveled in how good they made me feel. Yes, maybe I didn't feel like I'd become the exact person I was meant to be or like I was totally whole or like there wasn't still stuff I had to figure out. But I felt like I could get there. And I could definitely have a shitload of fun *while* I was getting there.

"Go wait for me out there," I finally said, pulling back from him. "I need a little moment alone."

"All right," he said, smiling and crossing over to the door. "But don't take too long or I'll have to come check on you and we'll end up kissing again. And then you'll definitely be late for your own party."

"Still so cocky," I said, rolling my eyes at him.

He just grinned and shut the door behind him.

I gave my makeup one last look in the mirror, my eyes wandering to the craft wall, to the words I'd written what seemed like eons ago.

I will be the greatest superhero of all time

I picked up a marker and crossed that out. Then I wrote an addendum.

I don't know exactly what I'm doing. I don't know exactly what I'll be. But I do know this.

I choose joy.

I choose love.

I choose hope.

And I can be anything I want.

ACKNOWLEDGMENTS

Big, sparkly, glitter-drenched thank yous to all the readers who have embraced the *Heroine Complex* series so enthusiastically—I love your cosplays, I love your fan art, I love your collage aesthetic inspiration pin boards, I love you. And it's because of you that this series is continuing past the first trilogy, with more adventures for Evie, Annie, and Bea (and all their friends!) on the horizon. I hope you're as excited as I am to follow my girls on their next epic quest.

Thanks, as always, to all my badass superhero teams: the Girl Gang, the Shamers, the Ripped Bodice writing crew, NOFXGVN, Heroine Club, the Cluster, and the incredible Asian American arts community of LA. I am honored to be in your company.

Thank you to my agent, Diana Fox, and my editors, Betsy Wollheim and Katie Hoffman, for always working tirelessly to help me make these books the best they can be. (Special thanks to Katie for knowing the power of a well-timed sign bunny.) Thank you to Alexis Nixon for all your publicity magic and SDCC superheroing, to Josh Starr for keeping everything on track and answering my weird questions with "NOT a weird question," and to everyone at DAW, Fox Literary, and Penguin Random House for all the care you put into getting these books out to the world.

Thank you to Rebekah Weatherspoon for being the best deadline buddy ever—we got our airplane pants, we got our Sprite, let's go. And for the record, I made it through because of that Tina Knowles quote.

Thank you to the proprietors of The Ripped Bodice, Bea and Leah Koch: your store, your pink couch, and you have all been there for me in more ways than I can count. It's Lit is not exactly your store, but its positive attributes (i.e. the parts that aren't infested with demonic porcelain unicorns) certainly took root there. And thanks to Fitzwilliam Waffles for allowing me to be so inspired by both your appearance and your demeanor—you are a natural star.

Thank you to Jenn Fujikawa and Tom Wong for always understanding me the very most—you are my favorite twins and I love you. Thank you to Jenny Yang for talking all-caps FEELINGS with me, to Andrea Letamendi for insightful Red Robin lunches that always make me cry (in a good way!), and to Christine Dinh and Mel Caylo for all those weekends of shoe shopping and brunch.

Thank you to Jason Chan for taking care of my girls again and making them look exactly as they should on the cover.

Thank you to Keiko Agena, Julia Cho, and Will Choi for being awesome friends and for your brilliant dramatic readings of these characters—that's how I hear them now in my head. Thank you to Amber Benson and Seanan McGuire, the most magical of magical girls. Thank you to Cindy Pon for being there for several crucial moments and for always being a rock star.

And thank you to everyone who fed this book in so many ways: Javier Grillo-Marxuach, Amy Ratcliffe, Christy Black, Sarah Watson, Liza Palmer, Erik Patterson, Phil Yu, Naomi Ko, Naomi Hirahara, Diya Mishra, Michi Trota, Alisha Rai, Sonjia Hyon, Jenelle Riley, Nick Brandt, Janet Eckford, and the Okamoto family (and the NERD HERD). Thank you to all the bookstores and booksellers who hosted me last year, especially Maryelizabeth Yturralde at Mysterious Galaxy and Jude Feldman at Borderlands—you are both so wonderful.

Thank you to my family for being my family: Dad, Steve, Marjorie, Alice, Philip, and all the other Kuhns, Yoneyamas, Chens, and Coffeys.

Thank you to Jeff Chen for everything—I will always share my okonomiyaki with you.

This book was, for many reasons, tough to write. Like Bea, I ultimately found hope in watching the people I love push past seemingly insurmountable odds to do the right thing. Thank you, everyone, for that.